The Alhambra

IN FOCUS

A COMPLETE NEW GUIDE
TO
THE ALHAMBRA
AND
GENERALIFE

Translated by Jon Trout

Published by EDILUX S.L.
Editor: J. Agustín Núñez
Original text: Aurelio Cid Acedo
English translation: Jon Trout
Photographs: M. Román and J. Agustín Núñez
Photographic composition: EDILUX S.L.
Layout, design and drawings: Miguel Salvatierra
Printing: Imprenta Comercial. Motril. Granada.
Digital redisign 2008: Portada Fotocomposición, S. L. Granada.
Binding: Hermanos Olmedo, S. L.
ISBN: 978-84-95856-15-9
L.D.: GR. 1.763-2007

Distribución: Edilux, teléfono y fax: 958-082000
www.andaluciabooks.com
E-mail: edilux@edilux.es
ediciones@edilux.com.es

CONTENTS

The names of the different areas of the Alhambra and Generalife have often been left in Spanish to enable the visitor to refer to the signs and locate his position more easily.

General information

OPENING TIMES

From 8.30 a.m. to 8.30 p.m. in summer and from 8.30 a.m. to 6 p.m. in winter every day of the year except 1 January and 25 December.

TICKETS CAN BE BOUGHT:

- At the **ticket office** at the entrance to the Generalife, just beside the car-park or
- **in advance** at some banks ***(La Caixa)*** and travel agencies.

The various palaces, towers and gardens of the Alhambra occupy a considerable area and you should allow at least half a day for your visit if not the entire day.

You must enter the Nasrid Palaces within half an hour of the time specified on your ticket. There are other parts of the Alhambra such as the woods, some of the gates and the Palace of Charles V which you can visit without charge and at your own leisure.

On Tuesdays, Thursdays and Saturdays in summer, and Tuesdays and Saturdays in winter there are late-evening visits to the royal palaces. During the rest of the week night-time visits and guided tours of parts of the Alhambra not usually open to the public can be organised by previous arrangement with the Alhambra administration (Tel: 958 22 09 12).

MUSEUMS

The Alhambra museum is on the ground floor of the Palace of Charles V. It contains many unique and fascinating objects from the Alhambra palaces and archaeological excavations in the precint. Entrance is free. The Museum of Fine Arts is on the first floor and contains interesting paintings, particularly from the Granadan school. The museums are closed on Mondays.

OTHER SERVICES

Medical assistance from the Red Cross is on hand during the summer months
(Tel: 958 22 20 24 / 958 22 22 22).

The Alhambra has a large staff of professional, multilingual guides who may be hired for any visit either by a group or by individuals (Tel: 958 229936)

Patronato de Turismo: 958 22 95 75

Smoking and eating are not allowed in the palaces and visitors are asked not to touch or lean against the walls and columns..

N.B. There is a special tourist voucher which allows access to many of the most important monuments in Granada, including the Alhambra, and also discounts on city buses., on sale at the ticket offices to most monuments and at the Caja de Ahorros savings bank in Plaza Isabel le Católica in the city centre.

HOW TO GET TO THE ALHAMBRA

Straight to the Alhambra from outside the city

Coming by motorway from Madrid, Córdoba/Málaga/Sevilla, or Almería/Murcia you take the Granada bypass (Circunvalación) heading south towards Motril/Sierra Nevada. Take the exit onto the southern ring road, signed to Sierra Nevada. You go through a tunnel (keep in the left-hand lane) and come to a roundabout, where you will see the signs leading you uphill (about 1 kilometre) to the car-park and ticket office at the Generalife. Do not be waylaid by illegal roadside car-parkers on the way up before you get to the official carpark, which is clearly signed.

To the town centre and from there to the Alhambra

Exits A and B from the bypass (circunvalación) will lead you by the routes indicated on the map to the public car-parks in the Avenida de la Constitución and San Agustín (just off the Gran Vía). Exits E and F lead to the car-park in Puerta Real in the city centre. Once in the city it is not really a good idea to try to drive up to the Alhambra; it is better to walk or catch a bus. It is possible, however, to drive via the Paseo del Salón-Cuesta Escoriaza-Vistillas-Caidero (see map on the next page). You must park in the car-park.

Pedestrian routes are shown in the plan overleaf.

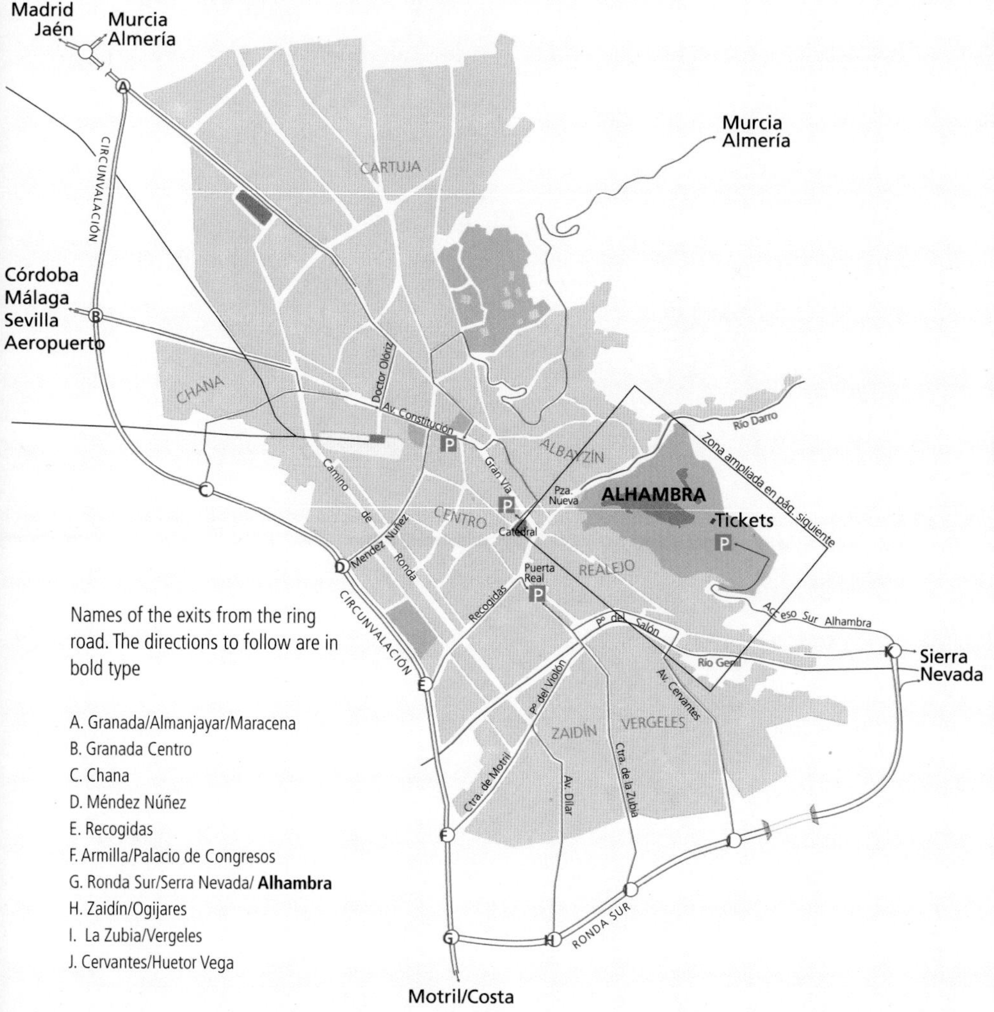

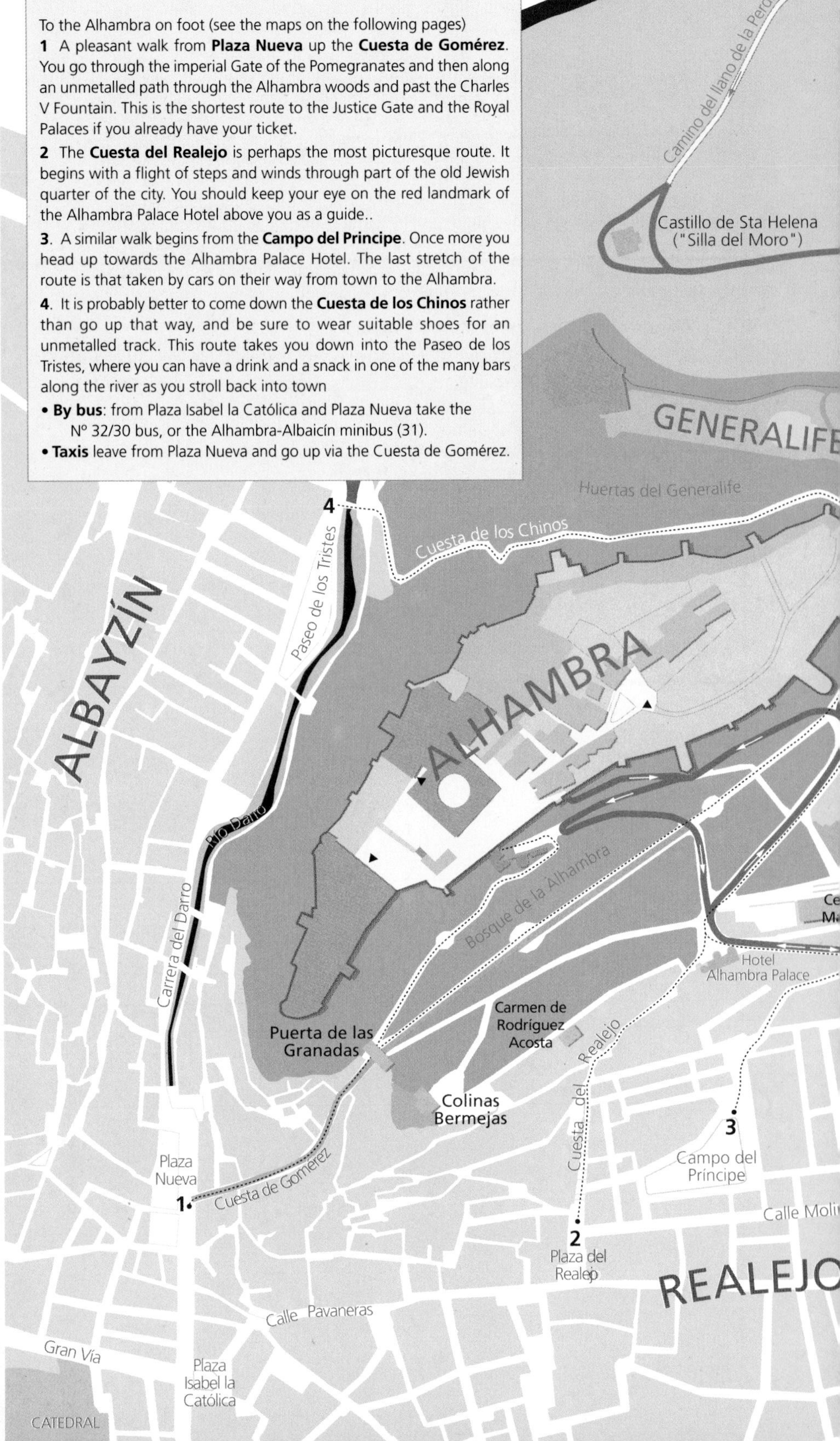

To the Alhambra on foot (see the maps on the following pages)

1 A pleasant walk from **Plaza Nueva** up the **Cuesta de Gomérez**. You go through the imperial Gate of the Pomegranates and then along an unmetalled path through the Alhambra woods and past the Charles V Fountain. This is the shortest route to the Justice Gate and the Royal Palaces if you already have your ticket.

2 The **Cuesta del Realejo** is perhaps the most picturesque route. It begins with a flight of steps and winds through part of the old Jewish quarter of the city. You should keep your eye on the red landmark of the Alhambra Palace Hotel above you as a guide..

3. A similar walk begins from the **Campo del Principe**. Once more you head up towards the Alhambra Palace Hotel. The last stretch of the route is that taken by cars on their way from town to the Alhambra.

4. It is probably better to come down the **Cuesta de los Chinos** rather than go up that way, and be sure to wear suitable shoes for an unmetalled track. This route takes you down into the Paseo de los Tristes, where you can have a drink and a snack in one of the many bars along the river as you stroll back into town

- **By bus**: from Plaza Isabel la Católica and Plaza Nueva take the Nº 32/30 bus, or the Alhambra-Albaicín minibus (31).
- **Taxis** leave from Plaza Nueva and go up via the Cuesta de Gomérez.

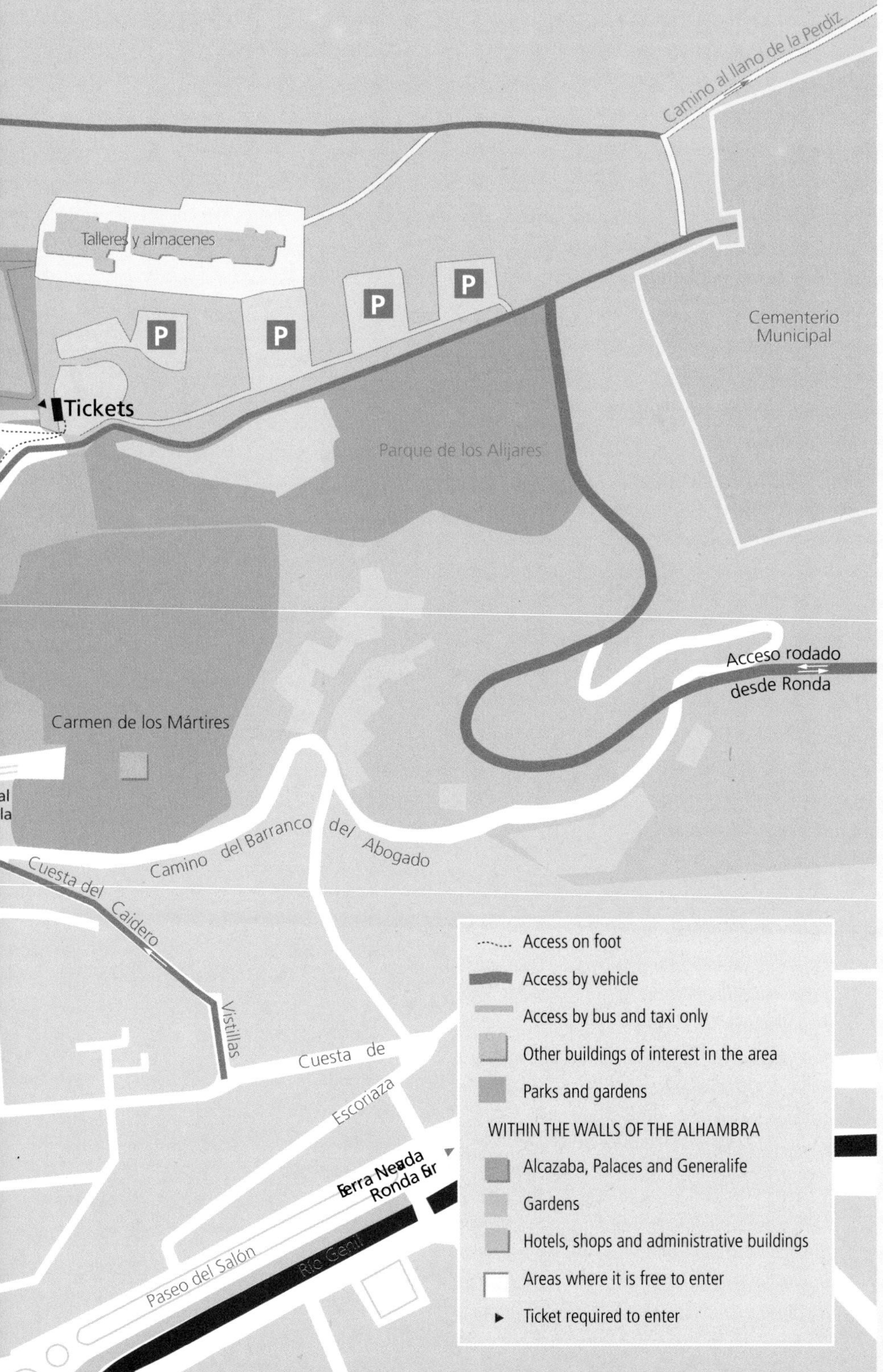
PARQUE DE INVIERNO
Camino al llano de la Perdiz
Talleres y almacenes
P
P
P
P
P
Cementerio Municipal
Tickets
Parque de los Alijares
Acceso rodado desde Ronda
Carmen de los Mártires
Camino del Barranco del Abogado
Cuesta del Caidero
Vistillas
Cuesta de Escoriaza
Paseo del Salón
Río Genil
Access on foot
Access by vehicle
Access by bus and taxi only
Other buildings of interest in the area
Parks and gardens
WITHIN THE WALLS OF THE ALHAMBRA
Alcazaba, Palaces and Generalife
Gardens
Hotels, shops and administrative buildings
Areas where it is free to enter
Ticket required to enter

Owen Jones y Goury, 1842

Introduction

Rising up above the Red Hill, the royal city of the Alhambra stands proud and eternal, one of the most important architectural structures of the Middle Ages and the finest example of Islamic art left to us in the western world.

The steep rise upon which the Alhambra sits forms a rough triangle; at its eastern end is the Cerro del Sol, the Hill of the Sun, crowned by the Generalife Palace and the Seat of the Moor; running beneath its abrupt northern flank is the valley of the river Darro; at its western extreme stands the Alcazaba citadel, and to the south it is bordered by a deep gully separating the Alhambra proper from the Mauror Hill and the Vermillion Towers, where a path climbs through the middle of the woods to the gates of the citadel.

The hill is composed of reworked detritus from the Sierra Nevada, mainly schists and quartz, redeposited some six million years ago in an alluvial fan delta. Subsequent tectonic activity fractured it into four distinct terraces.

Profile of the Alhambra drawn by Hermostilla, 1867

The Alhambra itself stands on the third one down. The deposits are in fact grey, the distinctive red colour which gives the hill its name being due to a thin covering of oxidised palaeosoil. At its highest point it is some seven hundred metres above sea level.

The shape of the whole citadel resembles that of a boat with its prow, the Alcazaba, set on a tireless course towards the city. It is seven hundred metres from its stem, the Alcazaba, to its stern, the Cabo de la Carrera tower, and two hundred metres in the beam at its widest.

In all it covers an area of some thirteen hectares and is enclosed by more than two kilometres of walls reinforced by some thirty towers, many of which are now in ruins. With the exception of occasional passing references no contemporary text speaks in any detail of the Alhambra as such. Occasionally one of the kings of Granada might make some such allusion as "I write to you from the Alhambra, may Allah preserve her!", but little else.

The Alhambra has not always been appreciated for the architecture itself. We all seem to become mere tourists in the Alhambra. A group of Spanish architects wrote in 1953 in the Manifiesto de la Alhambra that *"The Alhambra is a monument that has never been looked at properly from an architectural point of view; it is curious: not even by those architects who sharpen their professional eye (if we might put it like that) before the Escorial; when they come to the Alhambra they let go the reins of their critical perspicacity to become tourists like any others, even to the extent of excusing their complacency by alleging a clear distinction as far as their emotions are concerned: Yes, I like this a lot, but not as architecture." Later in the same text the authors add, "The relationship between this building of the XIV century and the most advanced modern architecture is in some respects astonishing: they coincide with us in their placing of things on a human scale, in their asymmetric yet organic way of laying out the different levels, in how they managed to incorporate the gardens and landscape into the buildings themselves, in their strictly uncluttered use of materials and in so many other aspects which would be laborious to enumerate."* And it is true, that the Alhambra, for all its great age, is in both conception and construction a very modern architectural complex.

The Swiss architect Le Corbusier found his view of modern architecture already defined in this monument as "the intelligent, just and magnificent interplay of volumes made harmonious by daylight ". He went on to express this as his ideal in his Cité Moderne (1922). They tried to bring the garden and the landscape into their buildings and they always kept their scale within human bounds.Francisco Prieto Moreno, who was for many years the architect in charge of restoring and preserving the monument, said, *"The Alhambra combines in its various buildings many architectural precepts which are still valid today, and are of course considered as masterpieces"*. Another great achievement in its construction is that although it was built over different periods and on a very uneven site the builders still

managed to keep the axes of its courtyards square, thus imparting an overall impression of complete regularity and harmony. And so it was: the Alhambra was not planned entirely from the start; it grew outwards gradually over the centuries from the original IX century fortress, the Alcazaba, increasing in splendour as the years went by.

In the XIV century, during the reigns of the great builders, the sultans Yusuf I and his son Mohammad V, the Alhambra stood out like a blaze of white light against the terraced gardens of the Generalife, and on the skyline the silhouette of the Hill of the Sun.
The most likely origin of the name Alhambra,is the colour of the oxidised soil covering the hill.
The name ***al-hamra*** probably contains a double allusion: to the colour of soil of the hill itself and also to part of the name of the founder of the Nasrid dynasty, Muhammed ibn **al-Ahmar** ibn Nasr.

Titus Burckhardt comments, "*The Alhambra was more than a palace, it was a complete city, albeit on a small scale, with its dwellings, administrative offices, garrisons, stables, mosques, schools, baths, cemeteries and gardens. Of all this there only remains the part corresponding to the royal palace itself. And it is almost a miracle that even this has survived, because despite its splendour it was built so insubstantially it almost seems that the builders didn't care. The fortifications as such are strong indeed - they had to be - but the buildings inside the city walls were not built to endure. This would reflect Muslim thought and their ideas about the transitory nature of things: the house of the king is only a temporary dwelling place. This is but one of the many contradictions that the Alhambra offers us if we look at it in the light of the rules concerning the construction of princely dwellings that we take for granted in the rest of Europe. But it is precisely in this "difference" that the hidden meaning of Granadan architecture lies.*

Panorama of Granada by A. Van der Wyngaerde, 1567

In contrast to all the royal residences in Christian Europe, the Alhambra has no façade; it has no main axis about which the buildings are disposed; the rooms are not aligned in such a way as to pass from one to another, from the prelude to the final apotheosis. Instead, at the ends of elusive corridors one finds oneself in hidden courtyards around which rooms are grouped as though by chance. One might never suspect what other worlds may still be concealed behind the walls. It is somewhat like the oriental tale of a traveller who is thrown into a salt quarry and finds there an underground palace replete with orchards and maidens, where he lives happily for twelve years, until one day he opens a secret little doorway which leads him into an even more magnificent palace."

Nothing of this sort can be seen in the Alhambra. Here, the smooth, weightless surfaces of the walls are perforated; the walls, windows and arches, which should manifest their own structural solidity, dissolve into subtle honeycombs, into shimmering light, and the columns in the arcaded rooms are so slim that the structures rising above them seem to be lighter than air.

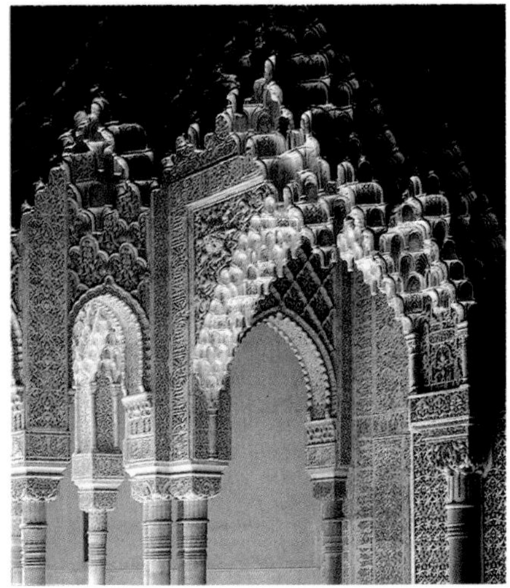

The same writer goes on to add, "*Classical European architecture always tries to involve the observer in the interplay of static forces, and to this end the chief component is the pillar, resembling the human form and giving proportion to what rises above it and what rests upon it; the plinths, pillars, arches and entablature also accentuate these forces, all of which form an integral part of the construction.*

The architecture of the Alhambra doesn't permit the visitor to enter with dramatic mien; it doesn't magnify the experience of power beyond the human scale; it is completely indifferent, limpid and serene, like geometry, of which Plato says that no-one should enter into the mansion of wisdom without it." (T. Burckhardt)

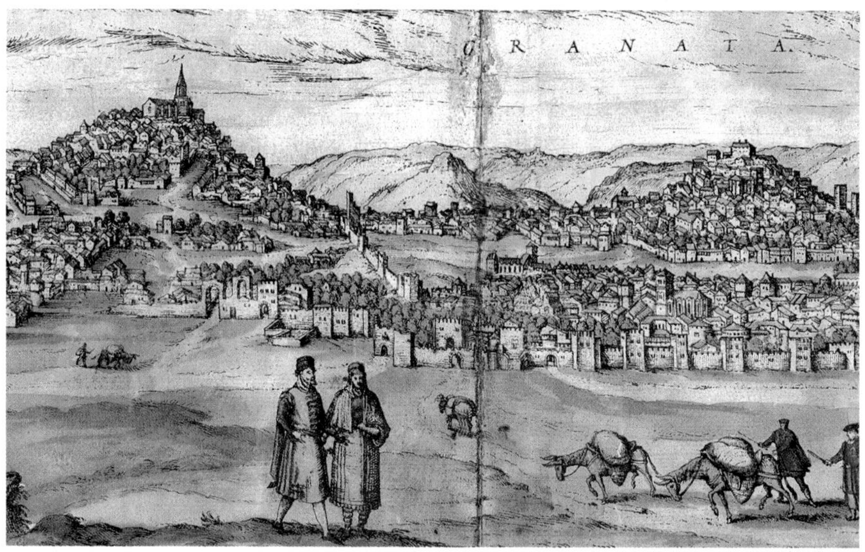

View of Granada in an engraving by Hoefnagel (1563)

At this juncture it might be worth mentioning the use of the term "Muslims", which we use throughout this guide to refer to the inhabitants of *Madinat Al-Hamra* rather than "Arabs". The concept of "Arab" tends to refer to nationality, whereas the builders of this mediaeval wonder were Spanish - grandsons and great grandsons of Spaniards - who spoke various dialects of Arabic and practised the Muslim religion, the product of a fortunate mingling of races that gave rise to a culture incomparable with any other in the world.

A suitable final word to this introduction may be the lines dedicated to the Alhambra by F. Villaespesa, which are written on a plaque beside the Gate of the Pomegranates:

Though the shadows of these walls have long since gone, the memory of them will live on as the final refuge of dreams and art. And then the last nightingale to breath on this earth will build its nest and sing its farewell song among the glorious ruins of the Alhambra.

History

The Alhambra and its Builders

The Alhambra is not a single building born complete and perfect at a particular moment in time; it is much more the product of three centuries of construction at the end of Muslim rule in al-Andalus, and continued throughout the Christian period almost until modern times. As the outstanding example of Islamic art it is a tree whose roots extend deep into times before al-Andalus, to earlier models in Persia and northern Africa. The Christian influence also began to be felt even before the conquest of the Catholic monarchs, during a period in the middle ages in Spain when the exchange of ideas between Christian and Muslim cultures was almost certainly not so radically proscribed as has often been suggested. Some knowledge of the history of the peoples who shaped the Alhambra is essential to an understanding of its multivariety.

TABLE OF CONTEMPORARY EVENTS IN EUROPE

Year	*Reign*	*Muslim Spain*	*Alhambra*	*Christian Spain*
889	*Abd-Allah in Córdoba.*	*Civil wars between Muslims and muladis*	*Sawar ben Handum reconstructs the Alcazaba.*	*866-910, Alfonso III "El Magno" "The Great"*
918	*From 912 'Abd-al Rahman III.*	*Umar b. Hafsun dies. 924, Battle of Valdejunquera.*		*914, León becomes capital of the kingdom of Asturias*
1212		*Battle of Navas de Tolosa.*		*1214, Alfonso VIII dies. Founding of the University of Salamanca.*
1238-1273	*Muhammad I founds Nasrid dynasty in Granada.*	*Conquest of Valencia, 1238, Sevilla, 1248 Niebla, 1262. (artillery used for first time in Spain)*	*The Alcazaba is rebuilt and extended.*	*1217-1252, Fernando III. 1252, Alfonso X. 1213-1276, Jaime I of Aragón.*
1273-1302	*Muhammad II*	*Benimerins arrive to help Muhammad II.*	*Construction of the Wine Gate(?) and Spiked Tower*	*1282-1302, Campaigns by Pedro III of Aragón and Roger de Lauria.*
1314-1325	*Isma'il I*	*Civil wars in the kingdom of Granada. 1319, Battle of Elvira.*	*1319, Earliest extant references to the Generalife. Building of the Mexuar.*	*1314-1325, Jaime II. 1324, Sardinia annexed by the kingdom of Aragón.*
1325-1333	*Muhammad IV*	*Muhammad reconquers Gibraltar with the help of the Emir of Morocco.*	*Tower of the Ladies 1348, The Justice Gate The Alcazaba and Royal*	*1312-1350, Alfonso XI of Castille.*
1333-1354	*Yusuf I*	*1348-1351, Plague in Europe. 1340, Battle of Salado. 1344, Alfonso XI conquers Algeciras.*	*Palaces are joined by a wall. The Palace of Comares is built and the Madrasa founded in Granada.*	*1348, Alfonso XI: Passing of laws of Alcalá. 1349, Alliance between Castille and France.*
1354-1359/ 1362-1391	*Muhammad V*	*1368, Muhammad V reconquers Algeciras.*	*The Comares Tower is decorated. The Palace of the Lions is built.*	*1350-1369, Pedro I. 1366, Rebellion by Enrique of Trastámara. Bertran Duguesclin.*
1392-1408/ 1408-1417	*Muhammad VIII Yusuf III*	*1410, Fernando of Antequera conquers Antequera.*	*The paintings of the Hall of Kings (end of XIV or beginning of XV century).*	*1394, Luna Pope. 1412, Accord of Caspe. 1414, Fernando of Antequera becomes king of Aragón.*
1429-1445	*2 reign of Muhammad IX*	*1431, Battle of la Higueruela.*		*1454-1474, Enrique IV.*
1445-1461	*Sa'd*	*1448, Battle of Alporchones, near Lorca.*	*Tower of the Princesses.*	
1464-1485	*Muley-Hasan (Mulhacén)*	*1481, Muslims conquer Zahara: The war to take Granada begins.*		*1474, Isabel I, crowned queen of Castille. 1469, marries Ferdinand of Aragón.*
1464-1485/ 1482-1491	*Abu-Abd-illah Muhammad XII (Boabdil)*	*1492, Granada falls and Muslim rule in Spain ends.*		*Isabel and Ferdinand named by the pope "The Catholic Monarchs".*

France	*England*	*Germany*
Arabs begin incursions into Switzerland	*878-900, Vikings settle in the north east. 871-900, King Alfred*	*900, Hungarians invade Baveria.*
924, Hungarian raids upon Burgundy and Languedoc.	*1066 Invasion by William of Normandy (William 1).*	*918, Heinrich I of Saxony is crowned king of Germany.*
1214, Phillipe Auguste: Battle of Bouvines.	*1213, King John swears allegiance to Pope Innocent III. 1215, Magna Carta.*	*1212, Freidrich II comes to the throne.*
1250, Crusade by Saint Louis to Egypt. 1265, Charles d'Anjou. 1270, Saint Louis.	*1261-1272, Henry III.*	*1241, Beginnings of the Hansard league. 1247, The Rhein league.*
Treaty of Caltabello. Charles d'Anjou is obliged to give up Sicilly.	*1272-1307, Edward I.*	*1248, Founding of Köln cathedral.*
1306-1311, Trial of the Knights Templar. Phillipe IV "Le Beau" "The Handsome".	*1314, The Scots defeat the English at Bannockburn.*	*1273, Rudolf von Habsburg is crowned Holy Roman Emperor*
1328, The direct line of the Capet dynasty dies out. Phillipe IV of Valois.	*1307-1327, Edward II. 1329, Recognition of Scottish independence*	*1316, Victoria von Brandenburg opposes a coalition between Poland and Scandinavia.*
1349, The heir to the throne is accorded the title of dauphin. 1337, The beginning of the 100 years' war.	*1320-1380, Wycliffe and the Lollards. 1346, Battle of Crecy. 1347, The English take Calais.*	*1331, The Swabian league opposes the ruling nobility.*
1358, "La Jacquerie" peasants revolt. 1355. Ét ts generales. (General States)	*1380, The English fleet is defeated in the Thames.*	*1337, Alliance between Ludwig of Baveria and Edward III of England.*
1393, Dynastic struggles between the houses of Orleans and Burgundy.	*1415, English defeat French at battle of Agincourt.*	*1349, Karl IV founds the University of Prague.*
1412-1431, Joan of Arc. 1428, Siege of Orleans.	*1435, Burgundy achieves independence from England.*	*1356, Karl IV and the "Golden Bull".*
1450, Charles VII regains Normandy. 1453, End of the 100 years' war.	*1455-1485, The War of the Roses.*	*1410-1473, Sigismund is crowned emperor. 1410, Defeat of the Teutonic Order in Prussia.*
1481, Louis XI incorporates Anjou and Proven e into France.	*1477, Willian Caxton starts the first printing press.*	*1411-1440, The Hoenzollern. 1438, The Hapsburgs.*
1483, Charles VIII.	*1485, Henry VII. 1509 Henry VIII marries Catherine, the youngest daughter of the Catholic Monarchs.*	*1477. Wedding of Maximillian I to Marie of Burgundy.*

AL-ANDALUS

In 711 Muslims from the north of Africa entered the Iberian peninsula ostensibly to support the followers of the Visigothic King Witiza against his kinsman Roderick. In the face of the military incompetence of the Christians and the complacency of the population as a whole, within three years the Muslims had taken possession of the entire peninsula except for a narrow strip of land in Cantabria in the north. Though led by Arabs the majority of the invaders were in fact Berbers.

Routes of the Muslim conquerors

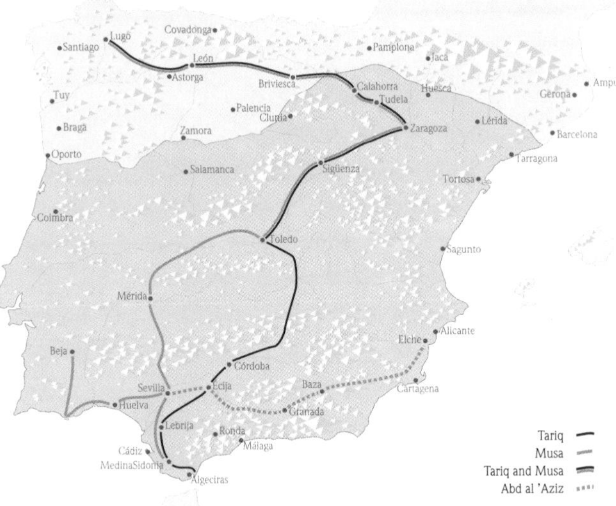

During the following **emirate**, subject to rule from Damascus, a semi-feudal society grew up around the old Christian lords (***muladis***), which at one and the same time incorporated the equalitarian structure of the Berber tribes and initiated attempts to form an Islamic state based on an urban society with a central administration and direct taxation.

'Abd al-Rahman III, founder of an **independent caliphate** in Constantinople, consolidated Islamic reforms, albeit in the face of opposition from the ***muladis*** and discontent on the part of Berbers left out during the redistribution of land. Thus began the age of greatest splendour in Islamic al-Andalus, which was reflected in the hugely impressive mosque at Córdoba and the caliph's capital, the royal city of Madinat al-Zahara. New cities were founded and military emplacements and civil buildings were erected. A well-disciplined army, courts of justice, where ***alfaquis*** applied the laws of the Koran to daily litigation, civil regulations within a central administration and a reasonable level of tolerance as far as a citizen's private life was concerned, all put al-Andalus centuries ahead of the rest of Europe of the time.

The first written reference we have to any construction on the hill of the Alhambra dates from the time of the fitna, *the social upheaval that preceded the Caliphate, when mention is made of a fortress at this place which had resisted a siege by the muladi Umar b. Hafsun.*

At the beginning of the XI century rivalry between groups eager for power divided the caliphate into the so-called **reinos de taifa,** small local fiefdoms which in social terms favoured a cultural and urban renaissance but militarily lost ground to the advancing Christian armies. When Toledo fell to Alfonso VI in 1085 the Muslims in al Andalus turned for help to the Almoravids, an emerging tribe in the Maghrib. Austere and warlike, the Almoravids quickly slowed the Christian advance but subjected the ***taifas*** to their dominion. Shortly afterwards, however, in 1146, they themselves were toppled by the Almohads, who followed them from north Africa. The Almohads recovered much of the lands lost to the Christians, until in 1212 they were heavily defeated by a combined army of Castillians, Aragonese, Navarrese and European crusaders at Navas de Tolosa, close to Bailén. This battle marked the beginning of a steady decline in Islamic power in the Iberian peninsula, interrupted only by the glorious interlude of the Nasrid kingdom.

Written sources mention a palace belonging to the Jewish vizier Samuel Ibn Nagrela at the beginning of the XI century somewhere on the Alhambra, but no remains of this building survive.

After an offensive by Alfonso XI in the XIV century, the kingdom was reduced to what are now the Provinces of Granada, Málaga and Almería, the mountainous areas of al-Andalus, from which it suited the Christians to exact tribute rather than attempt to conquer.

THE NASRID KINGDOM

Muhammad ibn al-Ahmar ibn Nasr was of aristocratic lineage from Arjona (Jaén), where he had fought against the Christian incursions at the beginning of the XIII century. Convinced of the impossibility of defeating the Christians, he first negotiated a pact between various aristocratic families along the frontier and then in 1246 came to an agreement with Ferdinand III, which allowed him to form a unified kingdom in the south of the peninsula with its capital at Granada and its lands stretching from Almería in the east to Gibraltar in the west. Its rulers were warrior families from the frontier to the detriment of the older local families, who had either to integrate into the new order or be dispossessed of their lands.

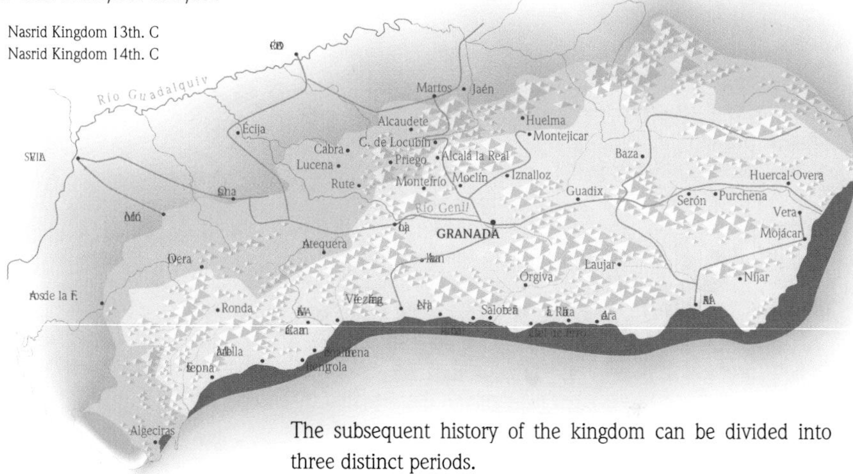

The subsequent history of the kingdom can be divided into three distinct periods.

1 Organisation and reinforcement: according to Manuel Acién, the period from its foundation in 1238 until 1325 exhibits many of the feudal, military characteristics (military equipment, coats of arms and so on) inherited from "contamination" by western customs at the frontier. A complete feudal system as such was never imposed but because of wholesale group migrations and extensive marriage outside the family unit, the age-old ties which had hitherto welded Arab and Berber clans so closely together had certainly all but disappeared by this time. This new society, arising some six hundred years after the first invasion, was organised upon economic and political principles and the ruling families became the founders of authentic noble lineages. Closely dependent upon this political system were the state functionaries and, related to these, the alfaquis, whose job it was to interpret the Koran and who saw their power increase considerably during this time.

The Alcazaba expresses the westernisation of this period. The watchtower (Torre de la Vela), built by Muhammad I, is a perfect example of a feudal residence. Other towers of the Alcazaba, such as the Torre del Homenaje (the Keep), were either rebuilt or reshaped at this time. At the same time, however, the first palaces, such as the Partal, and granges such as the Generalife were designed according to Islamic tradition

2 The **period of splendour** coincided with a movement towards a stricter interpretation of the tenets of Islam, instigated by **Yusuf I** (1333-54) and his son **Muhammad V** (1354-91). With the rise in influence of two lineages linked to alfaqui religious circles, the banu al-Sarray (Abencerrajes) and the banu Kumasa, there began a closer adherence to the traditional ways of al-Andalus. The sultan was an absolute monarch, although he might delegate some of his responsibilities to viziers or ministers. There was also a consultative assembly, the ***Maylis***, made up of prestigious figures in the kingdom, and a court of justice. A form of exchequer obtained its revenues both from direct taxation and indirect taxes on commerce, baths, inheritances and the like. Several typically Islamic buildings were erected in Granada at this time, including the ***Madrasa***, a school of Koranic studies, forebear to the later Christian university, and the ***Maristan***, a hospital devoted mainly to the care of the mentally ill. Commerce was encouraged by the construction of the ***Alcaicería*** (general market) and ***alhóndigas*** (mercantile exchanges), one of which, the ***Corral del Carbón,*** is still standing.

3 **Decline**: During the XV century the redistribution of power between warrior lineages led to the absence of any well-defined territorial administration and ever increasing inter-family feuding. This was the setting for the last civil war, between Muley-Abul Hassan (Mulhacén) and his son Abu-Ahd-Illah (Boabdil), kindled by Aixa, wife to one and mother of the other, in an attempt to thwart her husband's Christian concubine, Isabel de Solís, who had her eyes on the throne for her own son. At the same time they came up against the Catholic monarchs, Ferdinand of Aragón and Isabel of Castille, who, having pacified their own domains, were now intent on annexing the Kingdom of Granada to Christendom. They finally achieved their aim in 1492 and agreed to a treaty of surrender on the part of the Muslims that in principle respected the rights of the defeated citizens of Granada but which in practice was not fulfilled over scrupulously.

Yusuf I and Muhammad V converted the Alhambra into a palatine city, which could provide for the growing needs of the administration of their kingdom. The Alcazaba remained as a purely military citadel, divided from the private and governmental areas, which in turn were separate from each other. Under Yusuf I the council chamber of the Mexuar palace was separate from his private residence in the Comares palace, although some ambassadors were received in the great throne room in the Comares palace itself. This complete separation between the sultan's public and private life was completed by Muhammad V, who lived in his own Palace of the Lions, keeping the Comares Palace for state use. All around the royal palaces arose mansions belonging to important families, a mosque, the private houses of functionaries, soldiers and artisans, and public and private baths. Access to the city would normally have been via the northern Arms Gate to reach the Alcazaba and palaces, and via the Gate of the Seven Floors at the south to get to the residential areas.

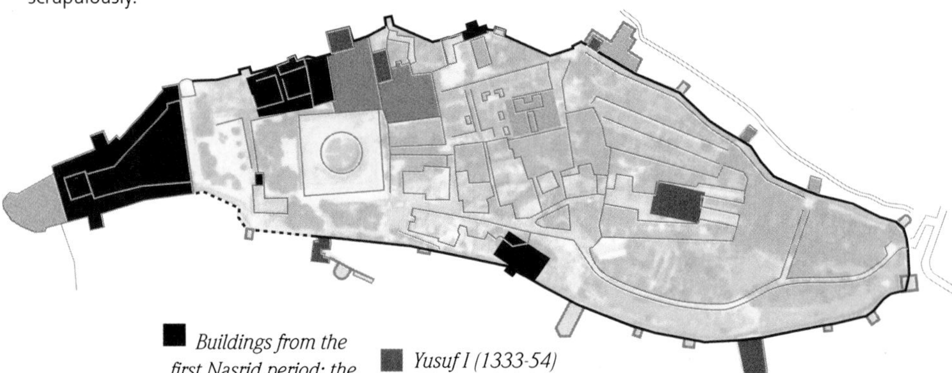

■ *Pre-Nasrid: the heart of the Alcazaba.*

■ *Buildings from the first Nasrid period: the rest of the Alcazaba; the Machuca-Mexuar zone; the Wine Gate; various demolished palaces; the Partal Gate, the Palace of the Abencerrajes; and a first phase of the Generalife.*

■ *Yusuf I (1333-54)*
■ *Muhammad V (1354-91*
The whole palace area was completed. The Gate of Justice and the Gate of the Seven Floors were built. Of the same period was a palace on the site where the parador stands today

■ *During this period Yusuf III built a palace (no longer standing) where the gardens of the Partal are now. Bastions were added to the outer walls and living quarters were built in some of the towers, such as the Tower of the Princesses*

The fortress was consolidated and adapted in general to new styles of military tactics. The royal palaces were refurbished to suit Castillian tastes. The whole orientation of life in the citadel was altered to fit in with the new road leading to it, which we today know as the Cuesta de Gomérez. The focus of attention was drawn away from the Arms Gate to the north and the main entrances became the Justice Gate and the Wine Gate to the south. The Gate of the Pomegranates and Charles V Fountain came to symbolise this movement in gravity towards the south.

THE CHRISTIAN PERIOD

In 1453 Constantinople fell to the Turks after centuries of siege. This was considered to be a grave blow to the whole of Christendom, so the conquest of the Alhambra, the last redoubt of Islam in the western world, was seen in Christian eyes as being a counterblow to settle the score. For the Catholic monarchs it was the culmination of a centuries-old Castillian dream, the capture of a most coveted prize, and as such it had to be preserved and adapted for generations still to come. It was for this reason that their grandson, Charles V, wanted to make the Alhambra the centre of his empire, an empire that looked towards Africa as a logical area of expansion against the might of the Turk Suleiman the Magnificent, who had the audacity to besiege Vienna.

The Mexuar was turned into a chapel, incorporating the small courtyard that had before afforded access to the Gilded Chamber (Cuarto Dorado).
The open garden outside the Lindaraja courtyard was surrounded by a covered gallery and the chambers of Charles V were added on to the Comares Tower.
In 1495 a Franciscan friary was built upon the ruins of a Nasrid palace.
The Alcazaba was finally joined to the rest of the city by filling the gully that separated them with a cistern covered by an open square. The perimeter was closed by repairing some of the towers in the outer walls and by adding the Torre del Cubo (The Tub) and Torre de la Tahona (The Mill Tower) in the XVI century.
The main mosque was converted into a Christian church dedicated to St. Mary of the Alhambra.
The Palace of Charles V was laid out but remained unfinished.

Nevertheless, the discovery of America shifted political and economic interests towards the Atlantic, particularly after the Turks were defeated at the Battle of Lepanto. King Phillip II continued his father's work to some extent but without enthusiasm. Thus the Alhambra as we see it today represents the sediment of many influences collected over the centuries, which have gradually altered its shape outwards from a

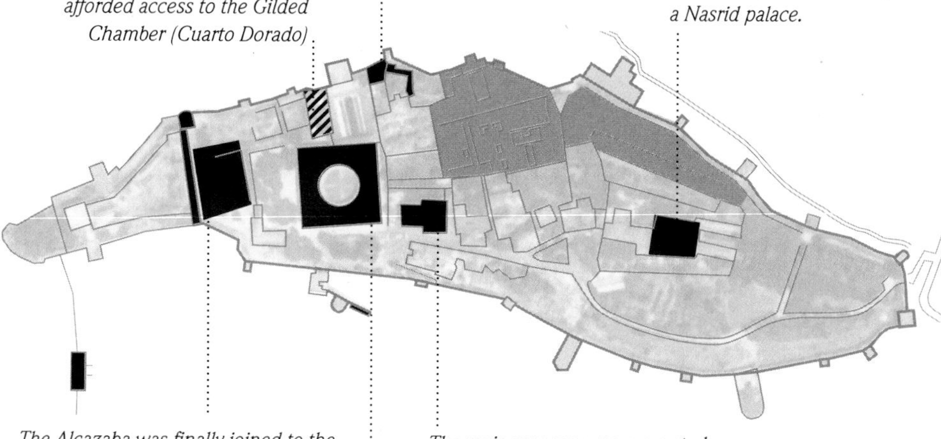

central core. To take a guided tour around its nooks and crannies, to view an entire cross-section of its structure, allows one to feel not only the splendour of any particular moment in the royal city's history but also to understand the succession of cultures that have gone to shape it over the centuries. It is well worth the effort, because understanding leads the mind on a journey that is both a delight for the senses and a stimulus to the imagination.

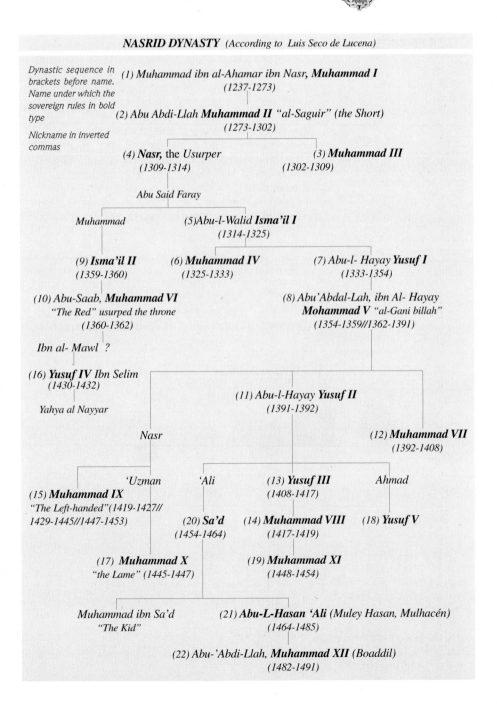

NASRID DYNASTY *(According to Luis Seco de Lucena)*

Dynastic sequence in brackets before name. Name under which the sovereign rules in bold type

Nickname in inverted commas

(1) Muhammad ibn al-Ahamar ibn Nasr, ***Muhammad I***
(1237-1273)

(2) Abu Abdi-Llah ***Muhammad II*** *"al-Saguir" (the Short)*
(1273-1302)

(4) **Nasr,** the *Usurper*
(1309-1314)

(3) ***Muhammad III***
(1302-1309)

Abu Said Faray

Muhammad

(5)Abu-l-Walid ***Isma'il I***
(1314-1325)

(9) ***Isma'il II***
(1359-1360)

(6) ***Muhammad IV***
(1325-1333)

(7) Abu-l- Hayay ***Yusuf I***
(1333-1354)

(10) Abu-Saab, ***Muhammad VI***
"The Red" usurped the throne
(1360-1362)

(8) Abu'Abdal-Lah, ibn Al- Hayay
Mohammad V *"al-Gani billah"*
(1354-1359//1362-1391)

Ibn al- Mawl ?

(16) ***Yusuf IV*** *Ibn Selim*
(1430-1432)

Yahya al Nayyar

(11) Abu-l-Hayay ***Yusuf II***
(1391-1392)

Nasr

(12) ***Muhammad VII***
(1392-1408)

'Uzman

'Ali

(13) ***Yusuf III***
(1408-1417)

Ahmad

(15) ***Muhammad IX***
"The Left-handed"(1419-1427// 1429-1445//1447-1453)

(20) ***Sa'd***
(1454-1464)

(14) ***Muhammad VIII***
(1417-1419)

(18) ***Yusuf V***

(17) ***Muhammad X***
"the Lame" (1445-1447)

(19) ***Muhammad XI***
(1448-1454)

Muhammad ibn Sa'd
"The Kid"

(21) ***Abu-L-Hasan 'Ali*** *(Muley Hasan, Mulhacén)*
(1464-1485)

(22) Abu-'Abdi-Llah, ***Muhammad XII*** *(Boaddil)*
(1482-1491)

THE TOUR OF THE ALHAMBRA

The various palaces, towers and gardens of the Alhambra occupy a considerable area and you should allow at least half a day for your visit if not the entire day. Your ticket is divided into three sections the **Alcazaba,** the **Royal Palaces** and the **Generalife**. The visit to the Alcazaba and the Generalife are unrestricted timewise but **you must enter the Nasrid Palaces within half an hour of the time specified on your ticket.** There are other parts of the Alhambra such as the woods, some of the gates and the Palace of Charles V which you can visit without charge and at your leisure.

The plan on the following double page gives you an overall view of the whole site of the Alhambra. Footpaths connecting the various areas are marked. It is important that you should check the time of your entry into the Nasrid Palaces printed on your ticket and organise the rest of your itinerary around this time.

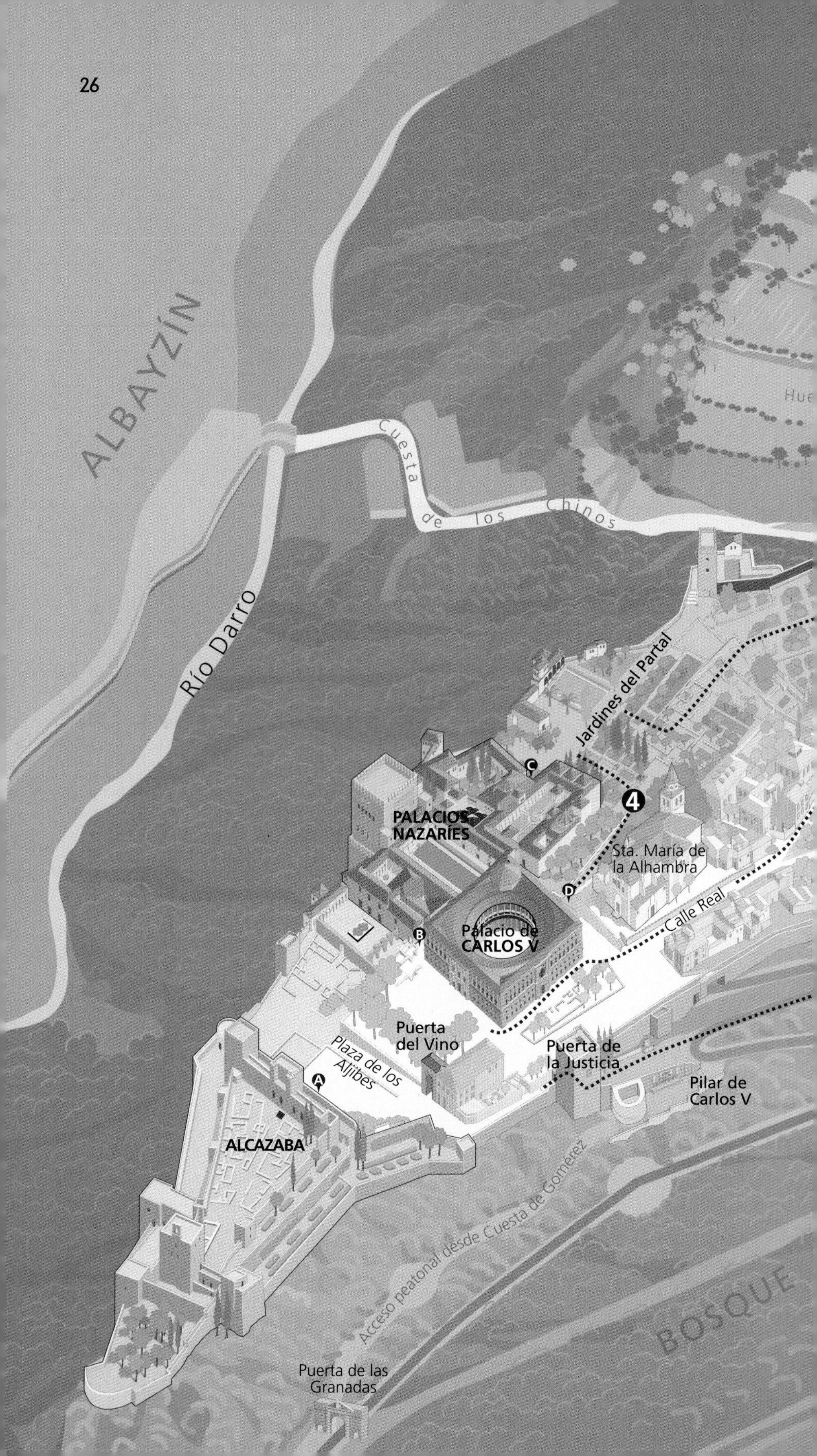

ALBAYZÍN

Río Darro

Cuesta de los Chinos

Jardines del Partal

C

4

PALACIOS NAZARÍES

Sta. María de la Alhambra

D

Calle Real

B

Palacio de CARLOS V

Puerta del Vino

Plaza de los Aljibes

A

Puerta de la Justicia

Pilar de Carlos V

ALCAZABA

Acceso peatonal desde Cuesta de Gomérez

BOSQUE

Puerta de las Granadas

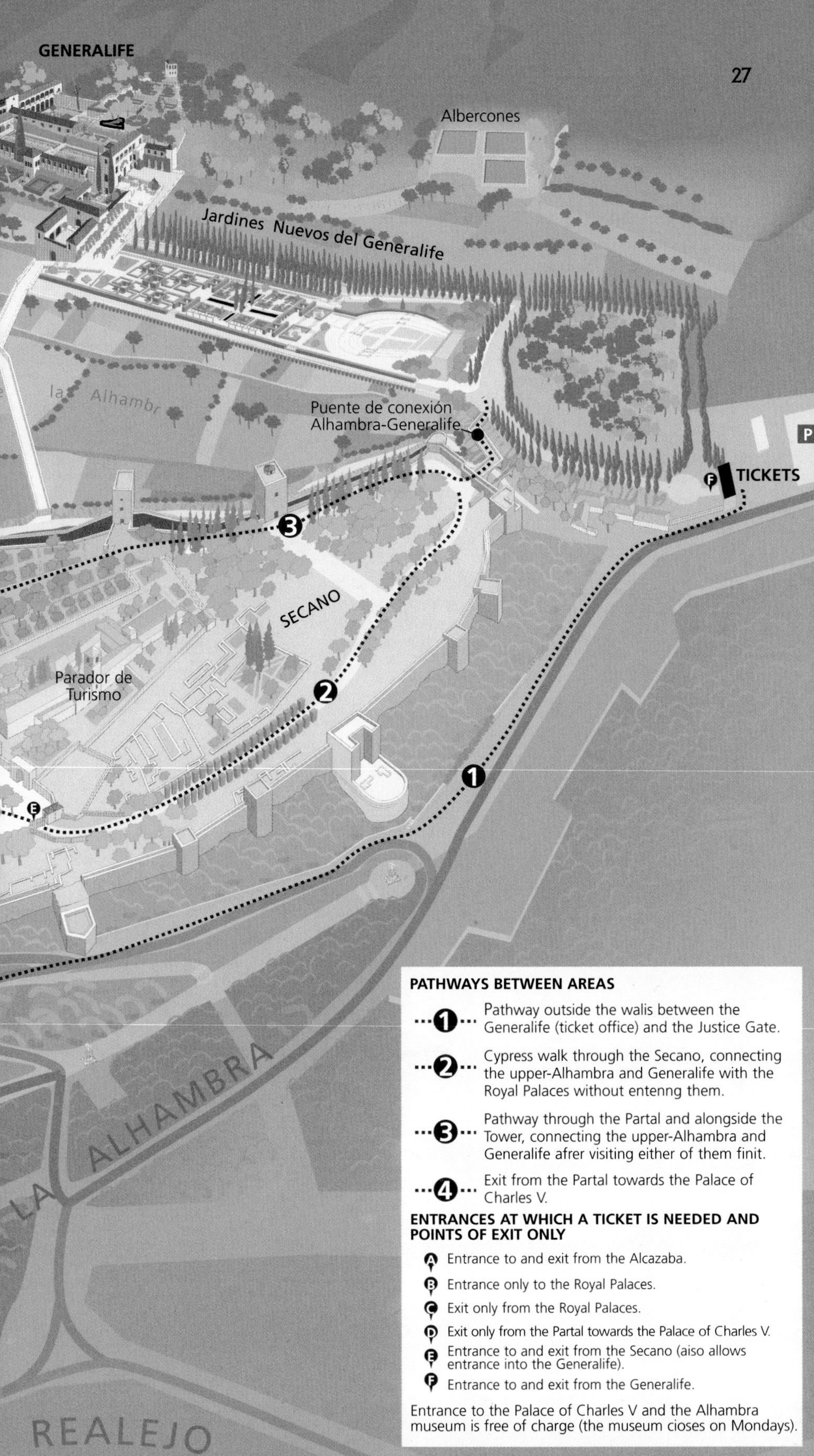
GENERALIFE
Albercones
Jardines Nuevos del Generalife
Puente de conexión Alhambra-Generalife
P
TICKETS
SECANO
Parador de Turismo
LA ALHAMBRA
REALEJO
PATHWAYS BETWEEN AREAS
1 Pathway outside the walis between the Generalife (ticket office) and the Justice Gate.
2 Cypress walk through the Secano, connecting the upper-Alhambra and Generalife with the Royal Palaces without entenng them.
3 Pathway through the Partal and alongside the Tower, connecting the upper-Alhambra and Generalife afrer visiting either of them finit.
4 Exit from the Partal towards the Palace of Charles V.
ENTRANCES AT WHICH A TICKET IS NEEDED AND POINTS OF EXIT ONLY
A Entrance to and exit from the Alcazaba.
B Entrance only to the Royal Palaces.
C Exit only from the Royal Palaces.
D Exit only from the Partal towards the Palace of Charles V.
E Entrance to and exit from the Secano (aiso allows entrance into the Generalife).
F Entrance to and exit from the Generalife.
Entrance to the Palace of Charles V and the Alhambra museum is free of charge (the museum cioses on Mondays).

HOW TO USE THIS GUIDE

This guide is organised to start from the Charles V Fountain, which is where you will arrive first if you walk up the ***Cuesta de Gomérez*** from the city, or walk down from the ticket office at the Generalife following footpath 1. It continues to the Justice Gate - Alcazaba - Nasrid palaces (Mexuar - Comares - Lions) and the Partal palace gardens, and then follows footpath 3 to the upper Alhambra (the Secano) and the Generalife. Finally you come back to the Palace of Charles V by footpath 2. You can, however, change the route to suit yourself and look for the information you require by consulting the contents, or finding the section you want according to the coloured edges to the pages. You may also refer to the subject index at the end of the guide

LAY-OUT OF EACH CHAPTER

Each chapter begins with an introductory page. ▶

Name of the area

Position of the area in relation to the monument as a whole.

Background motif for the chapter to be found on the edge of all the pages for rapid identification.

Introductory explanation to the chapter.

Followed by a detailed plan of the places described in the following pages of the chapter itself. ▼

Plan. The names in **bold type** refer to items explained in detail in the chapter.

Name of the chapter and its identifying symbol.

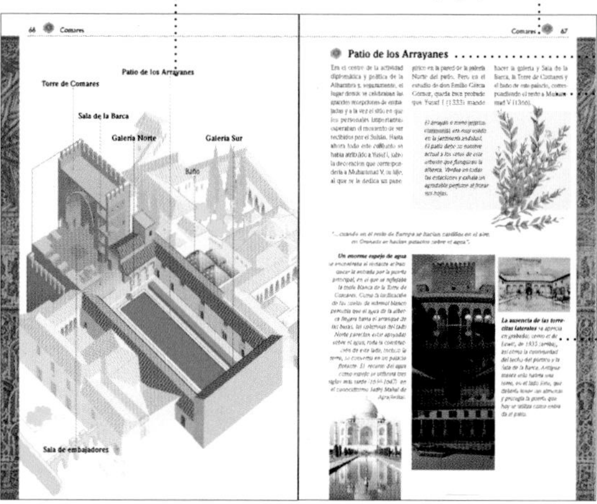

Name: corresponds to those features emphasised in **bold type** in the plan.

Introductory explanation: in normal type, provides general information about the feature in question.

Additional information: in italics, always associated to an image, diagram etc., which it explains.

Subjects of interest: in a coloured frame and different lettering, give extra information about subjects such as craftsmanship, engineering, social organisation and so on.

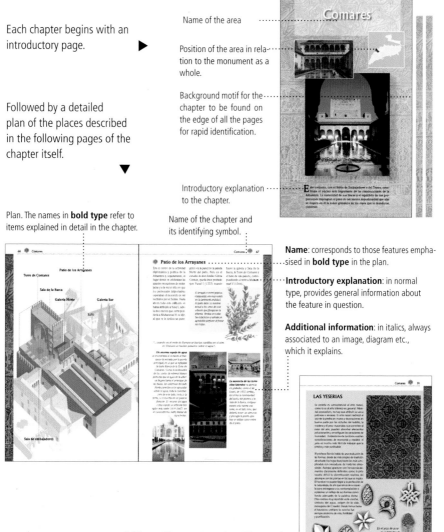

Charles V Fountain

The Charles V Fountain reflects the desire of the conquerors of Islam to christianise the Nasrid city without detracting from its past glory and to emphasise its importance as the new imperial capital. Within this context of respecting the old whilst affirming the reality of the new, this magnificent fountain was placed at the entrance to the Alhambra. It was designed by Pedro Machuca and sculpted by Niccolo da Corte in 1543 to fill a new space and define a new era.

Shield of the Tendilla family

Imperial shield *bearing the double-headed eagle of the Hapsburgs*

Pillars of Hercules

Pomegranate, *the symbol of the city.*

The shields of the city of Granada, the Tendilla family and the Hapsburgs are repeated throughout the ornamentation of the fountain, which is in the finest classical style.

It is not certain whether the mysterious masks are meant to represent Granada's three rivers, the Genil, the Darro and the Beiro, or three seasons, symbolised in the vegetal ornaments: ears of wheat for summer, flowers for spring and grapes for autumn. Whatever their intended significance, they are later baroque additions to the fountain.

The Alhambra woods

In order to facilitate its defence the hill surrounding the Alhambra was originally stripped of all vegetation, and thus it appears in contemporary engravings. During the reign of Charles V poplar trees were planted alongside the roads but it wasn't until the XIX century that the Duke of Wellington planted a woodland of new trees, including horse-chestnuts, elms and planes, which survive to this day to give welcome shade to those who walk up the hill to the Alhambra.

Puerta de la Justicia

The Justice Gate

This gate is today almost the only entrance to the walled confines of the Madinat al-Hamra (The Citadel of the Alhambra). It forms a projecting square tower with its rear edge butting against the city wall. Without doubt the most important gateway to the whole royal city, it rises up imposingly at the top of a long slope, defying time and successive generations. Neither centuries of neglect nor the holy-week processions of our own time have been able to reduce its majesty.

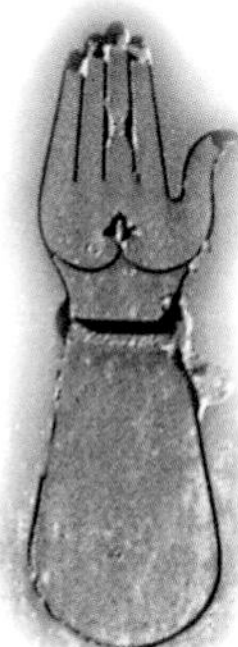

*The raised **open hand** carved into the keystone of the outer arch has been the subject of various interpretations; the most plausible of these would seem to be that it represents the five fingers referred to by Muslims as al-Hamza, the five basic precepts of Islam: a belief in one God and in his prophet Muhammad, to pray five times every day, to give alms, to fast during Ramadan and to go on a pilgrimage to Mecca at least once in one's lifetime.*

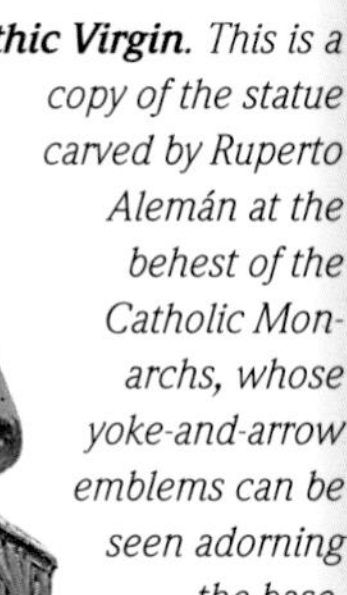

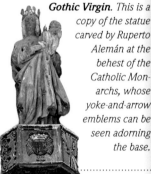

***Gothic Virgin**. This is a copy of the statue carved by Ruperto Alemán at the behest of the Catholic Monarchs, whose yoke-and-arrow emblems can be seen adorning the base.*

"This gate, called Bab al-Sari'a, [...], was erected by the emir of the Muslims, the righteous warrior sultan [...] Abu-l-Hayyay Yusuf [...]. The work was finished in the month of the Glorious Nativity of the 749th year. (June 1348)

*The **tasselled key**, carved on the inner arch, has also been interpreted in various ways, but it may well have been part of the arms of the Nasrid dynasty in Granada, as claimed by Hurtado de Mendoza, a Christian commander of the time. It is also to be seen on the nearby Wine Gate and in the Dismounting Yard at the entrance to the Generalife*

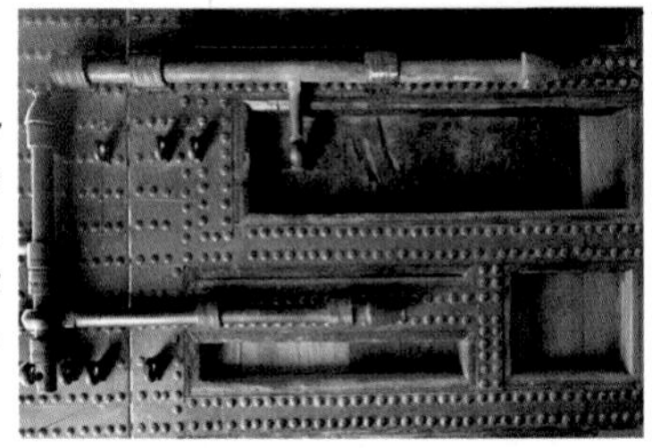

*Just inside the inner arch hang two massive **iron-bound doors**, with their original locks and bolts.*

***Marble Capital** belonging to the inner arch; in its day it would have been polychromed as would the rest of the doorway*

Between the outer arch, which was probably never closed by doors, and the inner arch there is a confined ***defensive area****, typical of Nasrid military building, where those defending the gate could hurl rocks, boiling oil or molten lead from the tower above onto any assailants trying to break down the door to the inner arch below them.*

Beyond these arches the ***entrance continues to rise in the form of a ramp*** *with four right-angled corners covered by squinched vaults containing lunettes.*

This way of ***breaking up a straight run into the city*** *is very much in character with the strategic nature of the gate; every corner provides a potential point of resistance. This feature is typical of Almohad military architecture.*

Once past the gate itself an assailant would arrive at the ***corraleta****, a wide passageway where horsemen would be arrayed waiting for the order to charge downhill against the uphill attack. To the right of the gate there is a pathway which runs between the parapets around the entire city wall, sometimes covered, sometimes open to the sky, but always protected sufficiently to allow the guards to make the rounds on horseback.*

Right: part of the wall, reconstructed with head-stones from a nearby Muslim cemetery.

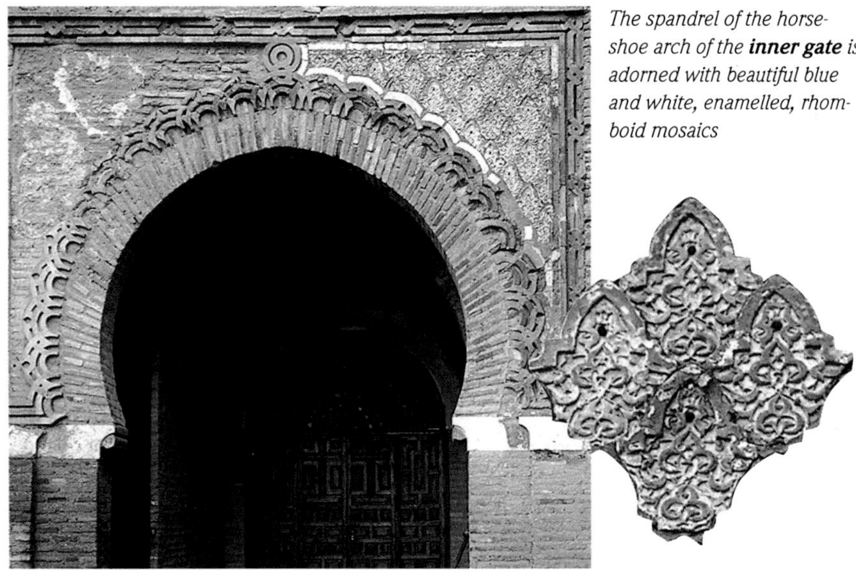

The spandrel of the horseshoe arch of the ***inner gate*** *is adorned with beautiful blue and white, enamelled, rhomboid mosaics*

The names Justice Gate or Gate of Law may derive from the inscription which reads, "May God allow the justice of Islam to prevail within". It has also been called the Esplanade Gate because of the esplanade that used to spread out in front of it before the two present-day roads were laid, one climbing to the left towards the Generalife and the other descending through the woods to the right.

The horseshoe arch

The art of the Goths tended to reflect their easily transportable possessions: swords, buckles, precious objects and the like, and it is these symbols which adorn their late-Roman architecture. One of the most fortunate contributions that the Visigoths made to Spanish architecture, however, was the horseshoe arch, which the Arab invaders took as their own and used extensively and with consummate skill (see the Grand Mosque in Córdoba, for example). The horseshoe arch became a symbol of Muslim architecture and was exported from Spain throughout the Islamic world.

Right: the VI century church of ***San Juan de Baños*** *in the Province of Palencia, where the Gothic horseshoe arch predates the first Arab invasion by 50 years.*

Puerta del Vino

The Wine Gate

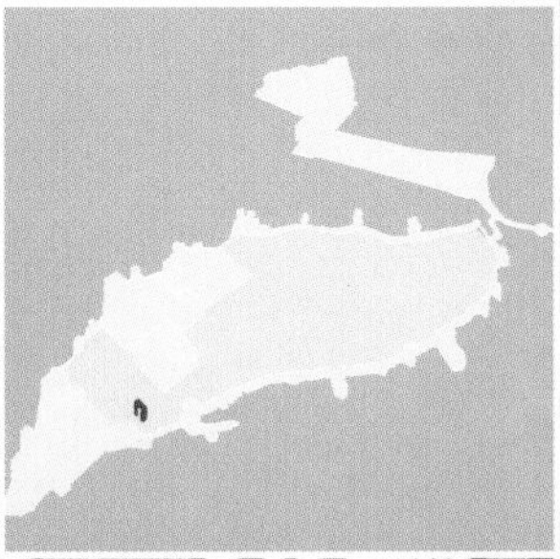

Grab. de Girault de Prangey, 1837

It is generally accepted that the name of this gate derives from the tax-free wine that was sold inside the portal from 1554. There were other gates nearby but within the intricate labyrinth of the mediaeval city this was the gate which gave most direct access to the higher reaches of the city, home to some 2,000 inhabitants. At this point the Royal Way, the main artery of the *medina* began; it was also a crossroads and the dividing line between the military and civil areas of the town.

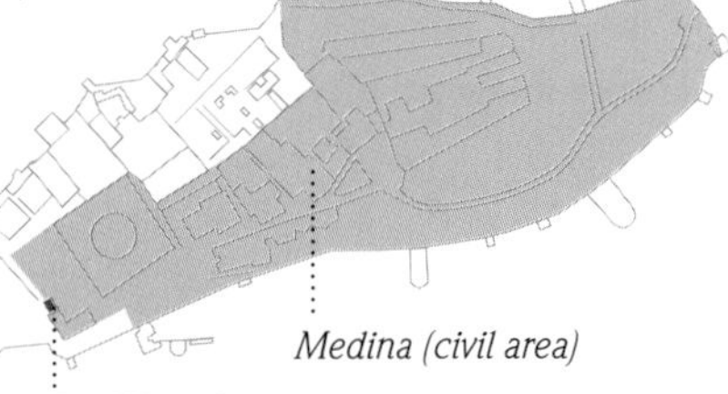

*The **eastern façade** is the most interesting and ornamental. It contains fine, ceramic tiling, painted and fired using the dry-cord technique (see preceding page), elaborate decorative gesso (left) and vestiges of stucco-work with hints of polychroming, which must at one time have covered many of the walls of the Alhambra.*

*The straight entrance through this gate with no corners to hinder an attacker and the **window with its jalousie** lend support to the idea that it was intended for civil rather than military use.*

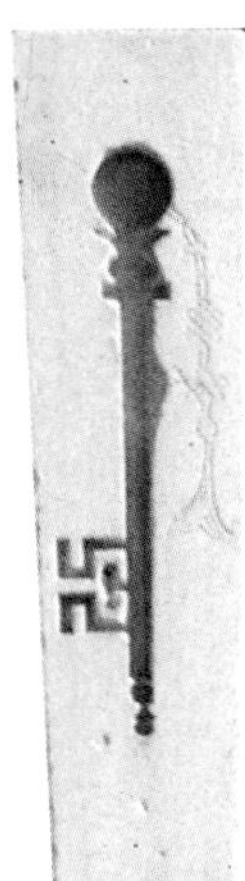

*The **western façade** (right) is older and more roughly executed. The gateway itself has one of the few still extant pointed horseshoe arches. It is also emblazoned with the mysterious symbolic key*

*Inside the **gate** are the typical benches where the guards would have sat, protected from the elements. The small room thus formed is covered by a magnificent groined vault similar to that in the Gate of Arms in the northern wall of the Alcazaba.*

Alcazaba

The Alcazaba
(The Old Citadel)

Laborde, 1812

The Alcazaba, unjustly forgotten by all those who after the Christian conquest wrote in dazzling terms about the Nasrid palaces, is the solitary forbear of an entire palatine city which would later come to be known as *Madinat al-Hamra* (The citadel of the Alhambra). It is referred to in the accounts of the civil wars in the IX century and battles against the invading Almoravids and Almohads by various different names such as the fortress of Elvira or Granada castle until, from the XIII century onwards, the name *qa'lat al-hamra* (the red castle) becomes fixed and it is by this name that we know it today.

Torre del Homenaje *(The Keep). This is one of the oldest towers of the Alcazaba, probably dating back to the caliphate. Archaeological comparisons of the building materials of the actual tower and those in its foundations suggest that it may have been rebuilt by Muhammad I upon the ruins of a previous IX century structure.*

Puerta de las Armas *(The Arms Gate). This gate used to be the main entrance to the Alcazaba. It butts onto the inner precinct of the Alcazaba as a flanking tower to the* ***Watchtower.***

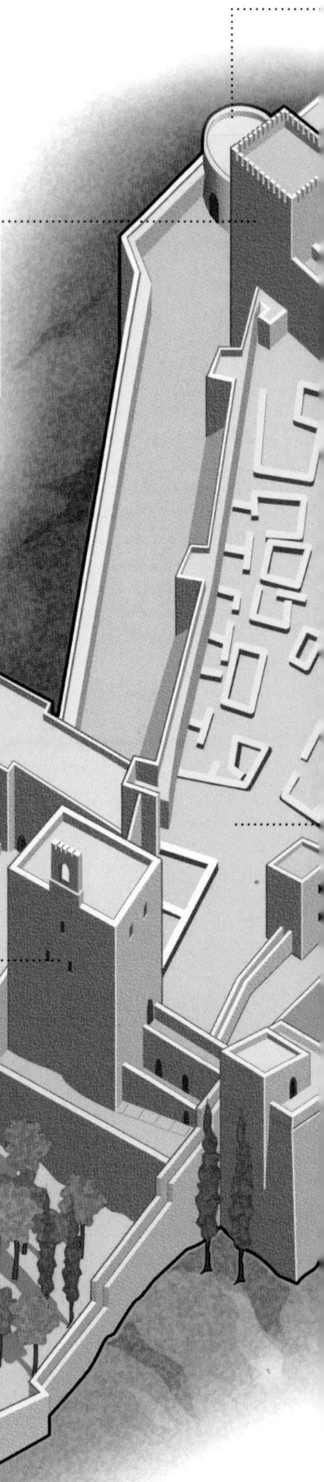

Torre de la Vela *(The Watchtower) This tower was originally built by the founder of the Nasrid dynasty, Muhammad ben Nasr "al Ahmar" (ruled 1238-73), as his feudal residence.*

Cubo de la Alhambra *(TheTub). This round, squat tower houses the Puerta de la Tahona (Gate of the Flour Mill), a XVI century renaissance addition after the Christian conquest.*

Torre Quebrada *(The Cracked Tower), known thus because of the great crack in its wall, stretching like a wound from top to bottom, which can be seen from the Plaza de los Aljibes. The tower has been filled in up to the height of the city wall but has two more floors above this level.*

Ticket The Cistern Square

Plaza de los Aljibes

Puerta del Vino

The Wine Gate

Plaza de las Armas *(The Arms Square). From the top of a cobbled slope a central street containing buildings of a multitude of uses led away from this square .*

Torre de la Sultana *(The Sultana's Tower). As the photograph below shows, this tower rises majestically above the Jardín del Adarve. It must have lost some of its slender elegance, however when the deep fosse was filled in to make the garden.*

Jardín del Adarve *(The Parapet Garden)A deep fosse separated the outer and inner ramparts until the beginning of the XVII century, when it was filled in with rubble and earth by the Marquis of Mondéjar to make this garden.*

Torre de la Pólvora *(The Gunpowder Tower). From here a pathway spans the deep ravine of the Cuesta de Gomérez across the top of a gate, thus linking the citadel to the Vermillion Towers on the other side.*

Plaza de los Aljibes.
(The Cistern Square)

For a long time, even after Muhammad ibn Nasr "Al-Amahr" arrived in Granada in 1238, the Alcazaba was an isolated fortress, separated by a deep gully from the plain to its east, where the royal palaces were later to be built.

During the reign of Yusuf 1 (1333 - 54) a long stretch of curtain wall and towers were erected along the edge of this gully, some of the remains of which can still be seen in the Cistern Square close to the Wine Gate.

*Yusuf also joined the walls of the Alcazaba to those of the royal palace by way of **a parapet walkway** along the battlements, which was reached via a stairway in the Mill Tower, rediscovered in 1955 below the so-called Tub Tower.*

*In 1494, two years after the Christian conquest, the Count of Tendilla, had the gulley filled in to make an **aljibe,** or water cistern, using the Cracked Tower as a filter for the water. He covered the cistern with the square that still exists today in front of the Alcazaba.*

Alcazaba

Palacios - Palace

*The Alcazaba comprises **two clearly distinguishable wards,** one within the other. The smaller of the two, the inner ward (coloured brown), may well be Roman in origin, as might be deduced from the stone blocks in the footings of the walls (below).*

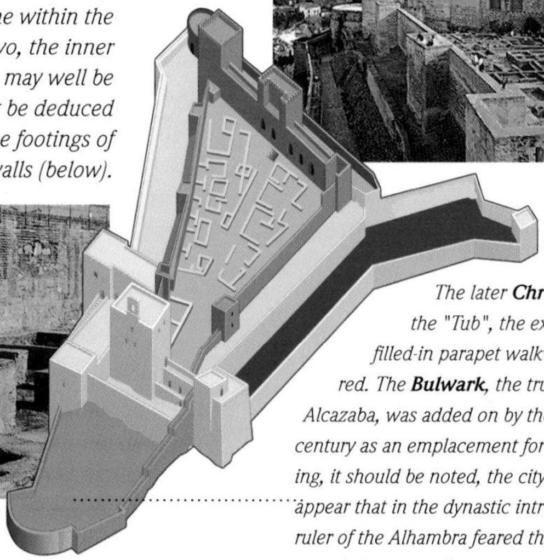

*The later **Christian additions:** the "Tub", the external wall and filled-in parapet walkway, are coloured red. The **Bulwark,** the true prow of the Alcazaba, was added on by the Nasrids in the XV century as an emplacement for their artillery, facing, it should be noted, the city itself. It would appear that in the dynastic intrigues of the time the ruler of the Alhambra feared the inhabitants of the town below more than any possible foreign invader.*

Torre y Puerta de las Armas

(The Arms Tower and Gate). This was the main entrance to the outer bailey and was equipped with a portcullis controlled from the floor immediately above the gate, which could only be reached from the battlements of the Alcazaba.

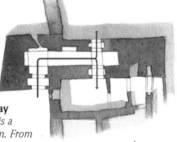

Beyond the entrance a wide **passageway** *turns sharply to the right, where there is a spacious room, obviously the guardroom. From here the path forks to the left towards the royal palaces and to the right to the Alcazaba.*

On the way to the royal palaces *a visitor, whether on foot or on horseback, had to cover a distance of some ninety metres with his unarmed right side (the shield was carried on the left arm) exposed to archers stationed on the inner wall or on the parapet of the keep (right).*

After passing another inspection in what is now ***the Tub*** *(above) he would arrive at the market, the remains of which are still visible. In consonance with its popular name, this Christian tower is round and squat, making it less vulnerable to the artillery fire that was being used to ever greater effect at this time.*

For anyone wanting to visit the Alcazaba the approach was no easier. He had to leave his mount at the stables next door to the Arms Gate and then follow a path so narrow that two people could hardly walk abreast, up and down steps and around corners, for a distance of at least three times the width of the Watchtower. All this time he was under the scrutiny of the soldiers on the ramparts, who could stop a whole army if they wanted to just by throwing rocks, boiling oil or molten lead down onto the tortuous passageway running below them

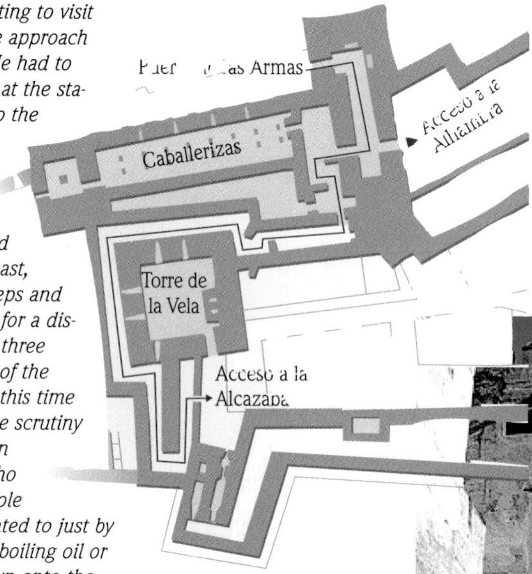

In the earliest extant painting of Granada, probably by the Flemish painter Petrus Cristus (ca. 1500), now in the Mateu collection (below), there is a ***door leading into the Alcazaba*** *which had been blocked up centuries ago. Through careful examination of the picture in 1894, Manuel Gómez Moreno was able to rediscover the door hidden within the wall (right).*

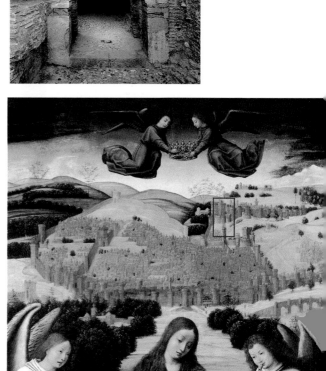

Plaza de las Armas (The Arms Square)

Within the inner precinct there still remain the foundations of a bath-house for the soldiers at the foot of the watchtower and small houses along each side of a main street, intended for officers of the garrison, armourers, blacksmiths and the such. There are also water cisterns, and a subterranean dungeon beneath the eastern wall, in which the prisoners' sleeping areas are laid out in brick.

View of the Arms Square from the Watchtower

Torre de la Vela

(The Watchtower)

The watchtower measures 16m by 16m and is 27m high. Its four floors underwent considerable transf ormation when they were converted into living quarters after the Christian conquest. The tower is not quite so high as it was originally, having lost its battlements in the various catastrophes that it has seen since the XVI century: first an earthquake in 1522; then in 1590 a gunpowder factory exploded in the valley of the river Darro just below, leaving it considerably the worse for wear; and finally in 1882 the bell gable was struck by lightning. This has since been replaced, but in the centre of the west wall rather than in its original position at the north-west corner of the tower.

*In the engraving by Doré (1862) shown above **the bell gable** can be seen still in its original position. The bell, founded in 1733 to replace the original, was rung to tell the smallholders in the vega (the fertile plain to the west of the city) when their irrigation turns began and ended. It has also sounded the alarm to the inhabitants of Granada at moments of danger or distress, such as the day the Alhambra itself caught fire in 1890. Nowadays the bell is rung electronically.*

The top of the Watchtower offers the visitor magnificent, uninterrupted views all around.

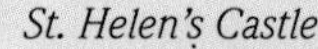

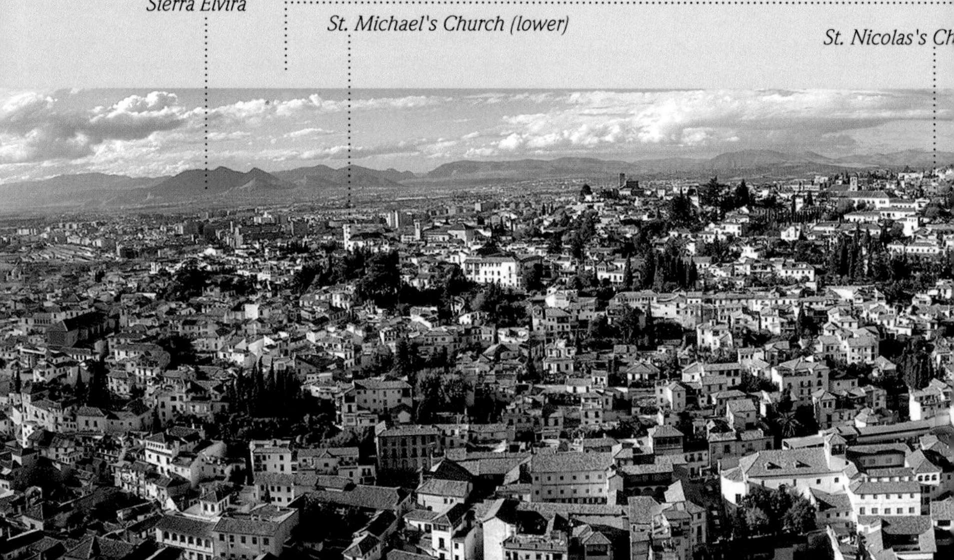

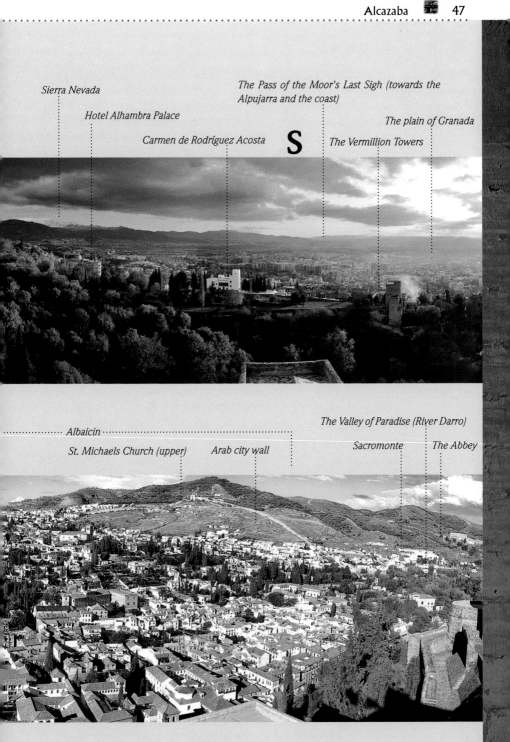

Sierra Nevada

The Pass of the Moor's Last Sigh (towards the Alpujarra and the coast)

Hotel Alhambra Palace

The plain of Granada

Carmen de Rodríguez Acosta

S

The Vermillion Towers

This is the Granada that Gautier called *"Celestial Jerusalem"* and that which the Córdoban al-Saqundi praised as being *"nourishing to the eye and uplifting to the soul"*.

Granada's city walls

The Alhambra represented a key element in a complex system of walls which surrounded the city of Granada, although its position is somewhat curious in that it really remained outside the main body of the town, as though fearing the inhabitants of Granada more than enemies from afar. When the new residential quarters that quickly grew up around the fortresses of the Albaicín began to block their way into the surrounding countryside, al-Ahmar and his descendants took to the castle on the red hill, which, although needing considerable repair, offered them open terrain if they ever needed to flee in a hurry.

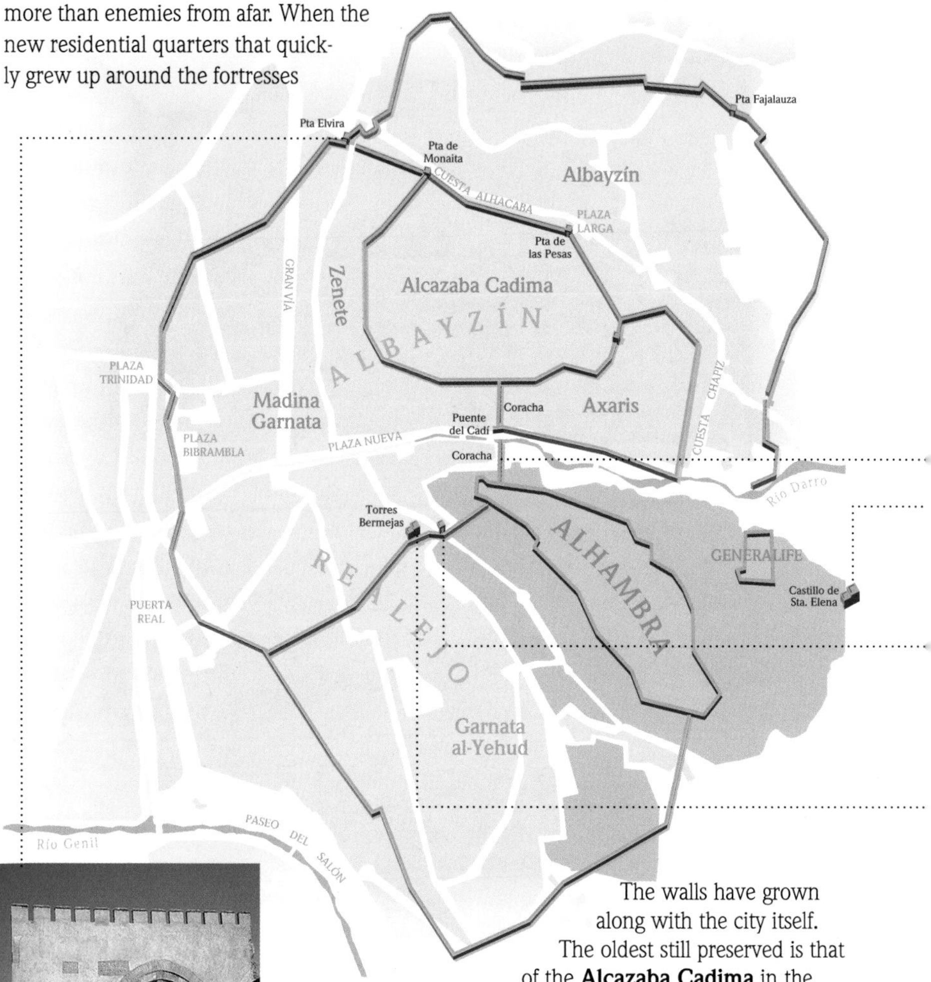

Just beyond the ***Puerta de Elvira*** *(The Elvira Gate) was an extensive cemetery, which took up all the area now occupied by the ornamental gardens and fountain of the Jardines del Triunfo.*

The walls have grown along with the city itself. The oldest still preserved is that of the **Alcazaba Cadima** in the Albaicín, from the Zirid dynasty (XI century), although there are remains of others built upon earlier structures dating from as long ago as Roman and even Iberian times. In the XII century what is now the centre of Granada was brought within the city walls and during the Nasrid dynasty the upper quarters of the Albaicín and the Jewish quarter, Garnata Al-Yehud, were also enclosed. Entrance could be gained through numerous gates, of which those remaining *in situ* are the gates of **Elvira, Monaita, Arco de las Pesas, Hizna Roman** and **Fajalauza**, all in the area of the Albaicín. A few others have been moved from their original positions and rebuilt elsewhere.

Before the construction of the Acequia Real (The Royal Waterway), which gave the Alhambra its own independent water supply, ***a wall, known as a coracha,*** *went down the hill from the Alcazaba to the river Darro to the point known today as the* ***Puente del Cadí*** *(The Judge's Bridge) or Puerta de los Tableros (The Woodworkers' Bridge) (left). It was here that the Alhambra's water supply was collected. This bridge may also have been a sluice gate designed to dam the river and release it suddenly downstream either to flush out the river-bed or to sweep away would-be assailants.*

El ***Castillo de Santa Elena*** *(St. Helen's Castle), also known as* ***Silla del Moro*** *(The Moor's Seat), was built to protect the orchards above the Generalife. In the XIX century the French used it as an artillery position, which helped in its general deterioration. It is in the process of being repaired.*

La ***Puerta de las Granadas*** *(The Gate of the Pomegranates) provides access from the Cuesta de Gomérez to the Alhambra woods. It was built in 1526 on the site of an earlier gate, la Puerta del Barranco (The Ravine Gate), along the top of which ran a pathway connecting the bulwark at the southern end of the Alhambra to the Vermillion Towers on the hillside opposite. This gate, together with the Charles V Fountain, confirmed the new orientation of the Alhambra facing southwards to the woods, which were also in the fee of the royal family.*

Las ***Torres Bermejas*** *(The Vermillion Towers) completed the defences of the southern edge of the Alhambra and protected the nearby Jewish quarter (or kept its inhabitants in check, depending upon which historian you choose to read). The ancient fortification was rebuilt upon its original foundations in the XIII century and joined to the Alhambra by Muhammad V in the XIV century.*

NASRID MILITARY FORTIFICATIONS

The Nasrid dynasty was immersed from the very start in constant frontier skirmishes and was besieged on all sides by the gradual advance of the Christian armies and the steady encroachment of their domains. This is manifest in the clearly defensive nature of its military structures, from its watch towers and frontier castles to the architecture of its very seats of power.

*In their military building techniques Nasrid architects adopted and refined all the advances made in Moorish Spain over the previous five centuries, and added some further touches of their own. The Almohads had introduced **barbican walls and towers, extra defensive towers along the main walls, and outlying walls to ensure their water supplies;** it was around this time as well that gates into the citadel began to be housed within towers rather than opening directly through the wall. The Nasrids improved upon these new gateways, equipping them with portcullises and incorporating easily defended corners into sloping passageways inside them. **Projecting wooden hoardings and machicolations with open-slatted floors** increased the security of the gates, allowing the defenders to rain missiles, boiling oil and molten lead down on besiegers. Building materials began to change from the stone blocks of the time of the caliphate to bonds of stone and brick, and above all tapial, a very strong mortar of stones, sand and lime.*

__Barbican tower:__ such towers were situated in front of the main wall, to which they were connected by a walkway. It was much easier from these vantage points to harass an enemy attempting to breach the main walls of the citadel.

__Main towers:__ positioned at intervals along the inner walls allowed troops to concentrate their defence in any required zone.

__Walkway:__ running around the walls between the battlements, allowed defenders to move quickly from tower to tower.

__No-man's land:__ a wide area in front of the walls cleared of all vegetation so as to offer no cover to an advancing enemy. The Alhambra in the middle ages was not surrounded by today's dense woods, which were planted by the Duke of Wellington at the beginning of the XIX century.

__Barbican:__ a lower wall built in front of the main wall as a first line of defence

__The Alcazaba at Almería:__ gives us an idea of what the Alhambra must once have looked like, dominating a hill stripped of all vegetation.

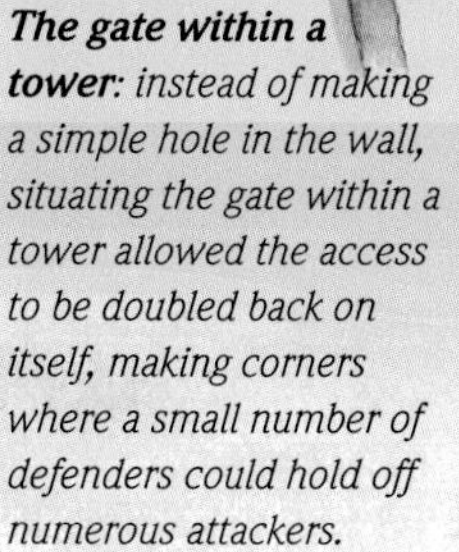

To the left, a plan of ***La Puerta de las Armas*** *(The Arms Gate) shows the characteristic double corner which an attacker would be obliged to negotiate. Below, a photograph of the stretch of ramp before the first corner inside the tower.*

The gate within a tower*: instead of making a simple hole in the wall, situating the gate within a tower allowed the access to be doubled back on itself, making corners where a small number of defenders could hold off numerous attackers.*

As can be seen in this Indian Muslim manuscript, ***tapial*** *walls were made in the same way that reinforced concrete walls are poured nowadays: wooden coffers were filled with a mortar of stones, sand and lime. The mortar is very homogeneous and with time gets extremely hard and resistant to impact. It will not crumble and fall down as a stone wall is wont to do; it has to be tunnelled through from side to side. Transverse ceiling beams which have either been taken out or have rotted in situ leave characteristic holes known as "****mechinales****".*

Projecting hoardings and machicolations*: structures made either of wood or masonry projecting from the walls above or beside the gates allowed the defenders to throw missiles, boiling oil or molten lead through gaps in the floor onto assailants below. The Spiked Tower and the* ***Justice Gate*** *still show where such structures were held in place.*

Coracha
is the name given to an outlying stretch of wall, occasionally just a simple palisade, built to allow access to a nearby spring, river or other watercourse to ensure the fortress's water supply.

The coracha *usually ended in a tower, a classic example of such a* coracha *being the famous* ***Golden Tower****, built by the Almohads in Sevilla.*

LOS PALACIOS NAZARÍES

THE NASRID PALACES

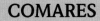

MEXUAR

COMARES

LEONES

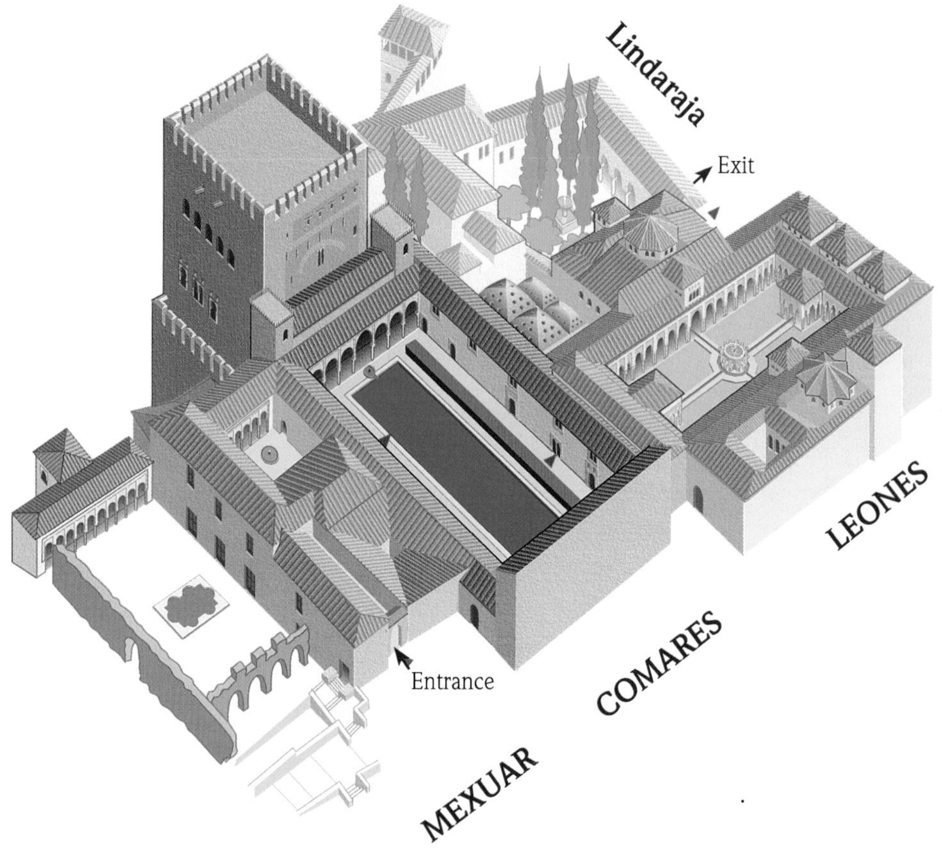

THE OLD ROYAL HOUSE

Not long after the Christian conquest the Nasrid palaces were referred to as the Old Royal House in order to distinguish them from the New Royal House, the palace that Charles V intended to build as the great residential, administrative and political centre of the new Spanish empire. This distinction implied a clear intention to integrate the Nasrid buildings into the projected scheme of the new Alhambra. The Catholic monarchs had no fixed residence and so when their grandson, Charles I of Spain, later the emperor Charles V, chose the Alhambra as the site of his own palace he unwittingly saved it for posterity.

The Old Royal House comprises today, as it did then, the most important focal points of the Alhambra: the Mexuar (council chamber) and the two palaces of Comares and the Lions, together with their annexes and outbuildings, all of which merit individual explanation within the context of the palace complex as a whole.

References have been made to seven palaces within the citadel and there is no doubt that only a small part of the original royal town and some vestiges of the *medina* remain today, but sufficient to give us some idea of the splendour and majesty of a civilisation at its cultural height, although politically in decline.

The Alhambra has justly been declared a monument of human heritage. Beyond the purely architectural it is a creation of space, air and light. But it is not a space filled within a void; it is rather a captured amalgam of brightness and shadow, streams and flowers, enveloped in verse and sensations which transcend time.

Mexuar

THE MEXUAR PALACES

Lewis, 1835

This is without doubt the area of the palace complex that has undergone most transformation since its earliest days, changes which were largely made by the Christian governors in the name of their king to adapt it to new roles and functions. Thus its original shape has been altered considerably, sometimes to the detriment of original structures, and so it is quite difficult nowadays to establish exactly where the entrances to this part of the palace really were.

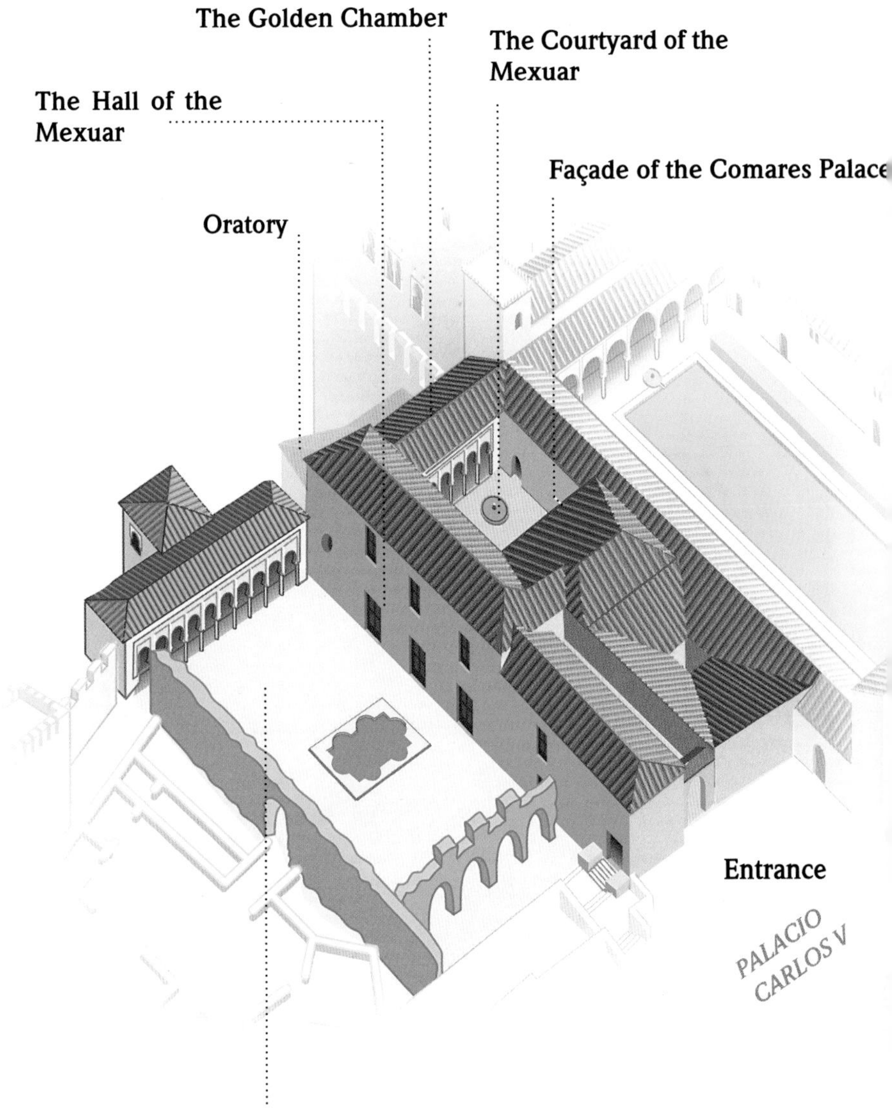

The Golden Chamber

The Courtyard of the Mexuar

The Hall of the Mexuar

Façade of the Comares Palace

Oratory

Entrance

PALACIO CARLOS V

Machuca's Courtyard

This courtyard is named after the famous architect Pedro Machuca, who designed the Palace of Charles V and lived in the tower with an arched portico on the north side of the courtyard overlooking the river Darro. On the opposite side of the courtyard there was an identical gallery, of which only vestiges remain in the ground, but an idea of its layout and form can still be seen in the arches of cypress trees growing where it used to be.

The Hall of the Mexuar

This is almost certainly the oldest surviving part of the royal palaces but it has undergone substantial alterations, either during the reign of Yusuf 1 or of his son Muhammad V. It was here that the royal court of justice is believed to have convened. After the conquest the Christian monarchs installed their chapel here, changing the shape of the room once again. A hypothetical reconstruction of its original appearance can be seen below.

The small door *guarding the entrance today is a later introduction brought from elsewhere. It has fine carved surrounds and is sheltered by overhanging eaves supported by elegant corbels.*

The original hall was illuminated by daylight filtering through the stained-glass panes of a lantern window in the roof. This was later replaced by an artistically carved, radial, wooden ceiling.

An ***original wall*** *at the northern end of the hall, which closed it off from either a small yard or a street, was demolished to amplify the hall. The decorative gesso covering the original wall was saved and used on the new wall, which contains a doorway leading to the erstwhile oratory, later used as a sacristy.*

The present-day wooden ***balustrade*** *represents the remains of a choir, which was added in the space gained when the exterior yard was included within the hall.*

The ***eastern wall*** *was reinforced to support the weight of a new floor added above the hall. Great windows with wrought-iron grilles were opened up to give more light to the room. It is impossible to determine what the surface of this wall might originally have looked like.*

The council met within the square formed by the four columns to decide upon important judicial matters. At the door there was a tile which reads,

"Enter and ask. Do not be afraid to seek justice for here you will find it."

Some of the ***elaborately adorned wooden, coffered ceilings*** (artesonados) *are original, recognisable as such by the darker hues of their polychroming. The higher reaches of the walls retain some of their original colouring, including giltwork in their gesso decoration.*

The ***capitals*** *were restored in 1995, when they were repainted in their original polychromed style.*

The whole room, including the part belonging to the yard, which was included into the Mexuar proper in Christian times, has a ***dado*** *of XVI century Morisco tiling. In the central stars the arms of the Nasrid dynasty alternate with those of Cardinal Mendoza, the double-headed eagle of the House of Austria and the Pillars of Hercules from the imperial shield, all of which suggests an admiration on the part of the Christians for things Muslim and a certain desire to integrate the two cultures.*

The present entrance was opened in modern times, disturbing one of the XVI century tiles showing the ***Pillars of Hercules****, which was moved to a position on the east wall, although the gypsum crown above it remains in its original position above the new doorway.*

The Mexuar Oratory

The oratory is situated at the end of the main hall overlooking the Albaicín. It is one of the rooms that suffered most damage from the explosion of the gunpowder factory in the valley below in 1590. Repairs were begun at once but it was not completely restored until 1917. In Nasrid times entrance to the oratory was by way of the Machuca gallery.

Along the northern wall are ***four arched windows,*** *three of which have marble-pillar mullions with alabaster capitals.*

The restoration work bears little in common with the original decoration and so the visitor need pay scant attention to the simplified ***mural adornments,*** *with the exception perhaps of some epigraphs around the mihrab, relating to Muhammad V, and one which says,*

"Do not be negligent: come to prayer".

Islam obliges the faithful to pray towards Mecca five times a day and so oratories of this sort are to be found everywhere throughout Muslim countries. Their main feature is the decorated devotional niche, the *mihrab*, which indicates the direction towards Mecca.

It can be seen that the orientation of this small oratory does not conform to the line of the battlements but slants to the south east in the direction of Mecca.

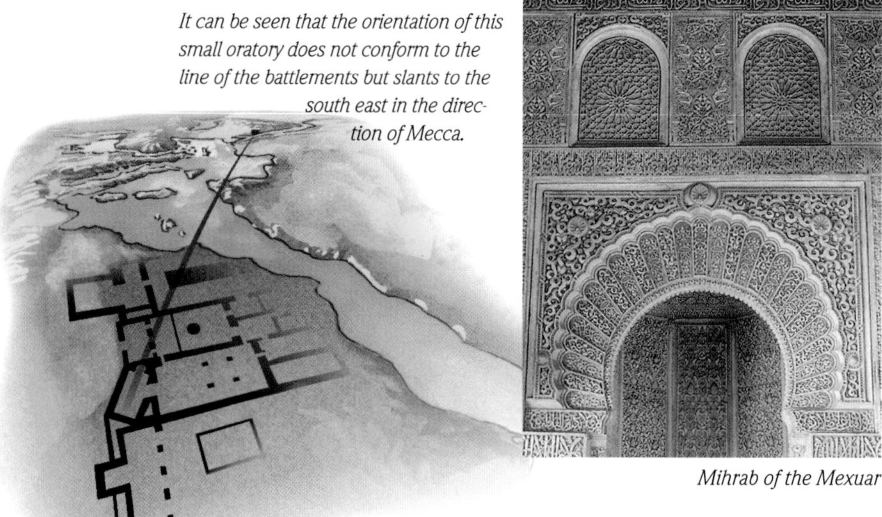

Mihrab of the Mexuar

The Courtyard of the Mexuar

This small courtyard used to be called, for no good reason, the Courtyard of the Mosque. On its southern side is an impressive façade, always accepted as having been the entrance to the Comares Palace. Opposite, on the northern side, with a ***portico*** in front of it, is the so-called **Golden Chamber.**

Engravings *of this patio from centuries past should be evidence enough to exonerate later restorers from any feelings of blame we might bear towards them; as far as this courtyard is concerned, the extensive restoration work has been well carried out.*

Above: a drawing of the Mexuar Courtyard by Owen (1842) and right: a lithograph by Taylor (1835)

The centre of the courtyard is occupied by a ***fountain*** *with a fluted trough of white marble, although only a copy of the original. The gallery at the entrance to the Golden Chamber is composed of three arches resting upon what may be Almohad white-marble capitals, crowning slender marble columns. The* ***two capitals with "handles"*** *could well be a stylised interpretation of similar zoomorphic capitals to be found in Persepolis (below).*

The eastern wall of the courtyard houses the entrance to a long tunnel, which leads eventually to the Comares Palace bath-house after passing small rooms on either side that must have served as soldiers' quarters or guard rooms.

The Golden Chamber

Behind the gallery lies the Golden Chamber. Here a gothic window looks out across the woodlands beyond. The mullion of this window has a capital bearing the emblems of the Catholic monarchs. It has been suggested that in Nasrid times this was where visitors waited to be admitted to the sultan's presence in the palace beyond.

The original ceiling, fastened onto a hipped roof (see below), was restored during the reign of the Catholic Monarchs, who included Gothic motifs and copious gilt-work in the decoration, whence the name of the chamber.

MUDEJAR WOODEN ROOF FRAMEWORKS

Carpentry attained new heights of magnificence in Andalusia in elegantly carved wooden ceilings, which, like the stuccoed and tiled walls of the rooms they covered, combined practicality with artistic and symbolic beauty.

Many of the building techniques of al-Andalus were kept up by skilled Moorish craftsmen who chose to stay in Spain after their lands had been conquered by the Christians. They were known as Mudejars (from the Arabic mudajjan, meaning "permitted to remain") and were responsible for the construction of many of the new building projects embarked on in the recently conquered cities, among which were the churches erected in the name of the new faith. In this way the term Mudejar came to represent an architectural style in its own right.

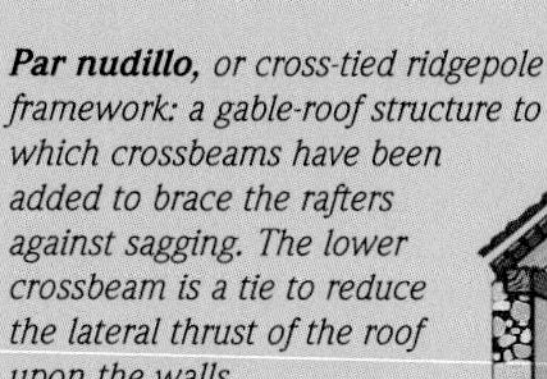

***Alfarjes**, or panelled framework: a flat structure comprising either one or two sizes of beams. The thick beams underneath, known as summers, are set at right angles into the walls.*

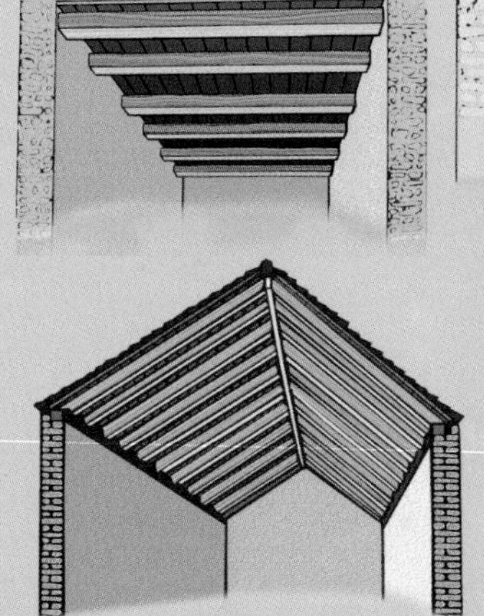

***Par hilera**, or ridgepole framework: a gable roof, the lower ends of the sloping rafters being butted against a beam engaged lengthways in the wall and the top ends fastened to the ridgepole.*

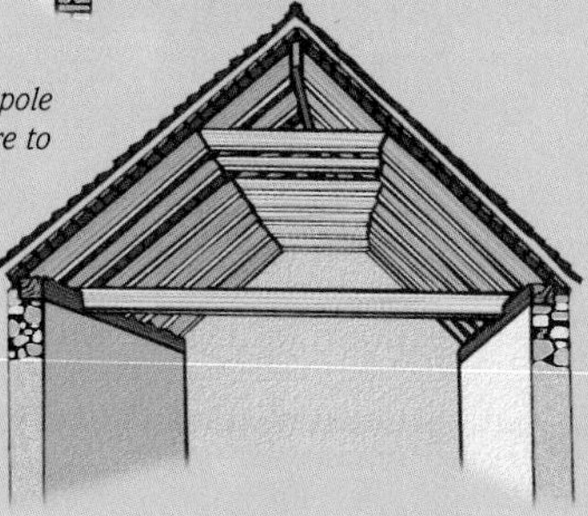

***Par nudillo**, or cross-tied ridgepole framework: a gable-roof structure to which crossbeams have been added to brace the rafters against sagging. The lower crossbeam is a tie to reduce the lateral thrust of the roof upon the walls.*

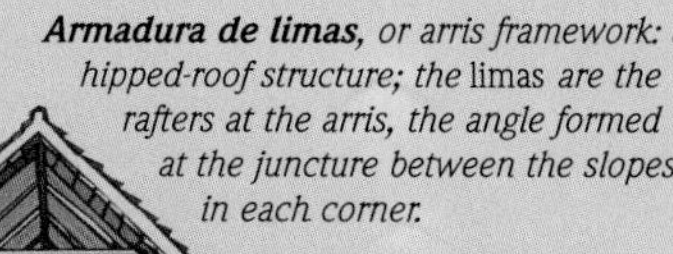

***Armadura de limas**, or arris framework: a hipped-roof structure; the* limas *are the rafters at the arris, the angle formed at the juncture between the slopes in each corner.*

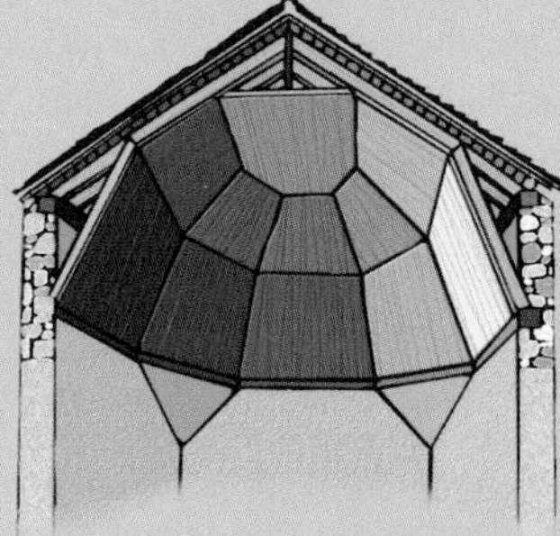

*Additional panels could then be pinned onto these frameworks when necessary to give the basic structure for **vaulted ceilings** of various shapes.*

Fachada de Comares

The Façade

This façade of the Comares Palace was considerably restored in the XIX century. The entrance is raised above the level of the courtyard upon a plinth of three white marble steps. Its ataurique (foliate and vegetal) decoration becomes more intricate as it goes upwards, possibly in imitation of the ascending order of classical design

"My position is that of a crown and my door is a parting of the ways: the West believes that in me is the East. Al-Gani bi-llah has entrusted me to open the way to the victory that has been foretold

The façade to this palace, at least in the form in which we know it today, was made to commemorate the successful siege of Algeciras by Muhammad V in 1369. The inscription quoted here would seem to refer to its unusual construction with two doors

and I await his coming just as the horizon ushers in the dawn. May God adorn his works with the same beauty that resides in his countenance and his nature.

(Inscription within the frieze on the façade)

The overhanging wooden eaves are supported by wooden corbels and a frieze. Their fine, elaborate carving is generally considered to represent the apotheosis of Spanish-Muslim carpentry.

The motto of the Nasrid dynasty, "The only conqueror is God", *(right) is repeated in Maghrib script around the two arched windows at the sides and above the smaller central window.*

"The only conqueror is God"

*Above the door lintels there are vestiges of the **original tiling,** which has been continued in modern stucco-work down the door jambs to the dado, which has also been restored.*

***Façade of the Alcazar in Sevilla,** dating from the time of the Almohads, and, according to Rafael Manzano, possibly even preceding this.*

According to some expert commentators on the subject this beautiful façade is not in its original position. Thus Oleg Grabar states, *"It is too big and elaborate to be a simple doorway; looking at the overall composition the façade is out of balance with the tiny courtyard which precedes it and lacks any clear visual role; although the inscriptions do emphasise its pivotal position within the internal organisation of the palace."* Whatever the truth of the matter and wherever this monumental façade may originally have been, it must have been very impressive: multicoloured like a Persian carpet, the eaves and the stucco reliefs gleaming with gold leaf and the huge bronze doors themselves burnished to shine like gold.

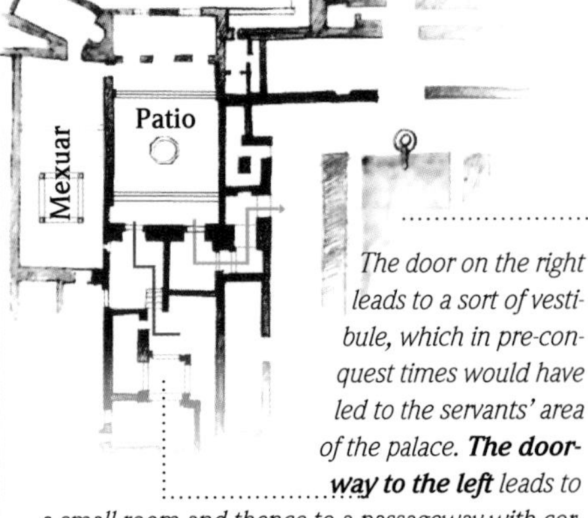

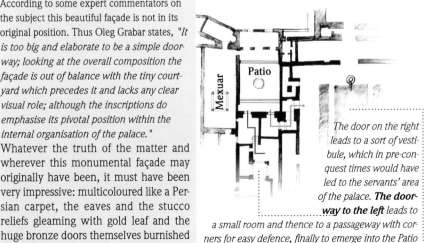

*The door on the right leads to a sort of vestibule, which in pre-conquest times would have led to the servants' area of the palace. **The doorway to the left** leads to a small room and thence to a passageway with corners for easy defence, finally to emerge into the Patio de los Arrayanes (**The Courtyard of the Myrtles**).*

Comares

Taylor, 1832

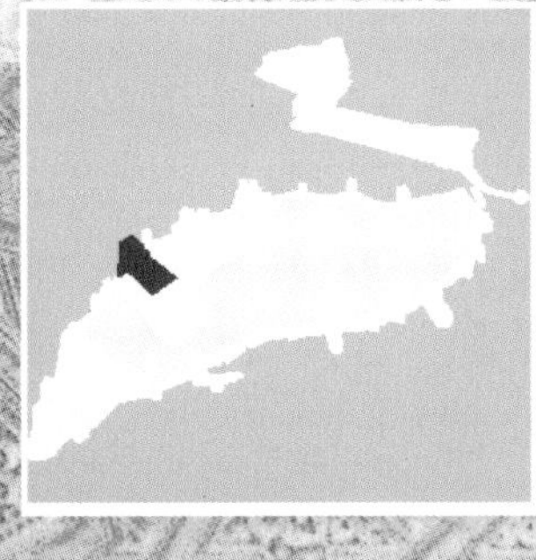

This palace complex, including the Hall of the Ambassadors, or Throne Room, forms the most important nucleus of the Alhambra. The simplicity of its lines and its balanced proportions lend the courtyard a feeling of such serene majesty that we still breath in the air of noble grandeur of the kings who presided over its building.

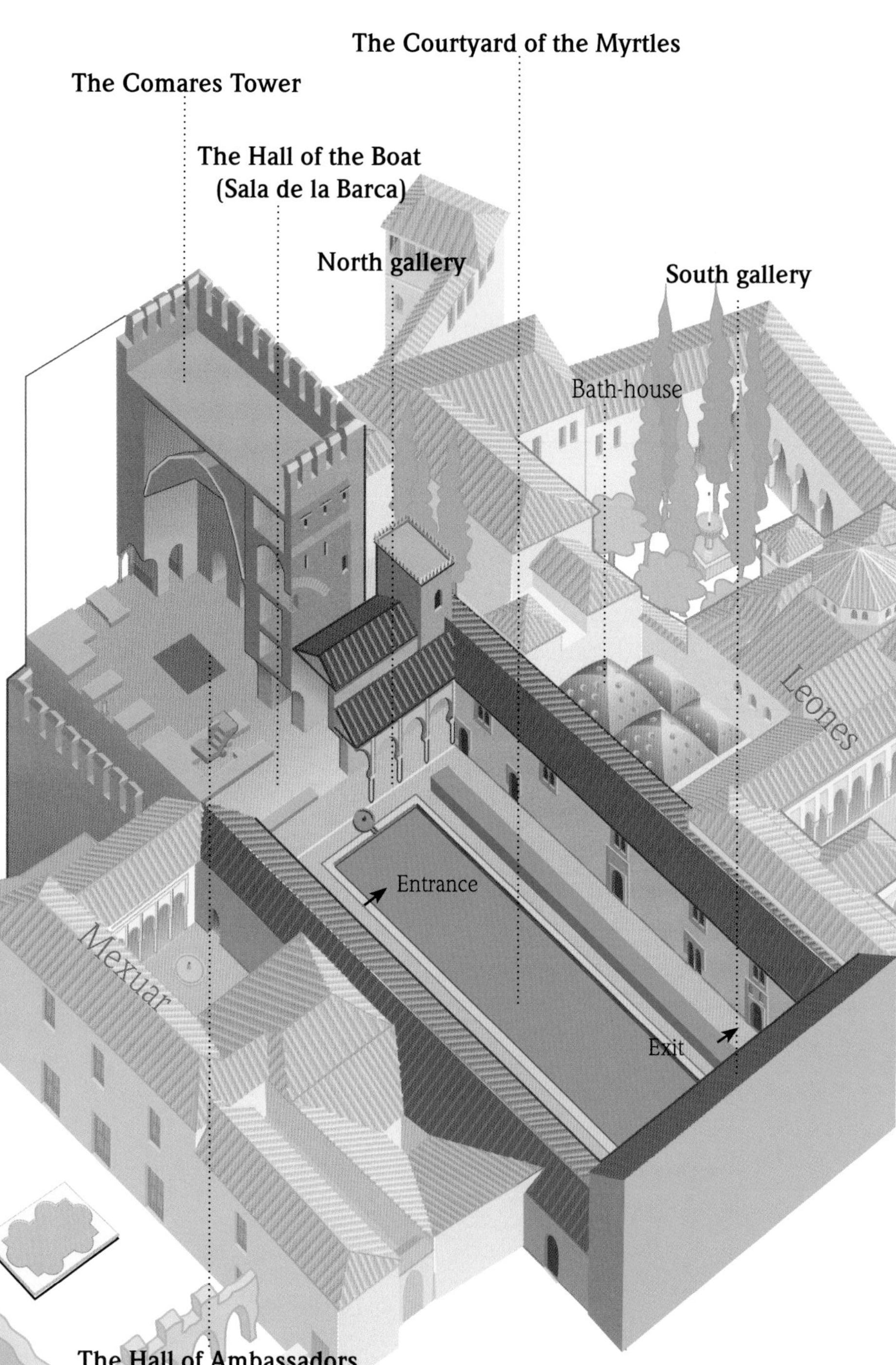
The Courtyard of the Myrtles
The Comares Tower
The Hall of the Boat
(Sala de la Barca)
North gallery
South gallery
Bath-house
Leones
Entrance
Mexuar
Exit
The Hall of Ambassadors

The Courtyard of the Myrtles

This was the focal point of diplomatic and political activity in the Alhambra and without doubt the place where great receptions for ambassadors were held. It was also where important visitors waited to be received by the sultan. Until recently the whole of this part of the building, apart from some of the decorative work corresponding to his son Muhammad V, to whom there is a panegyric on the wall of the north gallery, had been accredited to Yusuf I. A study by Emilio García Gómez, however has shown fairly convincingly that Yusuf I (1333-54) built the gallery and Hall of the Boat, the Comares Tower and the baths, whilst the rest was built during the reign of his son Muhammad V.

The myrtle (myrtus communis) was frequently found in the gardens of al-Andalus. This courtyard owes its name to the myrtle bushes that border the central pool. They are evergreen and give off a very pleasant smell when their leaves are rubbed in the hand.

"...when the rest of Europe was building castles in the air, in Granada they were constructing palaces upon water." (Jesús Bermúdez Pareja)

When a visitor crossed the main threshold he was confronted by a ***vast mirror of water*** *reflecting the solid white bulk of the Comares Tower. The slope of the white marble floors allows the water in the pool to reach right up to the plinths of the columns on the north side of the courtyard and so the whole palace, even the tower itself, seems to be floating on water. This use of water to mirror the structure above was used some three centuries later (1630-47) in the Taj Mahal at Agra in India.*

It can be seen in engravings by XIX century artists, such as that shown above by Lewis (1835), that there were ***no small turrets*** *flanking the main tower and that the roof of the portico did not run smoothly and uniformly into that of the Hall of the Boat. Originally there was only one such tower, to the east, which would have served to protect the door that nowadays allows access to the courtyard. At the time of the engravings this tower was not crenellated, although it may have been in earlier times.*

Water forms the mysterious life of the Alhambra: it allows the gardens to grow exuberantly green, it gives birth to the splendour of flowering shrubs and bushes, it rests in the pools reflecting the elegantly arcaded halls, it dances in the fountains and murmurs in rivulets through the very heart of the royal residence.
Just as the Koran describes Paradise, "An orchard flowing with streams."

(Titus Burckhardt)

If God is the eternal One, so all of creation is but a part of the whole: fragile, mortal, deceptive. This concept of the elusiveness of reality and its constant flux became almost an obsession, both because of its religious significance and the effects it had upon artistic creations of the time, to the extent that an architect would construct only half of what was to be seen: the reflection of reality, a transient lightness, reality's other face.
The tangible has no greater substance than its reflected image, although the latter may be an optical illusion. In the desert the horizon also seems to be continuously shifting, forming unattainable mirages.

There has been some debate as to whether the ***skirting of the walls*** *around this courtyard was tiled. The way in which the decorative door embrasures stop short before floor level would seem to confirm that they were. Their style was almost certainly similar to the rest of the mediaeval tiling, traces of which remain in the niches and jambs of the arches at the ends of the north gallery, which imitate the reflections of the water in the pool. To the right is a picture of the mosque at Marrakesh (XIV century), showing a similar design.*

Tiling (alicatado)

Alicatado tiling, a sort of marquetry in stone, derives its name from the type of pincers, *al-qata'a*, or *alicate* in modern Spanish, used to trim the edges of the tiny ceramic pieces used in its make-up. These were put together on a flat surface like a jigsaw puzzle, but face down, and then covered in gypsum plaster. When the composition was dry it was cleaned and smoothed off before being put into place on the wall. When the pieces formed part of a repetitive pattern they were probably moulded and their edges clipped clean with pincers and sanded smooth. Alicatado tiling in the true sense of the word, however, was the technique of taking a simple piece of fired ceramic and shaping it with the alicate and a fine chisel. Although this craft has fallen into disuse in Spain it continues to this day in Morocco, where craftsmen have inherited the artistic skills once common to al-Andalus and northern Africa.

The process of making ceramics begins with collecting the clay: in Granada this probably came from the banks of the river Beiro. Afterwards it has to be ground, suspended in water, filtered off and then trodden and kneaded into the shape required. Colours were obtained for mosaic tiling by melting siliceous sands, lead sulphide and other mineral-bearing ores in ovens and pounding them to obtain a fine powder, which, when mixed with water and other dyes, was painted onto the tiles before being fired.

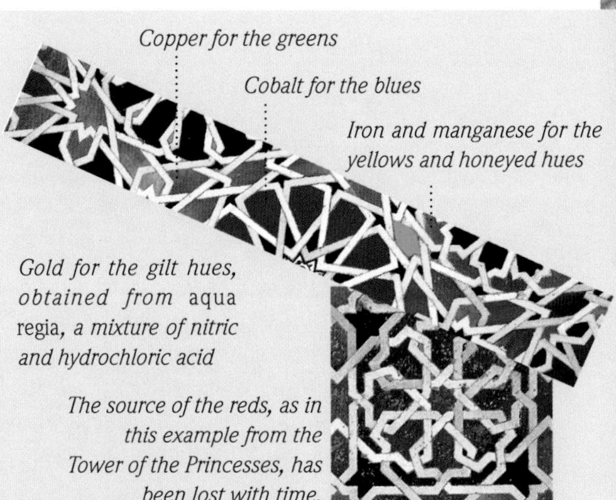

Copper for the greens

Cobalt for the blues

Iron and manganese for the yellows and honeyed hues

Gold for the gilt hues, obtained from aqua regia, *a mixture of nitric and hydrochloric acid*

The source of the reds, as in this example from the Tower of the Princesses, has been lost with time.

The ceramics were ***fired*** *in ovens divided into three sections: firebox, baking chamber and outer heat chamber. Using bushes and shrubs such as gorse for fuel, temperatures of up to 900 degrees could be reached. The baking process consisted of 24 hours' heating plus a similar period for slow cooling, two days and nights in all.*

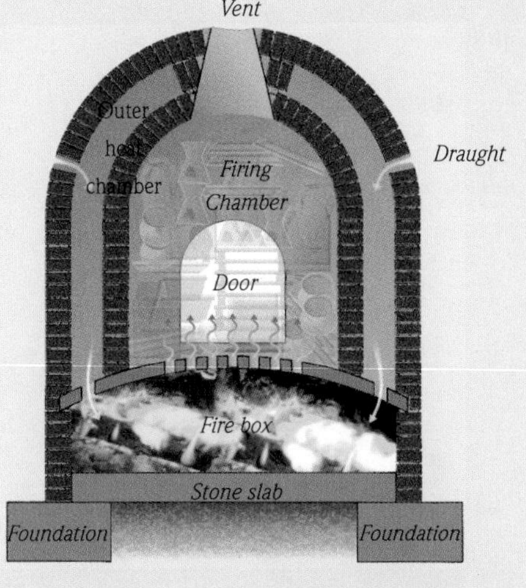

Virtuosity and refinement *in the art of tiling is to be seen in the pillars in the Throne Room, where the tiles are moulded to the curvature of the columns.*

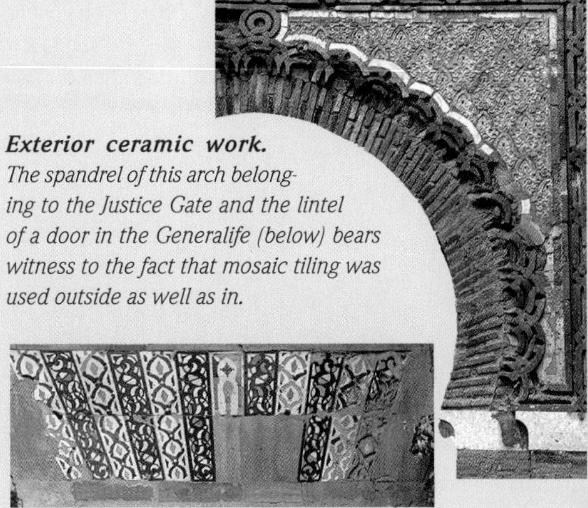

Exterior ceramic work.
The spandrel of this arch belonging to the Justice Gate and the lintel of a door in the Generalife (below) bears witness to the fact that mosaic tiling was used outside as well as in.

Mysticism and mathematics

The compositional principles which guide the Islamic ornamental code can be reduced to stylised, repetitive rhythm. Such rhythm is the basic com-positional element in all Islamic art, including poetry and music. In their art ornamental designs and motifs follow each other in reiterative rhythms towards infinity as a metaphor of eternity, which fills the whole of space. It consists of formulas created by the multiplication, division, rotation and symmetrical distribution of basic, deceptively simple themes. A fascination for repetition and symmetry and the continuity of motifs is the prime motivation in Islamic art. This produces an effect which is dynamic and at the same time immutable, in which each concept of the overall design pre-serves its own identity without holding sway over any of the others. No detail dominates the whole: it is unity formed from mul-tiplicity and multi-plicity in one. The result is complete harmony and tranquillity, an art at rest where all tension is dissipated. (Prof. C. Borrás).

There are two distinct types of design discernible in the ceramic tiling in the Alhambra:

- *Mosaics, in which one or more elements are repeated. These are generally moulded and cover the wall at measured intervals in the form of a basic shape which is reproduced in two axes to produce the overall design.*

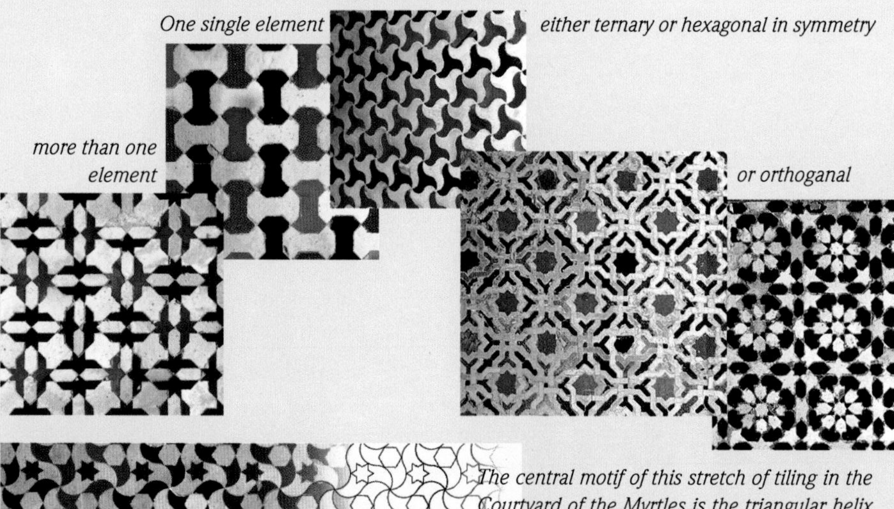

One single element

either ternary or hexagonal in symmetry

more than one element

or orthoganal

The central motif of this stretch of tiling in the Courtyard of the Myrtles is the triangular helix but it is broken up by the addition of stars and hexagons. The hexagons are left in white and thus they appear to form a background, leading the eye to see the convergence of the three horns of the helices. One single element of the design is now one thing, now another. This is a magnificent illustration of the mutability of creation, symbolised primarily in water and also in this tiling, which both reflects and explains it.

- Alicatado *tiling in which no general matrix can be discerned, the effect depending upon the rotation of shapes, alterations in scale and leaps in optical perception of the indivisible depth of the pattern, all of which go to make a whole.*

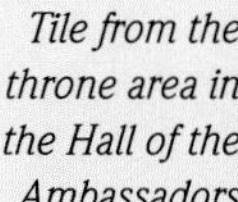

Tile from the throne area in the Hall of the Ambassadors

Tower of the Captive Princess

One of the most important aspects of the alicatado *tiling is visual symmetry in one. two, three, four or even six axes and the way in which the smallest elements combine to form others of a higher dimen-sion, such as this example from a jamb in the Lindaraja tower, which includes three increasing dimensions of stars, each including the smaller dimension within itself.*

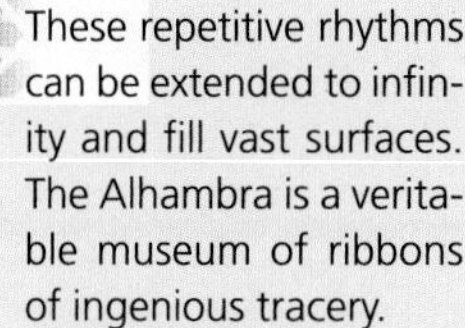

These repetitive rhythms can be extended to infinity and fill vast surfaces. The Alhambra is a veritable museum of ribbons of ingenious tracery.

The mathematical complexity of the tiling has always fascinated artists and researchers. One of these was the Dutch artist Maurits C. Escher, whose famous visual experiments with tessellation and the interplay of background and geometric design were inspired by the tiling in the Alhambra, which he first visited in 1926 and again ten years later in 1936, the date of this sketch.

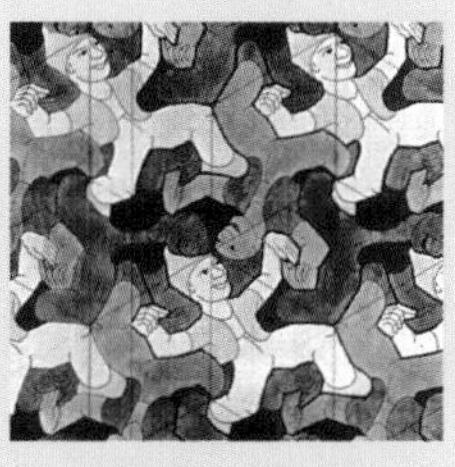

Drawing by Escher in crayon and watercolour (1938).

The courtyard was an open esplanade during the reign of Yusuf I. His son, Muhammad V, built the gallery to enclose its southern end and thus make a private courtyard similar to the Greek megaton and Roman atrium.

The juxtaposition of the cornice of the Palace of Charles V intrudes upon the delicate, insubstantial lines of the Courtyard of the Myrtles, bearing witness to two completely different ways of understanding shape and space.

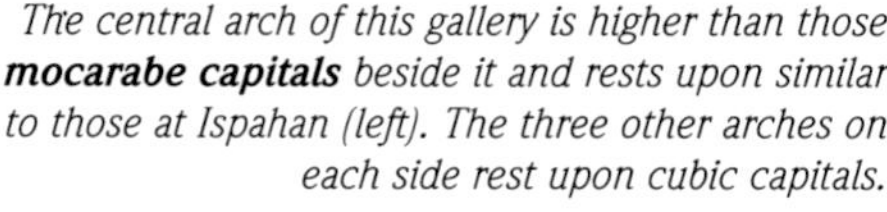

The central arch of this gallery is higher than those beside it and rests upon similar ***mocarabe capitals*** *to those at Ispahan (left). The three other arches on each side rest upon cubic capitals.*

Most of the inscriptions in gesso and wood in the south portico are in praise of God and, apart from those dedicated to the sultan, are mainly copies from the north side of the courtyard.

The ***intrados*** *of the arch behind the portico is covered in intricate leaf motifs in delicate shades of blue. Above the arch there are three windows with gypsum jalousies.*

Modern ***dado tiling*** *copied from original XVI century ceramics.*

Behind the central arch is the so-called ***Crypt of the Emperor's Palace,*** *preceded by the remains of a hall bisected diagonally by the stone wall of the Palace of Charles V. Nowadays it is inaccessible from the Courtyard of the Myrtles.*

*The **third floor** consists of a gallery covered by a ribbon-work, coffered ceiling. During the XIX century all the openings between the pillars in this upper gallery were closed off by **wooden jalousies in the form of a balustrade.***

*Above the gallery is a **long room** with seven windows opening onto the courtyard. The central window has a mullion and they are all protected by modern wooden jalousies. This room, which connects with the higher part of the Courtyard of the Lions, was a concession to the ladies of the palace, who might use it to observe the comings and goings in the courtyard below without their being seen.*

*The **two walls along each side** of the courtyard contain five doorways opening into small rooms. All these rooms have two floors, the upper one receiving daylight through arched windows, but it is not clear what these rooms were used for. The presence of brick daïses on the floors of some of the rooms has led authors to claim that they were set aside for the women of the palace. Nevertheless, functionaries at this time also used to work sitting on such daïses and they may equally have been used for administrative purposes.*

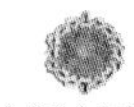

The North Gallery

This gallery is very similar to the one on the south side and many of the decorative elements and epigraphs found in the south gallery were copied from this one.

Above the XVI century tiled dado is a poem by Ibn Zamrak written in cursive script, which refers in one of its verses to the heroic deeds of Muhammad V.

"You conquered Algeciras with the might of your sword, opening a secret doorway to our victory."

*The **tree of life** crowns the line of epigraphic verses written around the wall. This type of design, in which* ataurique *motifs spread downwards from an apex is an allusion to the inverted tree that sustains the celestial bodies in the firmament and buries its roots in paradise.*

*The **coffered ceiling** of this gallery was destroyed in a fire in 1890 along with that of the Hall of the Boat beside it. It has been very skilfully repaired, however, making use of many of the burnt pieces (as can be seen in the photograph on the left).*

*The **door**, which was carefully restored in 1954, is a tribute to the minute care and skill of the Nasrid carpenters.*

*A **detail** of the geometry of the stucco decoration*

Sala de la Barca — The Hall of the Boat

This long room lies behind the gallery and serves as an anteroom to the Throne Room. At each end it has two alcoves framed by stilted arches and also a water closet on the west side.

Right: entrance arch in an engraving by Taylor (1855).

The Hall of the Boat

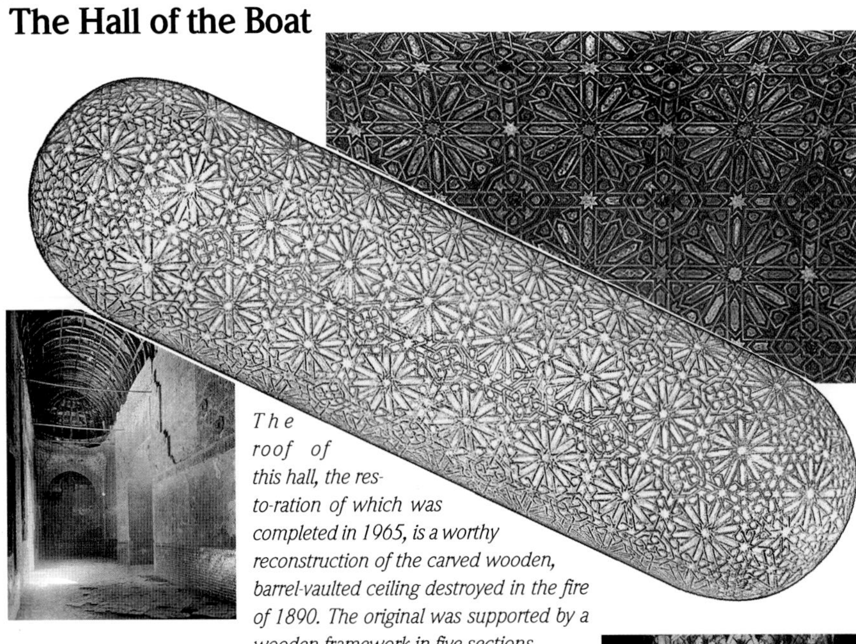

The roof of this hall, the res-to-ration of which was completed in 1965, is a worthy reconstruction of the carved wooden, barrel-vaulted ceiling destroyed in the fire of 1890. The original was supported by a wooden framework in five sections.

The greeting **"baraka"**, "a blessing on you", *appears everywhere among the inscriptions on the walls and it has been suggested that the name of the hall, 'barca', or boat, may well derive from the phonetic mutation of this oft repeated word. Nevertheless, its ceiling in the shape of an upside-down boat might have provided added visual support for the term.*

The muted tones of the ***ceramic*** *tiles in the dado dates the construction of this hall to the first half of the XIV century.*

Remains of polychroming are visible on ***the entrance arch*** *(right) just as they are on the arch which leads into the Hall of Ambassadors*

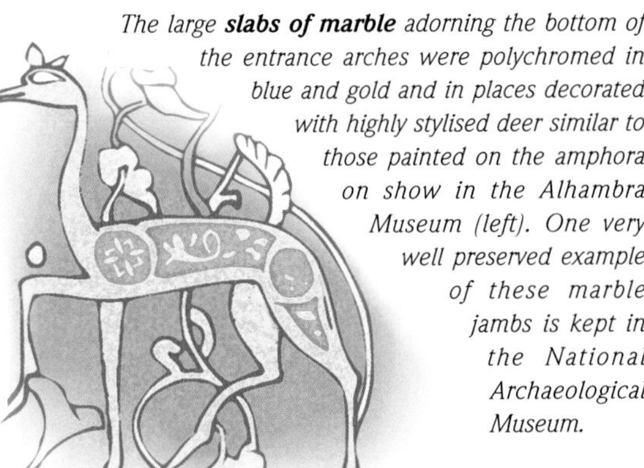

The large ***slabs of marble*** *adorning the bottom of the entrance arches were polychromed in blue and gold and in places decorated with highly stylised deer similar to those painted on the amphora on show in the Alhambra Museum (left). One very well preserved example of these marble jambs is kept in the National Archaeological Museum.*

The small, beautifully sculpted marble or gesso niches in the jambs of the arches were for keeping jars of water, perfume or vases of flowers, but almost always water as a symbol of hospitality, according to the verses written around them.

"Praise be to God. My finery and my diadem dazzle those already endowed with beauty, for the brightest stars have descended on me from their highest mansions. The jar of water standing inside me resembles one of the faithful who, deep in prayer facing the mihrab, is completely absorbed in God. Throughout the pass of time my generosity will continue to give relief to he who is thirsty and shelter the needy.... The fingers of my maker set the stones in my crown and shaped me subtly. I appear to be the throne of a wife, but indeed I am far more than that because I contain the whole joy of the bride and groom. Whoever should come to me thirsty I shall lead him to a place where he will find clean, fresh water of the sweetest purity. For I appear as a rainbow and the sun is our Lord Abul Hachạch."

The Hall of the Ambassadors

This is the symbolic centre of Nasrid Power; in it is concentrated the magnificence of the last Muslim court in Europe. Everything here speaks of splendour and refinement, from the gold leaf that can still be made out on the entrance arch and the intricate mosaic tiles to the magnificent ceiling covering the entire hall.

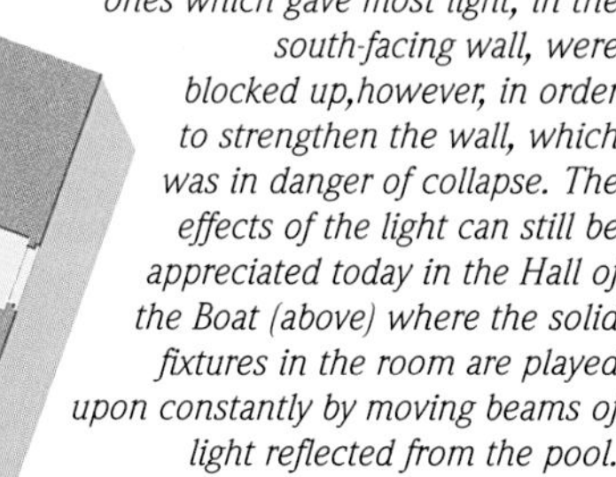

*The **overall plan of the Tower of Comares** reveals the deceptive nature of its design; 45 metres in height, it would appear to be a military tower, but the three deep alcoves in the walls on three sides would have greatly weakened its defensive capacity and reveal it for what it really was: a palatial reception hall. The alcoves themselves are covered with elegant, wooden, coffered ceilings.*

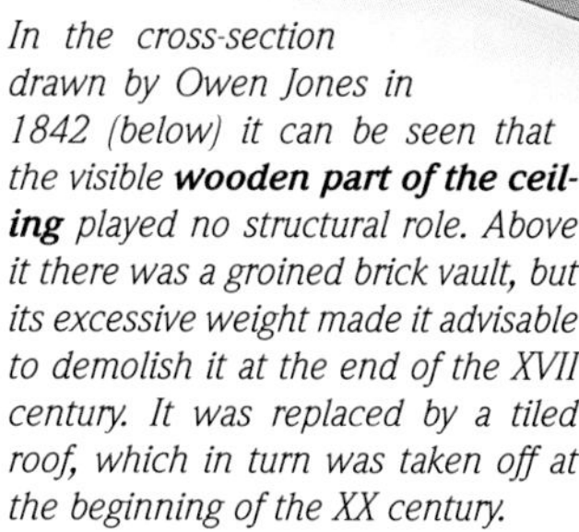

The five windows in each wall of the tower are reminiscent of desert architecture. The ones which gave most light, in the south-facing wall, were blocked up,however, in order to strengthen the wall, which was in danger of collapse. The effects of the light can still be appreciated today in the Hall of the Boat (above) where the solid fixtures in the room are played upon constantly by moving beams of light reflected from the pool.

The Throne Room, or Hall of Ambassadors, is also called the Hall of Comares, deriving from the Arabic, "*qamariyya*", meaning "stained glass". The alcoves, swimming in colours pouring through the stained-glass windows, were favourite places for dignitaries and important visitors, who, just as they would in a desert tent, always sat in the corners of a room.

*In the cross-section drawn by Owen Jones in 1842 (below) it can be seen that the visible **wooden part of the ceiling** played no structural role. Above it there was a groined brick vault, but its excessive weight made it advisable to demolish it at the end of the XVII century. It was replaced by a tiled roof, which in turn was taken off at the beginning of the XX century.*

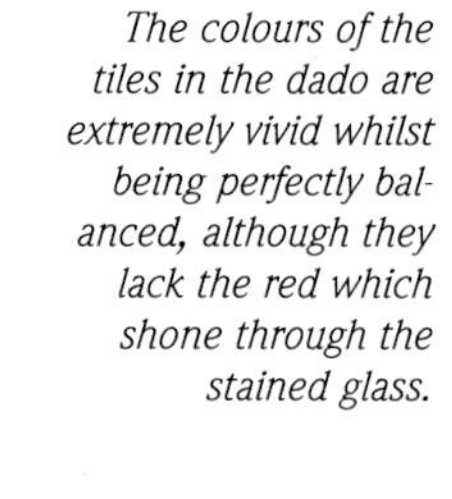

The colours of the tiles in the dado are extremely vivid whilst being perfectly balanced, although they lack the red which shone through the stained glass.

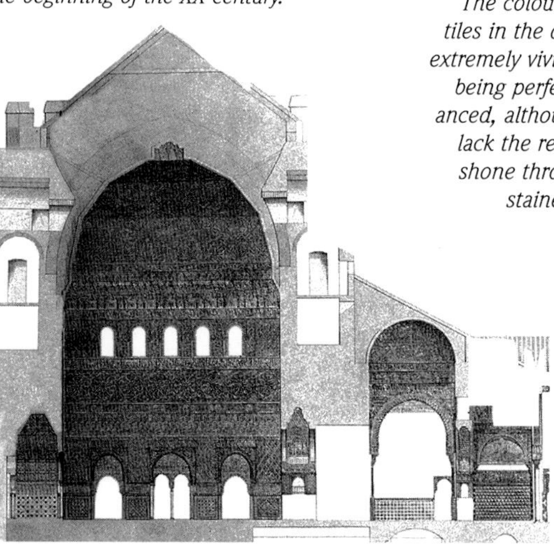

According to the inscriptions that run along the wall above the tiling in the alcove itself, the central alcove on the north side of the hall was reserved for the throne:

[...] Yusuf [...] chose me to be the throne of the kingdom.

From here the sultan had a psychological advantage over his subjects, who would have felt themselves at one and the same time under the commanding but protective gaze of the political, military and religious leader of their kingdom. Foreign ambassadors too, as they crossed the threshold of the Hall of the Boat and walked towards the throne room, surrounded by brilliant colours and gleaming gold, would have felt intimidated by the scrutiny of the sultan, silhouetted against the more mysterious light of the stained glass behind him. The sultan himself, lying on his throne, could enjoy the view of Granada and its elegant houses and gardens, the sky and water, which was offered to his eyes like a mirror in the Courtyard of the Myrtles.

The stained glass windows of the throne room were destroyed by the explosion of a gunpowder magazine in 1590. The geometric design of these windows were a transparent continuation of the tiled dado. In the windows; the fine straight lines that criss-cross the ceramics were represented by the thin strips of lead holding each coloured pane in place. The light thus filtered through the stained glass fell upon a blue and gold tiled floor, some vestiges of which remain, roped off in the centre of the hall. The originals are those tiles in which the blues surrounding the dynastic shields are painted right to the edge and are completely flat, so as to be smooth for unshod feet. The later, post-conquest imitations stick up slightly around the edges of the colours

The **roof of the throne room** is the culmination of Nasrid carpentry. It is composed of 8,017 separate pieces of wood in seven concentric circles with superimposed cedar-wood adornments and crowned in the centre with a sumptuous mocarabe boss.

During repair work on the ceiling ***a wooden peg*** *was found sticking out farther than those around it. Written on it were all the notes referring to the colour scheme of the ceiling. It seems to have been an* ad hoc *painter's crib. Darío Cabanelas, who initially studied this tell-tale scrap of wood, found that the order of colours originally used on the ceiling was first white, then red, followed by walnut, light green, another red, green again and finally a different red. His study has enabled modern scholars to make a scale model of the ceiling in its original polychromed finery. Below is the ceiling in its present condition.*

Written within a surround of epigraphs supporting the ceiling are the words,

"...He who created seven heavens, one above the other; you will find no discord in the creation of the Merciful One..."

Korán. Sura LXVII

This allows us to interpret the ceiling as representing the seven heavens of Islamic belief. This geocentric concept visualised a flat earth, above which were the seven concentric heavens crowned by paradise, wherein were buried the roots of the tree of life, which sustained the stars and the galaxies. This belief was founded in the legendary journey that the prophet made to heaven upon a white horse, accompanied by the Archangel Gabriel. In his description of these seven heavens Ibn 'Abass wrote that the first was made of emeralds, the second of red pearls, the third of rubies, the fourth of white silver, the fifth of gold, the sixth of white pearls and the seventh of brilliant light.

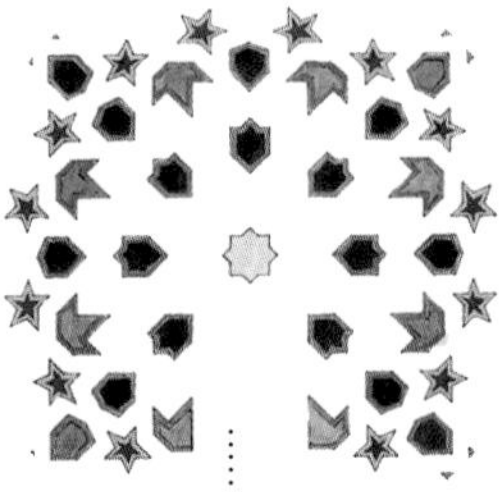

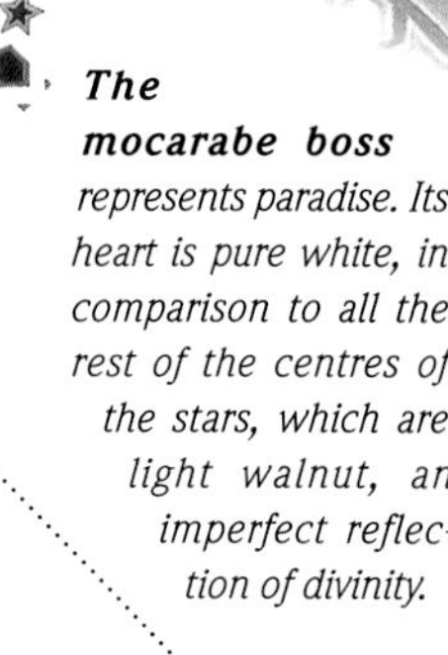

7

6

5

4

3

2

1

The mocarabe boss *represents paradise. Its heart is pure white, in comparison to all the rest of the centres of the stars, which are light walnut, an imperfect reflection of divinity.*

The ***ribbon-work stars*** *of both eight and sixteen formal elements were drawn according to the precise rules of a strict mathematical code. Nevertheless, Gómez Moreno inclines to the belief that their drawing can be put down more to the skill of artisans using compasses and set- squares than to numerical calculation.*

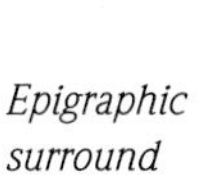

The walls are veritable tapestries of delightful stucco motifs and epigraphs which border on perfection.

The inscriptions in Kufic script and Maghrib and Andalucian cursive characters recite mainly religious themes and praise to the sultan Yusuf I. Oft repeated is the oration,

"***The only conqueror is God.***"

A panel from the intrados of the entrance arch to the throne room.

An almost imperceptible inscription upon the capital of one of the arches to an alcove confirms the public nature of this hall:

"Be brief and leave in peace."

Epigraphic surround

Ribbon-work stars

Kufic inscriptions, difficult to distinguish at first glance from the interplay of the purely geometrical design.

Interweaving of curved arches and other forms similar to those found on the Justice Gate reveal a clear Almohad influence.

Epigraphic surround between two different motifs.

Below, floral motifs in the niche at the entrance to the Hall of the Boat

ARABESQUE

The artistic intention of the rhythmic repetition of the arabesque design is very different from that of figurative art; it might almost be said to be the contrary. It doesn't try to imprison the gaze and direct it to some *ima-ginary* world but rather frees it from all the impediments of thought and imagination, in the same way as when we look at running water, the wind blowing a field of wheat, falling snow-flakes or flames flickering up the chimney.

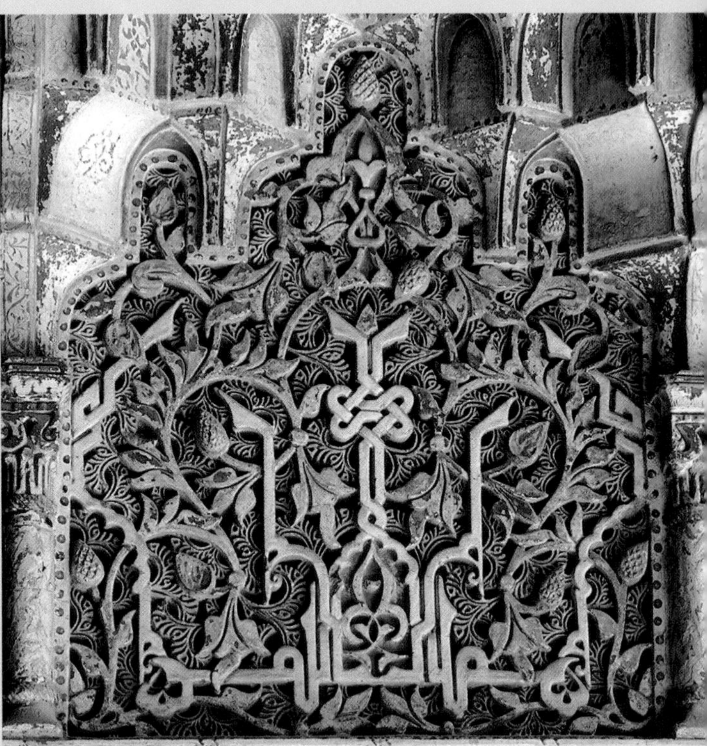

Incription on the jamb of the entrance to the Comares Tower.

It produces in us no fixed idea, just an existential condition, a feeling of tranquillity combined with an inner sense of vitality. It is abstract art, but nothing about it owes its origin to a stru-ggle between the subjective and the conscious; it obeys the precepts of total consciousness alone. The arabesque grows from the shoots of plants and obeys the laws of pure rhythm, hence the uninterrupted flow, its opposing phases, the balance between its fully expressed forms and those left almost blank. The Alhambra arabesques combine abstract palm fronds with stylised flowers interlaced with geometric design. Tongues of flame, jasmine blossom and snowflakes form together an infinite melody of divine mathematics, or, to quote the words of Muslim mystics, "drunkenness *and sobriety* combined". Lines of religious verse are interspersed or intertwined within these designs, and among it all, pointed arches rise from slender pedestals like blazing candle flames.

The geometrical roses and stars which join together and spread out from each other reflect the quintessential spirit of Islam. They are the purest symbol of the manifestation of divine reality, which is the centre of every place, of every being and every cosmos, and no thing or being can aspire to this divinity, only to be its image. Thus it is reflected from centre to centre towards infinity. The unity of being is expressed in this divine lacework in two ways: woven from one single thread and radiating from many centres. This arabesque concept sa-tisfies the Muslim artistic spirit as does no other. Because of its abstract nature and forms this artistic style has sometimes been referred to as "dehumanised", but in fact it gives mankind a frame to measure his own dignity; it places him at the centre whilst at the same time reminding him that he is only God's curator on earth.

(Titus Burckhardt)

STUCCO

Stucco is essential to Nasrid art, as it is to most Islamic art. The fact that it is an insubstantial medium should not be put down to poverty or the scarcity of firmer materials. Nasrid builders rejected stone in their walls and decorations in favour of brick, wood and gesso, materials which allow air to pass through them, absorbing contaminating elements and balancing any brusque changes in seasonal dampness. Nevertheless reasons of economy and speed did play some part; stucco work is much more malleable than stone and much easier to repair.

Carlos Borrás writes about an evolution in form, from the simpler Almohad tradition of smooth unadorned leaves to the more intricate veined shapes of the Almorávids. Although some elements such as the pineapple are fairly clearly identifiable, the majority of the plants which inspire the ataurique design are difficult to make out with any certainty. Man cannot hope to copy the perfection of nature and thus should not try to copy it but be content to contemplate it or use its form as a mere reflection or background to the word of God.

Another oft repeated motif is the shell, the symbol of water, the origin of life, belonging to the Creator alone. From Venus to Christian baptism the shell has always been synonymous with life, fertility and purification.

This strange hand is perfectly incorporated into the design of the entrance arch to the Mirador of Lindaraja.

MUSLIM EPIGRAPHS

Muslim epigraphs were executed in many different media: metal, stone, wood, gesso, ceramic and textile, and a diversity of styles, but they were all designed with the dual intention of symbolism and aesthetic beauty. Calligraphy is the most important artistic form in Islam and so the calligrapher is highly respected in society (He whose letters are beautiful deserves respect.). Because letters give form to the word of God and have the same iconographic function as images in western art. *"Muslim writings are comparable to holy images in Christian art and represent them in Muslim tradition."* The importance of the epigraphic inscriptions makes the Alhambra a complete, brilliantly lettered book. According to C. Borrás it is, *"the most luxurious edition in the world"*.

Stucco inscription in the Tower of the Captive Princess

In wood in the same tower

In stone in a niche in the Palace of Comares

In ceramic in the Tower of the Captive Princess

The fact that Arabic was the language in which the Koran was written conferred upon it a certain holiness and made it a symbol of the Moslem civilisation to such an extent that Arabic script came to be used to supplement and comment upon other languages such as Persian, Turkish, Afghan and many African dialects.

Right, Nasrid Koran, manuscript on vellum (XIV century).

Arabic script in principle only had letters to represent consonants and long vowels, and the same graph might represent various sounds. This difficulty meant that whilst official epigraphs were written in the accepted, uniform Kufic style, practical needs encouraged the development, of a more utilitarian script, which included diacritic marks and auxiliary vocalic signs. From the X century onwards this new graphic style began to be seen in epigraphs as cursive, or Naskhi, script and eventually it replaced Kufic script altogether.

The various styles of Arabic script can be seen to have evolved chronologically in the following way:

*In **old Kufic** the bottom of the line is always completely straight and the shape of the letters is very geometrical. Any spaces are left blank.*

Funeral plaque (854 a.d.)

*In **florid Kufic** the graphs are more stylised and there are many floral swashes and embellishments to the script. This style seems to have been developed by the Abbas dynasty but appeared in al-Andalus with the Omeya caliphate.*

A detail from Madinat al-Zahara.

***Simple script** is a variation introduced by the Córdoban caliphate of al-Hakam (961). It does away with the vegetal swashes but continues with the development of the linking forms.*

Funeral plaque from Córdoba (1103 a.d.)

From a devotional niche (mihrab) in the Aliafería at Zaragoza

***The taifas**, or small local kingdoms, which grew up after the initial Arab conquest, developed a great range of local variations of both the original Kufic script and its "florid" counterpart.*

Almohad Mqabriyya (1221 a.d.) Málaga Museum.

***Almohad Kufic** existed alongside the cursive style and was enriched with cursive links between the bottom of letters, decorative swashes and vegetal backgrounds in the blank spaces.*

*The most widely used and legible script was **cursive**, which became popular with the increasing use of more malleable writing surfaces, such as stucco and wood.*

The preference shown for any particular style or formula depended in the final instance upon the ideological bent of the ruler of the time and often a case can be made out for the propagandist role of the epigraph. Thus, whilst the Omeya caliphate and the local taifas preferred to use Kufic and relied on formulas praising the sovereign, the Almohad reform heralded the use of cursive script and a more religious orientation to the writings. It is evident from the epigraphs how political and religious power have always been intimately linked in the world of Islam.

*In their inscriptions the **Nasrids** revived the old formulas of the caliphate whilst at the same time maintaining the cursive, with an enormous array of vegetal backgrounds, as can be seen in this example from the Courtyard of the Myrtles. The formula is the Nasrid motto,* "The only conqueror is God." *(below)*

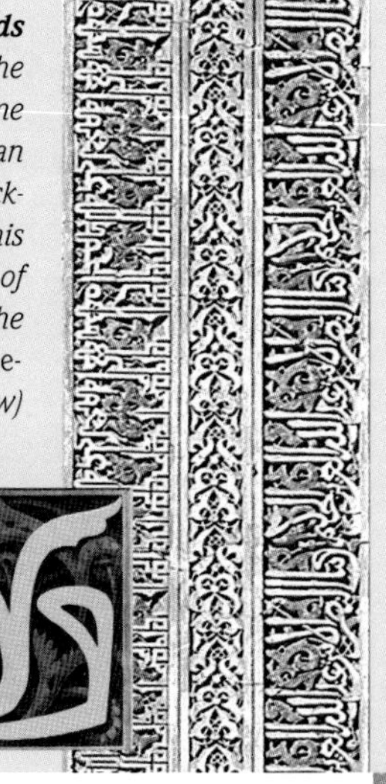

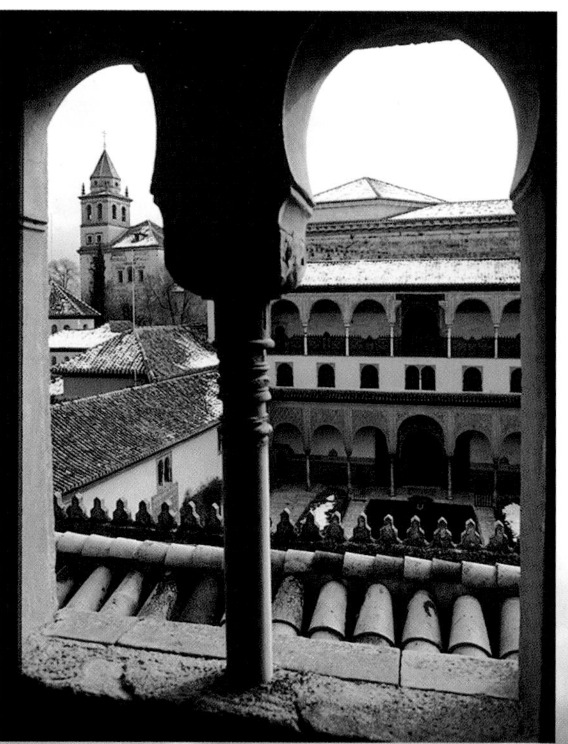

*The **rooms in the upper four floors** of the tower are contained within the thickness of the south wall. The most spacious is on the third floor; its ceiling is a barrel vault with wooden beams and it also has attractive twin windows with a pillar mullion (left). This room was possibly part of the sultan's private quarters, from where he would have had a view of the Courtyard of the Myrtles and indeed most of the citadel itself*

The view from the Comares Tower is explanation enough for why the Nasrid sultans chose the Sabica hill as the diadem of their kingdom. The traditional, limitless space of the desert, the nomad's tent joined with the elegance and grandeur of the tower itself is open to all four horizons, blown by the four winds, and lies beneath an entire hemisphere of stars. Proud and watchful, from the outside it shows only the rough skin of a tropical fruit, jealously guarding the sweet flavour of its inner wisdom.

I am a wife in my bridal gown, sublime in my perfection. Look at this jar of water and you'll understand how true my words are. Look too at my crown; it will seem to you like the new moon..."

Niche made of Macael marble in the intrados of the arch leading from the portico of the Courtyard of the Myrtles into the Hall of the Boat.

Patio de los Leones

The Palace and Courtyard of the Lions

Roberts, 1835.

This was the focal point of the sultan's private dwellings, within which there were areas set aside for the women of the house. It cannot be called the harem because it wasn't reserved exclusively for female use but was also probably used for some aspects of the sultan's political and diplomatic affairs. It is recorded on December 30 1362 that during the second reign of Mohammad V nothing more existed of the Courtyard of the Lions than the Sala de las Dos Hermanas (The Hall of the two Sisters) and so the buildings that surround it today must have been constructed after this date.

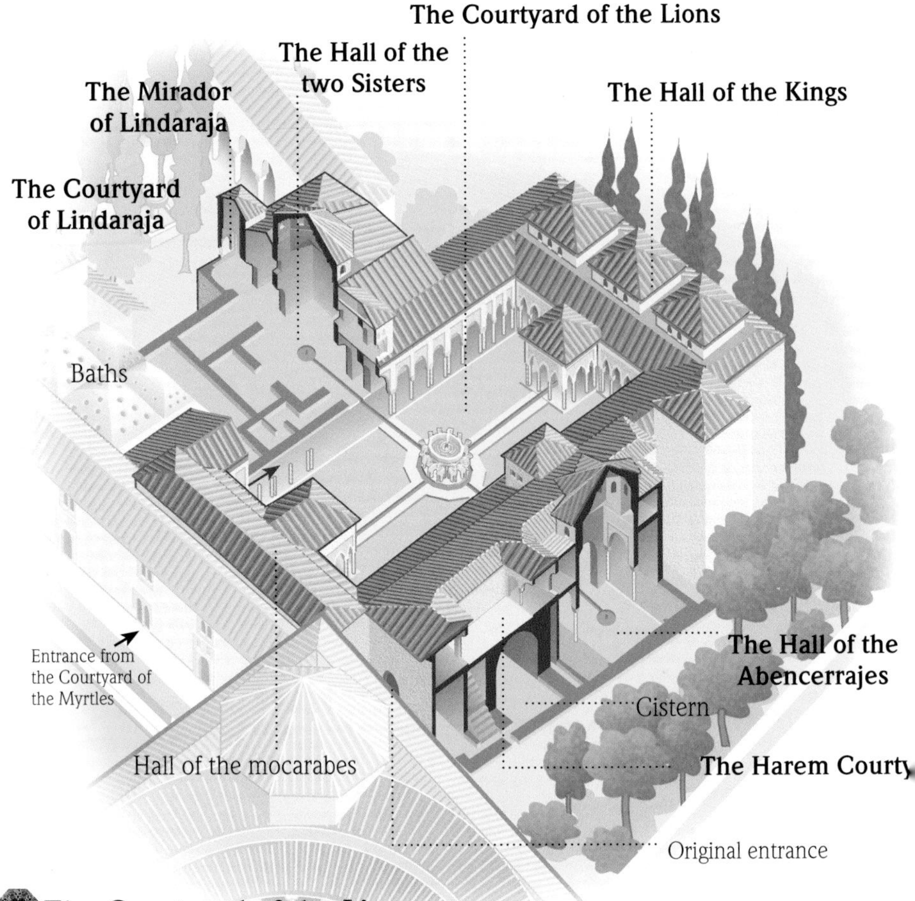

The Courtyard of the Lions

The Hall of the two Sisters

The Mirador of Lindaraja

The Hall of the Kings

The Courtyard of Lindaraja

Baths

Entrance from the Courtyard of the Myrtles

The Hall of the Abencerrajes

Cistern

Hall of the mocarabes

The Harem Courty

Original entrance

The Courtyard of the Lions

From the original entrance, shown here in the lower corner of the plan, the beauty of this patio progressively revealed itself to the visitor. In either direction that he chose to take around the cloister, he found himself walking through a forest of gilded pillars, which little by little began to appear like *"gold fringes of lace hanging from the sky"*.

The overhanging carved wooden eaves with beautifully sculpted corbels, which were originally polychromed, protected the adornments of the arches and columns below.

The Nasrid motto, ***"The only conqueror is God"*** *is repeated throughout the epigraphic surround.*

The columns support ***pilasters,*** *which in turn hold up lintels supporting the upper structure of the walls. The spandrels between the pilasters are filled by small, purely decorative, open-work, or "curtain" arches.*

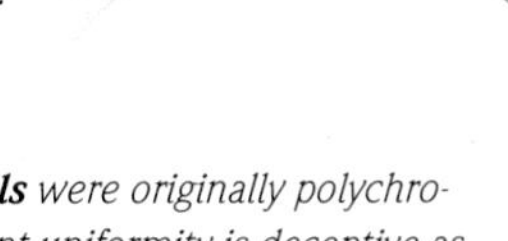

The ***cubic capitals*** *were originally polychromed. Their apparent uniformity is deceptive as their motifs are in fact considerably varied*

"The integrity of Granadan art can be seen in the artistic saturation of many single forms, such as the capitals on the columns in the Courtyard of the Lions. Ever since the Egyptian lotus capitals, never have columns been crowned more elegantly, if by elegance we understand simplicity combined with the finest degree of development of the artistic forms." (Oleg Grabar).

The ***jambs*** *of the columns are connected both to the capitels and plinths by lead joints to assure the perfect seating of all three parts of the column and also to allow them a suitable degree of expansion and contraction.*

Space in the Alhambra *is as open as in the desert, where intimacy itself is to be found beneath the stars. The Courtyard of the Lions isn't a house with a garden but a garden containing a house, which should be looked at from its corners at floor height; thus the photograph on the left, which complies more accurately with the viewpoint of its builders.*

There has been interminable discussion about the original appearance of this courtyard, with decisions appealing to all tastes.

An inscription in the Hall of the Two Sisters asks,

"Have you ever seen such a beautiful garden?"

"We have never seen a garden with greater abundance of fruit, nor sweeter, nor more perfumed..."

but today its flowers no longer form a carpet on the earth, nor do they climb and twine around the marble columns; what we see is no more than a magnificent skeleton, a dry framework to which greenery once gave meaning and life.

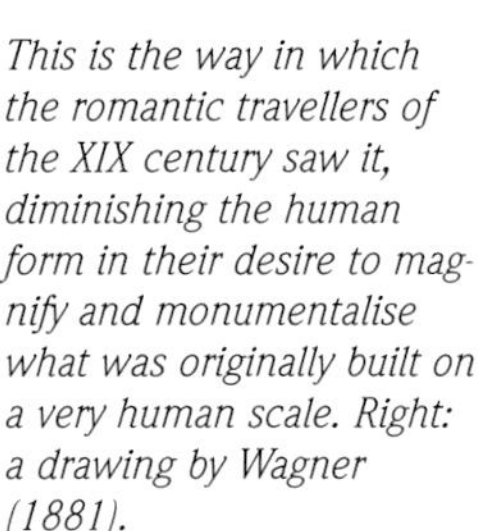

This is the way in which the romantic travellers of the XIX century saw it, diminishing the human form in their desire to magnify and monumentalise what was originally built on a very human scale. Right: a drawing by Wagner (1881).

Interest in the Alhambra aroused by authors such as Washington Irving led to the first restorations, in which there was a certain tendency towards adorning the original monument according to not very accurate guesswork

Thus in 1858 Rafael Contreras embellished the eastern chamber of this courtyard (below) with a ***dome*** *and glazed tiles to give it the appearance of similar buildings in Persia.*

The dome was taken off in 1934 by Leopoldo Torres Balbás, who initiated a programme of preservation which confined itself to keeping what was already there and not reconstructing a hypothetical monument where there was any doubt as to the original design. The only exception to his policy was to make clearly new innovations in places which had been left completely abandoned, such as the gardens of the Partal Palace.

To get an idea of the original appearance of this courtyard a visitor must have some understanding of the ***symbolic points of reference*** *of its designers. Thus, from certain angles the forest of columns reminds us of the palm trees surrounding an oasis, as suggested by Francisco Prieto Moreno in this drawing. Streams always flow along the shady floor and it is sheltered by leafy greenery. Below is a photograph of one of the many "adaptations" or "trials" to which this courtyard was subject during the XX century.*

According to Islamic tradition, the hortus conclusus *or walled garden is an image of* ***paradise****, the name of which in the Koran is* al-Yanna, *a word which embraces the two meanings of "garden" and "secret place". A visitor today must allow his imagination to see the four areas between the streams, today covered with sand, as beds full of flowering bushes and aromatic herbs. The four streams symbolise the four rivers of paradise that run towards the four points of the compass, or flow from them towards the centre* (R. Manzano).

Evidence from other similar courtyards suggests that ***the floor level*** *may well have been lower than the pathways, in such a way that the plants would have formed a living carpet. Tapestry came from the East and is an expression of the garden taken into the house.*

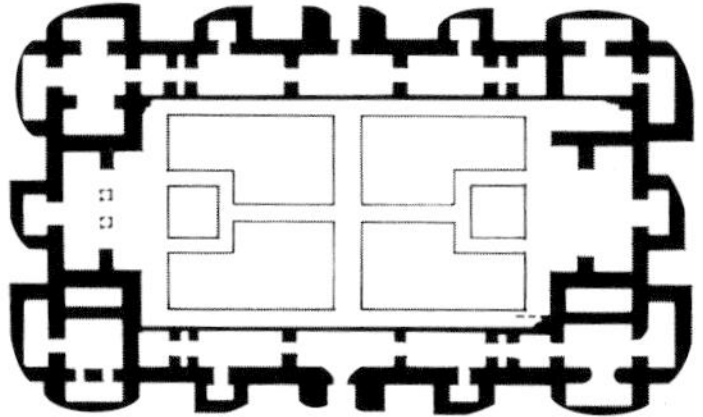

Plan of the ***Monteagudo*** *Palace in Murcia (XII century), which, according to some authors may have been the inspiration for the Courtyard of the Lions.*

***Similarities** have often been drawn between the Courtyard of the Lions and Benedictine cloisters, which abounded in the middle ages (such as in this photograph of the monastery of Seo Urgell). It is known that when Mohammad V, the builder of this courtyard, was dethroned by his cousin for two years he spent his exile in the court of the Castillian King Pedro the Cruel, his friend and protector, who eventually helped him to regain his throne. Upon his return in 1362 he started work on this courtyard and, according to documents in Fez, he was always smothered in lime and plaster while he personally supervised the building work. This was a period of tolerance and the exchange of cultural ideas between Christians and Muslims. In Castilla noblemen contracted Granadan artisans to decorate their towers and carve their wooden ceilings, which led to "Mudejar" art becoming fashionable throughout the Castillian Christian world. At the same time in the most beautiful dome of the Alhambra, that of the Hall of the Two Sisters; the most prominent design is the* fleur de lys *of King Pedro. Although there may be similarities in the earlier courtyard in Murcia, the uniqueness of the Courtyard of the Lions in the Alhambra lies in its synthesis of all the old traditions, resulting in the expressive culmination of an entire culture.*

*The **present-day layout** is quite modern and replaces the last garden, which had to be taken out to prevent its roots and the dampness from affecting the fragile structures of the palace itself. Four cement basins with their own drainage have been constructed below floor level to accommodate any future damp and even the four orange trees growing here today are planted in large pots below ground.*

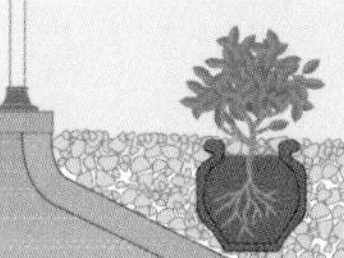

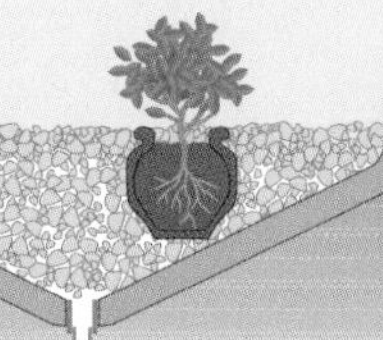

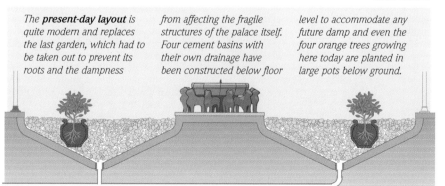

The two small pavilions jutting out into the east and west sides of the courtyard, each housing a small fountain, also play a part in the Islamic image of paradise as the high tents *(rafraf)* or canopies described in the Koran. The model for these pavilions floating above delicate columns derives from further east, in Persian art, of which this part of the Alhambra is so reminiscent.

The ***coffered ceilings*** of these two pavilions are two perfect hemispheres constructed with pieces of flat wood. Originally they were polychromed as were the majority of the Alhambra's ceilings.

*Refreshing water springs from the mouths of twelve white marble lions in t***he Fountain of the Lions** *in the middle of the courtyard. Placed in a circle and bearing on their backs a twelve-sided bowl, their gaze embraces every part of the courtyard. Some experts say that at one time the whole fountain was polychromed, and indeed there is evidence to suggest that the lions have been scraped clean at some time in their lives. It is also believed that the lions may originally have come from a palace belonging to Samuel Ibn Nagrela, which is thought to have existed in the precincts of the Alambra. What is generally accepted is that they were sculpted between the end of the X and beginning of the XI century.*

XIX century engravings reveal the presence of an **upper bowl** *to this fountain, which today is to be found in the Adarve gardens in the Alcazaba (right). To the left is an illustration by Nicholas Chapuy (1844).*

The original fountain represents an ancient symbol that arrived in Granada from pre-Christian civilisations in the East: the lion spewing water from its mouth is the sun, from whence all life springs. The twelve suns of this fountain are the twelve suns of the **zodiac**, the twelve months in which we all exist simultaneously. They uphold the sea like the twelve iron bulls in Solomon's temple, and this sea is the basin of heaven's waters. To what extent the nasrid builders of the Alhambra were aware of this ancient symbolism, however, is impossible to say. (R. Manzano).

Around the edge of the bowl there is a beautiful poem by Ibn Zamrak which gives us considerable insight into many details of the courtyard and its fountain.

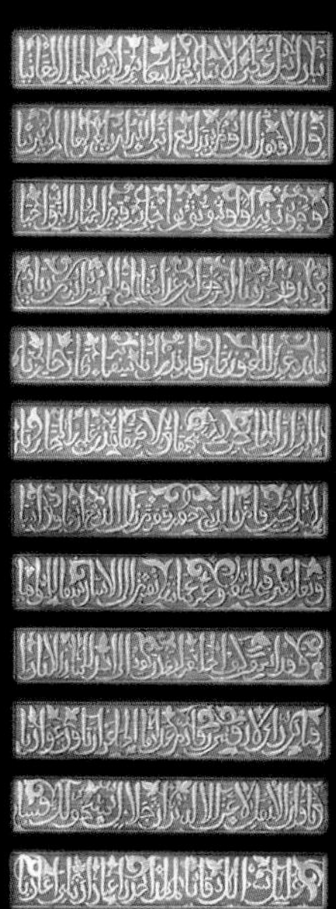

"Blessed be He who gave to the Iman Mohammad mansions adorned so magnificently. Do we not have here in this garden a work so beautiful as to be unrivalled in all God's creations. The glistening pearls of which she is made have overflowed into her very substance. Liquid silver, incomparable in its whiteness and brilliance, flows between her jewels. To the eye the molten silver and the solid jewels become entwined so that it is impossible to say which of the them is flowing. See how the water laps against the rims of the channels, to be hidden moments later underground, just as a lover tries to keep the tears in his eyes from betraying him. And truly, is she not like a cloud who pours down her beneficence onto the lions. And in the same way, the hand of the caliph, from the first light of dawn, does he not also pour his bounty upon the lions of war..."

The Fountain of the Lions is the best example of one of the most important contributions that the Nasrid era gave to Granada: water engineering of the most ingenious subtlety. Until then irrigation was based on the traditional flooding system and water was often supplied by means of Roman aqueduct-type canals, which carried water constantly. The network of water channels in Granada, which relied on the natural flow of water from the surrounding mountains, brought a real social and agricultural revolution to the city, the marvel of all visitors to the kingdom. As did the rest of the citadel, the royal palaces received their water from the Royal Waterway, which was kept in a reservoir at its highest point above the city to give sufficient pressure to supply the whole town. It is most likely in fact that the royal palaces were not built higher up on the Alhambra hill, which today is known as the Secano, or dry area, precisely in order to take advantage of the water pressure lower down to run the fountains and streams that were so essential to Nasrid architecture.

On the right is a bird's eye view of the cross section of the bowl of the fountain

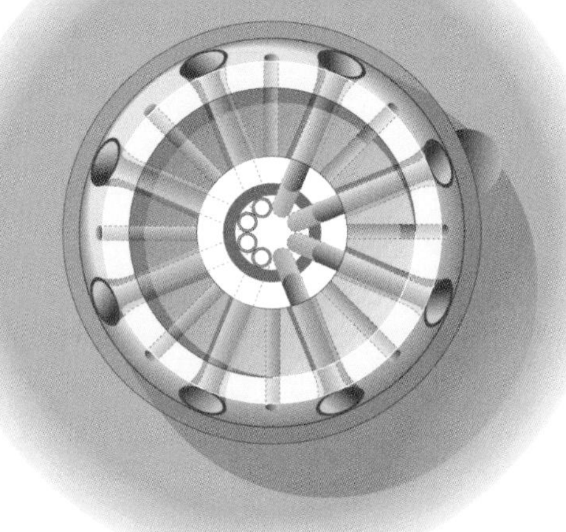

The water arrived under considerable pressure due to the height of the reservoir. As it rose through the wide pipes to the main fountain and bowl it lost pressure to give a gentle curtain of water. The water which spouts from the lions' mouths comes from a sump beneath the fountain and then not far away from the fountain the flow of the slimmer drainage channels is calculated to be such that the water level in the fountain is always constant and the balance of flow and escape always the same. The water fell in a glitteringly smooth curtain to shatter into gleaming pearls and re-emerge through the mouths of the lions. Today the Arabic hydraulic system has been dismantled and part of it is on display in the exhibition hall of the Alhambra (left).

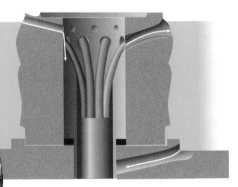

DAYLIGHT AND THE ALHAMBRA

It is well known that the orientation of the palaces makes each column the hand of a sun dial (see the drawing to the right). This is the result of all the rooms' being aligned from north to south, even to the extent of filling in gullies in the case of the Comares Tower and the Tower of the Ladies in order to keep this orientation to within tenths of degrees. Neither is it mere chance that all the rooms receive much more light in winter than in summer, mainly thanks to the wide overhanging eaves and cornices. Particularly favoured are some secluded corners, warmed by the slanting winter sun but sheltered from the wind. During the hottest months, however, the sun is so high that its rays scarcely reach these hidden nooks enough to warm the marble walls and floors. The places that receive most sun in winter stay in the shade in summer and many of the south-facing rooms remain as cool as they would with any modern air conditioning.

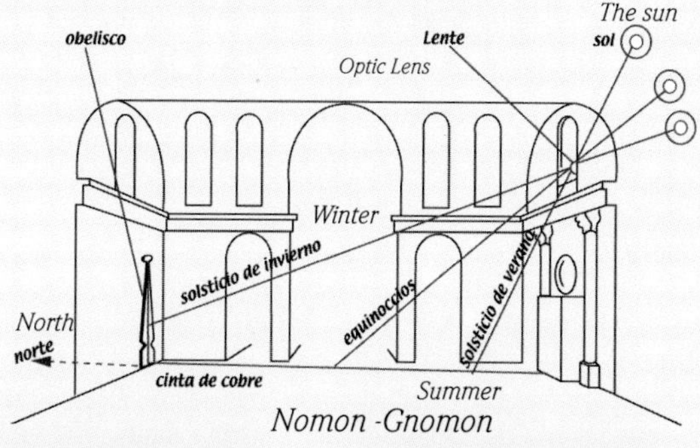

Above, the sun at midday in the Hall of the Two Sisters, which in Granada is 2 hours and 14 minutes post meridiem Greenwich time, allowing for European summer time and Granada's longitude, nearly 4 minutes west of Greenwich.

Midday: Stunted shadows in the north gallery of the Courtyard of the Myrtles at the summer equinox.

Above, sun dial at the Carthusian Monastery

 The Hall of the Abencerrages

It has been said that in Granada legend and history are so interwoven that it is impossible to distinguish between the two. The name "Abencerrage" is a mutation of banu al-Sarrya, *the name of a family who played an important role in the politics of their day. Legend has it that a rival family, the "Zenete", engineered a conspiracy involving the sultana in an amorous affair and that in a fit of jealousy the sultan invited thirty-six men of the Abencerrage family to a celebration in this hall and had them all cut down in front of him. In fact it is not clear when this is supposed to have happened and the story has also been attributed to various sultans.*

***Mariano Fortuny,** a painter of the romantic period of the end of the XIX century, portrayed the slaughter of the Abencerrages in this painting of 1871. A lot of what many visitors to the Alhambra expect to see, and so believe they are seeing, has been created by the imagination of romantic writers and painters.*

The story affirms that the russet veins in the marble in the bottom of the fountain are the bloodstains of the murdered courtiers.

They are of course oxidisation in the marble itself.

This hall is an ideal refuge in the heat of summer. When the doors are shut the only light to enter the room filters in through the high, star-shaped, lantern windows in the cupola, which also draw out the hot air from below. The water in the fountain, emerging chilly from underground, always keeps the air fresh and cool. Its thick, windowless walls let in no heat and turn it into a pleasant cave in which the temperature of its alcoves never rises much above twenty degrees even during the hottest months of the year.

***The alcoves**, set apart by pillars from the rest of the room, were couches and divans. The step up into these alcoves accentuates their separation from the rest of the room. They usually open onto a courtyard or another room but would have been curtained off for privacy.*

A romantic impression of the Hall of the Abencerrages by Chapuy (1840).

*The **"alicatado"** tiling was stripped from this hall and taken to the Alcázar in Sevilla (above); the present-day tiles (right) date from the XVI century.*

*From behind the fountain **the perspective** is one of a series of different brilliantly lit optical planes. Right in the background, through the The Mirador of Lindaraja in the Hall of the Two Sisters there was a view of the old city framed against the sky. The surface of the fountain reflects the magnificent coffered ceiling, the mocarabes of which form an enormous eight-pointed star (see the following page).*

Two passageways lead out of the Hall of the Abecerrages: the one to the left gives onto a vestibule, which was the entrance to the palace in Nasrid times, and the one to the right takes you to a stairway leading up to the first floor, where the women and younger children probably lived.

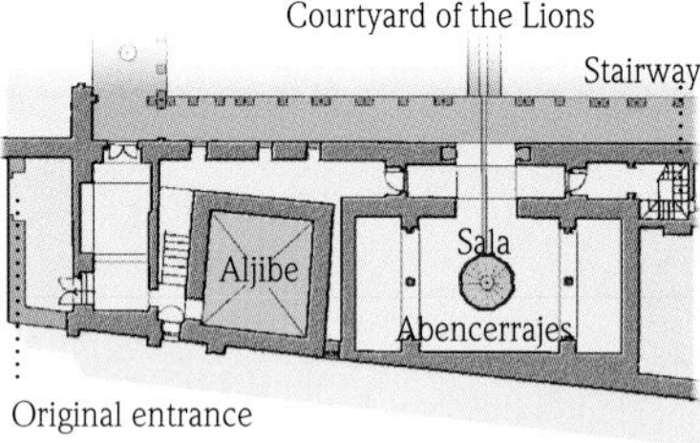

The Courtyard of the Harem

The central area of this upper living space was the Courtyard of the Yannan, *or* Harem, *built over the cistern that provided water for the baths in the Comares Palace. The courtyard still has vestiges of painted dados and black marble capitals, found nowhere else in the Alhambra.*

From behind the jalousies the women, hidden but ever present, could see all that happened in the courtyard and so were aware of the daily goings-on in the palace.

Domestic objects

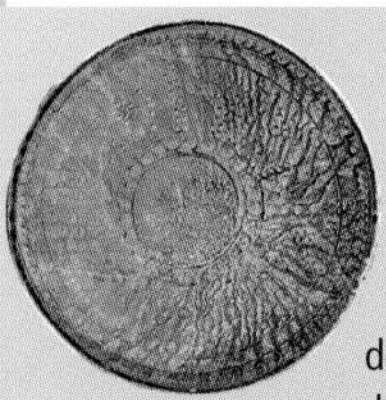

It is quite clear that these rooms were never intended to be filled with furniture in the western style. In desert culture furniture consists of carpets, cushions, tapestries and a few ornately decorated cabinets, divans and mats laid on the floor beside the odd low table: everything easy to be collected up to turn whatever space into a dining room or reception room according to need. Very little of this survives in the Alhambra but we do have other types of objects belonging to the daily life of the people of this time: ceramics, iron, stone and wooden utensils, ivory and bone adornments, jewels and so on.

A woman's place in Muslim society

Islamic culture preaches the equality of men and women at the moral and religious level but at the same time maintains the pre-eminence of men in public and political life. Women should be kept safe and looked after by men and devote themselves to affairs inside the home and the care of their children, whilst men rule outside the home and take care of their businesses.

The anthropologist Pierre Guichard points out how the dwelling tells a lot about the structure of the family in those days: turned inwards upon itself around a central courtyard with many rooms opening onto it; one room for the head of the family to receive visitors, and upper lodgings for the women and children. This separation is not so much one of space as of time. When the husband is away the home belongs to the wife, who runs the household from around the courtyard. But when strangers visit the house the women are kept apart from their gaze. Differences also existed according to social class; a servant would obviously have been admitted to the presence of a visitor in order to carry out her duties whilst the wife or daughter would remain hidden. The reason for this was that inheritance was always via the male side in these communities and women were a valuable property to be exchanged with care. Added to this was the strong sense of "self" compared to society as a whole, with all the fear of ridicule and social rejection which this implied. This is why personal intimacy was valued above many other things: high walls, gates with hidden corners, discreet entrances, and all that is mentioned elsewhere in this guide about Muslim architecture.

Within the house women might receive visits from other women belonging to their family or women from outside such as those coming to sell household wares, healers or their children's teachers, all of whom would have kept them up to date with affairs of the world. There were also certain places in the town permitted to them: the part of the mosque set aside for women, the market and the baths, during the hours reserved for them, when they became a popular feminine meeting place.

A special case in palaces and noble households was that of the slave girls (yariya), whose job it was to provide pleasure for the lord and his guests. They were instructed in many arts; we find them playing the lute, reciting poetry or pouring wine, while the wife remained in her rooms. Often Christians who taught Castillian to the lord's children, these slave concubines might sometimes be chosen as second or third wives and history is full of tales to suggest that some of them did not hesitate to use their influence on their lord to meddle in state affairs.

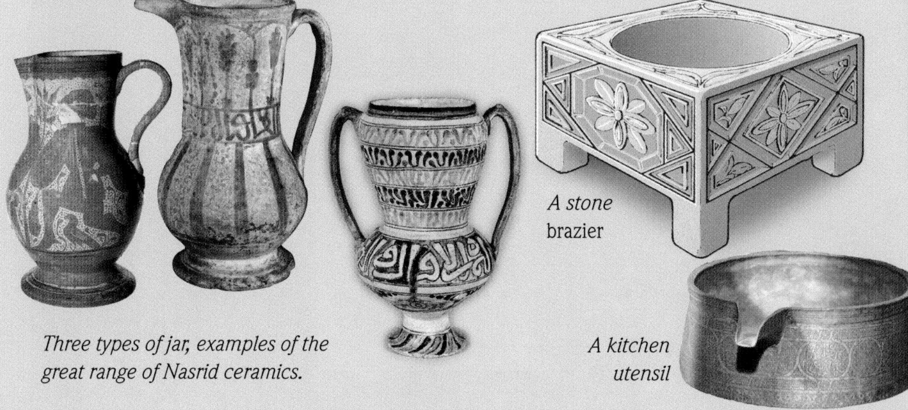

A stone brazier

Three types of jar, examples of the great range of Nasrid ceramics.

A kitchen utensil

The Hall of the Kings

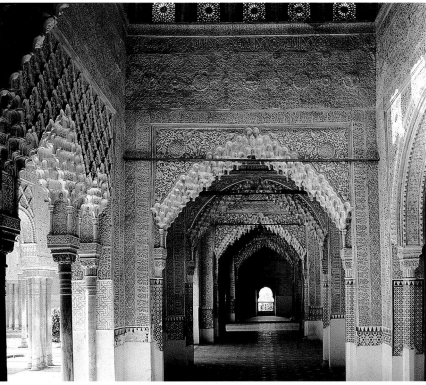

This hall occupies the whole of the east side of the courtyard. It is divided into five separate areas; three of these are chambers illuminated from porticos giving onto the courtyard and separated from each other by the other two transitional areas, which lie in deep shadow. From either end the hall appears to be a succession of light and shade. Each room is defined by high, pointed stucco arches, all elaborately decorated in different styles. This variety in adornment and the alternation of light and shade renders even such rich and complex decoration soothing to the eye, without producing the fatigue which Baroque design can cause when repeated incessantly.

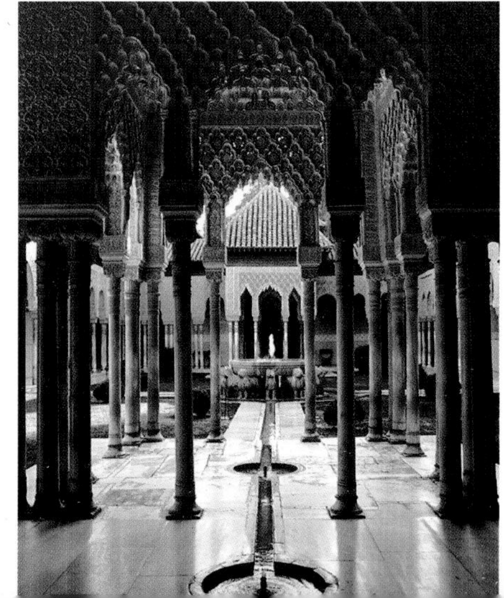

*The alcove of **the central chamber**, due to its privileged position, was without doubt that of the sultan and his retinue. Sitting here the view of the courtyard appears to be one of an oasis seen through a grove of palm trees with the fountain of the lions at its centre.*

The ceilings of the alcoves at the back of the three principal chambers are painted with pictures of seated kings and other human and animal forms. It is generally accepted that they date from the end of the XIV or beginning of the XV centuries but, given the Koranic prohibition against the representation of living beings, argument still goes on as to both their origin and supposed symbolism. Nevertheless, since inves-tigations by Massignon, the French specialist in Arabic matters, the tendency is to agree that they are of Muslim origin, although highly influenced by occidental taste. In fact what Sura V of the Koran prohibits is the *anzab*, or idol, which may become an object of worship. This prohibition is not in fact exclusive to Islam, it is also intrinsic to the Old Testament and the Talmud.

The paintings are on ***sheep skin*** *stuck to wooden frames with starch glue and small bamboo pins to prevent their coming unstuck because of differences in expansion rates and also to avoid any damage that might be caused by rusty nails.*

On the ceiling of the ***central alcove*** *is a painting of ten seated men, who, according to tradition, are the first ten rulers of the Nasrid dynasty.*

The paintings on the ceilings of the two side alcoves seem to share certain similarities in theme. In one of them, two characters, a Muslim and a Christian, are engaged in acts of prowess, ostensibly with the intention of winning the love of a Christian lady. The tale continues in the south alcove, where the Muslim runs his Christian rival through with his lance, before gestures of supplication from the lady, who is watching the tournament from a tower. Almost all experts in the subject point to a clear early Tuscan influence on the style.

The Hall of the Two Sisters

Contrary to what was believed until recently, it is now known that this hall is the oldest of all the rooms surrounding the Courtyard of the Lions. What this room was called originally is unknown but its present-day name, the Two Sisters, refers to the twin pair of Macael marble slabs that lie in its centre.

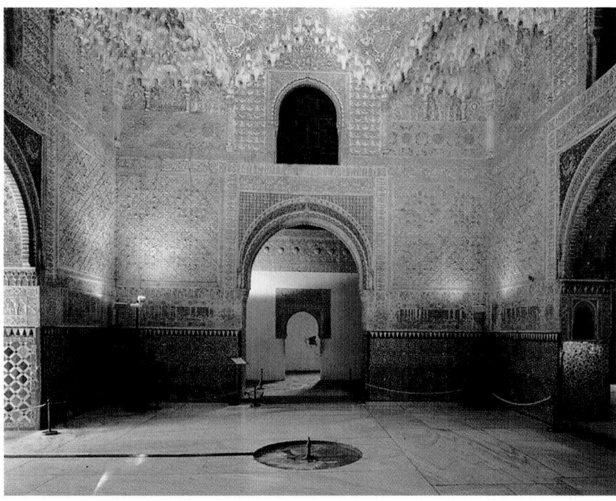

On entering this hall from the Courtyard of the Lions, just as in the Hall of the Abencerrages, one narrow passage branches to the right and another to the left. The one on the right leads to a stairway to the **upper rooms** and that on the left to a **water closet.**

The Muslims were far ahead of the rest of Europe in the design and use of lavatories flushed by water. ***The latrine*** *itself was a tile perforated with a long hole. The closet also contained a separate wash basin and ventilation.*

Two sturdy ***arches*** *on each side of the main entrance from the courtyard provide access to bedroom alcoves. The arch opposite leads out of the Hall of the Two Sisters proper into the Chamber of the Ajimeces (referring to the beautiful mullion windows), which itself serves as an anteroom to the Mirador of Lindaraja. Above these arches there are four more smaller ones, which provide light for the rooms above.*

The pattern and metallic lustre of the tiles adorning the dado of this room are some of the most original and beautiful to be found in the whole of the Alhambra. The general pattern is one of small shields within a labyrinth of interwoven ribbons without beginning or end. As a counterpoint to this, the jambs to the arches (right) are decorated with circular motifs.

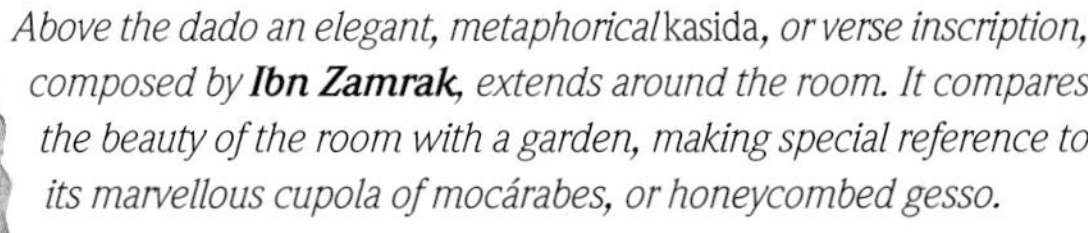

Above the dado an elegant, metaphorical kasida, *or verse inscription, composed by* ***Ibn Zamrak****, extends around the room. It compares the beauty of the room with a garden, making special reference to its marvellous cupola of mocárabes, or honeycombed gesso.*

"I am a garden adorned with beauty; you will understand me if you gaze at my harmony. Through the generosity of my lord Mohammad I am superior to all that is noble both now and in the future. A sublime creation, Fortune wishes me to surpass all other monuments.

How much pleasure there is here for the eyes! In this place the soul will find idyllic reveries. The dreamer will be accompanied by the five Pleiades and will wake to the gentle morning breeze. An incomparable cupola shines with beauties both hidden and open to the gaze. Seduced, Gemini holds out her hand to you and the moon comes with her to converse. And the brilliant stars themselves want to remain fixed in your cupola rather than continue their course through the vault of heaven and wait submissively like slaves in either courtyard, vying in their desire to serve you:

It is not to be wondered at that the very stars err and pass their appointed limit, ready to serve my lord, for whosoever serves the glorious himself achieves glory.

The portico is so elegant that the palace itself challenges the celestial firmament.

So many arches rise up in its vault, resting upon columns embellished by light.

Like the celestial spheres that form a vault across the brilliant pillar of the dawn!

All the columns together are so lovely that their fame has been spread abroad by many tongues: the marble throws its serene light to brighten the dark corners hidden in shade; and despite their size their reflections appear to be pearls in their iridescence.

Never has such a magnificent palace been seen before, of such clear and ample lines.

Never before has such a florid garden been contemplated, full of the most fragrant and succulent fruits.

The judge of beauty has decreed she be paid a double tax in double coinage, for if at dawn the hands of the zephyr are full of drachmas of light to satisfy her, in the evening the sun decks out her gardens, filling them with golden dihram through the branches of the trees.

The ***cupola of mocárabes*** *(previous double page) is an amazing composition of 5,416 pieces. To the right are both the plan and the cross-section, as drawn by Owen Jones in1842.*

At the top of the walls, the square ground-plan of the room becomes octagonal by the use of mocárabe pendentives, upon which rests the octagonal ceiling, which has two high windows in each plane of the octagon.

Until 1590 light fell onto the mocarabes through stained-glass in these windows. The effect of the light upon the mocárabes was to give a sensation of movement, which the light imparted to the ceiling according to its angle of incidence at any moment. There are no two seconds in the day when the cupola looks exactly the same and its eternal mutation within unity represents a metaphor of the stars in the firmament circling around their northern axis.

Relationships between Muslims and Christians at this time were not always so tense as we are led to believe. At times they made alliances to help each other against third parties of either persuasion. A detail that reveals the importance of cultural exchange during the reign of Mohammad V is this **fleur de lys,** *the Bourbon symbol that Pedro I added to his arms when he married Blanche de Bourbon. It appears here either as a symbol of friendship or homage. This friendship caused the Castillian king, known as The Just, considerable problems during his reign.*

Mocárabes

According to Muslim tradition the prophet Mahoma received his inspiration for the Koran directly from the Archangel Gabriel in the famous cave at Hira, where he had sought refuge while fleeing from his enemies. A spider's web miraculously sealed the entrance to the cave to confuse his pursuers and since then it has been an important place of pilgrimage for all Muslims on their journey to Mecca some 30 km away. In celebration of this event stalactites became an essential decorative element, imbued with religious connotations, throughout the world of Islam, a tradition persisting even to this day.

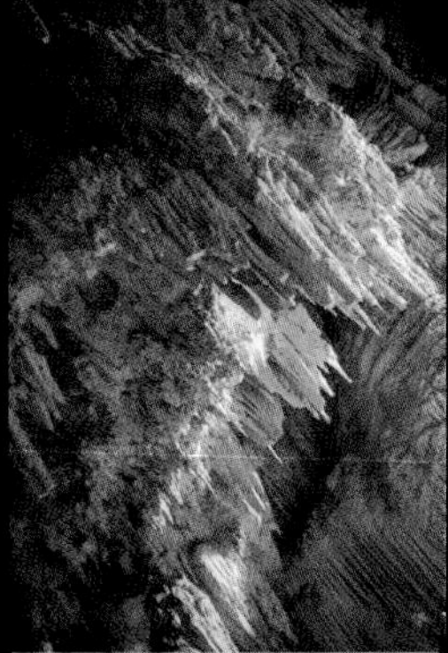

The caves at Nerja (Málaga)

Early mocárabes dating from the X century are to be found at Nisapur (Iran), and from the XI century at la Oal'a de Beni Hammad (north Africa). After this their use became widespread throughout Islam, reaching levels of great architectural splendour in cities such as Isphahan. (To the right, a ceiling in the caliphal mosque in Isphahan.)

Mocárabes

Mocárabes are essentially a combination of stucco elements with prismatic or triangular sections, which can be joined together in an infinite number of ways.

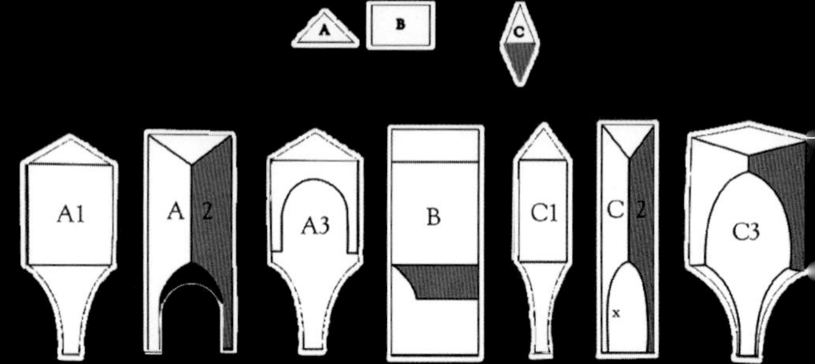

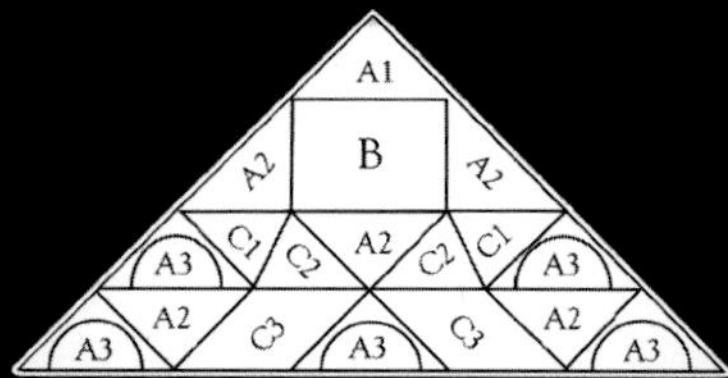

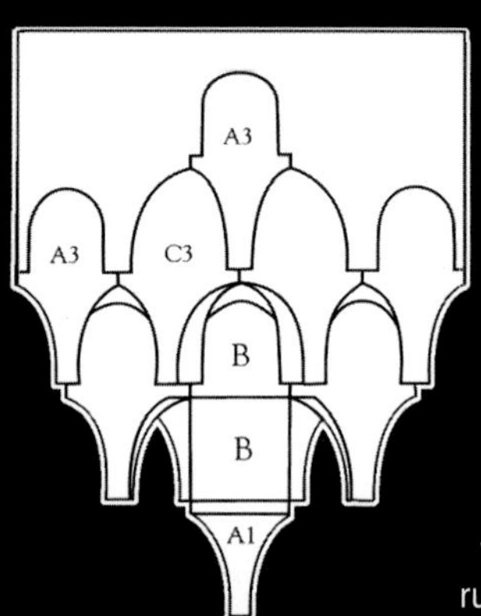

To the left, a pendentive from the Hall of the Two Sisters, as analysed by Owens and Gury. Although they have no structural role, Muslim builders used mocárabes in profusion to resolve the visual problem of the transition between upright surfaces and the cupola (right), which western architecture tends to resolve with a curvilinear trian gle.

"From the cosmological point of view th hemispherical cupola represented the sky with it constant spinning motion, whilst the cube-shape of th walls and room below it represented the earthly worlc ruled by contrast. The sky is ether. The cells comprising th mocárabes that form the transition from the undivided cupola to the square walls freeze the liquid ether of the sky into th solid forms of the earth. The stalactite effect is obtained b accentuating and elongating the groins of the vault, in whic there may be several honeycombs of mocárabes Furthermore, the honeycombs or individual cells o the design can be assembled in a multitude o ways, with both convex and concave shape Granadan artists have dissolved entire vault into mocárabe honeycombs, the honey o which is the sky itself. A similar effect i produced by the plaster networks anc grilles moulded into the front walls o the halls; the wall seems to be sc transparent that it might be made of cells filled with light".
(Titus Burckhardt)

Ceilings in the Hall of Kings, revealing the great diversity of form which mocárabes can express. In fact the same element seems to alter throughout the day as the light thrown upon it changes in colour and angle. In this way the light becomes a primary component of the architecture itself.

".... in the light all the materials shine and gleam; they glow luminously. As every individual note of colour in the decoration is quite small, the chromatic effect is one of pointillist fragmentation, weightless, absolutely incorporeal, the pure vibration of light in a diaphanous mantle, constantly changing its shape and colour .... the light as it shines on the surfaces from different angles creates contrasts in planes and textures and generates mobility in form. Artistic reality here, like reality in nature, appears at every moment to be newly shaped from myriads of atoms." (C. Borrás).

Ceiling at the north-east corner of the Courtyard of the Lions with vestiges of its original polychroming

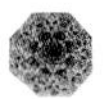 The Mirador of Lindaraja

"All the arts have enriched me with their own special beauty and given me their splendour and perfection. You who would see me, judge through me the beauty of a wife who walks towards this jar and asks its favour. When you watch me and contemplate my beauty attentively your eyes are deceived by a vision. Because when you look into my splendid depths you believe that the full moon has abandoned her mansions to live in mine and keep here her dwelling place. I am not alone for from here I look over a lovely garden; no eyes have ever beheld anything similar to it. This is a crystal palace, although there are those who on seeing it have pronounced it a storming, surging ocean.

Here breathe fresh breezes; the air is healthy and the zephyr agreeable. I join together all beauties in the same way that the stars in the high firmament steal their light from them.

Surely I am in this garden an eye filled with joy and the pupil of this eye is veritably my lord."

Poem inscribed above the mirador.

The name, "Lindaraja" would seem to derive from the phonetic mutation and semantic misunderstanding of three Arabic words, "ain-dar-Aixa" (the eyes of the house of Aixa). The mirador, in which the window sills are still at their original height, has a beautiful mullion window in its north wall, overlooking the garden of Lindaraja. Before the addition after the Christian conquest of the gallery that now encloses the garden the whole city could be seen beyond and below the wall.

View of the garden from the ground floor.

Crowning the mirador a ***stained-glass, lantern window*** *(below), enclosed in a delicate wooden frame filled this small room, once the throne room, with multicoloured light.*

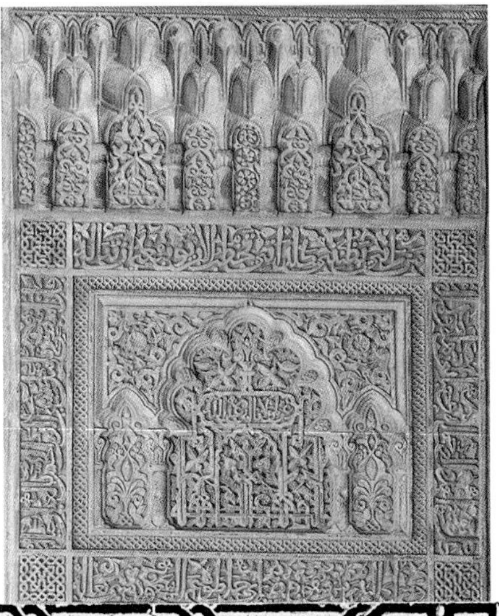

All the ***dados*** *in this room are made out of tiny hand-made tiles. In the embellishment covering the jambs of the arch are splendid inscriptions in black ceramic fixed upon a white background. They allude to Muhammad V and are without doubt the finest and most laboriously executed in the palace, a masterpiece of Muslim art.*

The centre of this intricate jewel of ceramic art is composed of only three black pieces, which fit into the white background, moulded to the millimetre to accomodate them.

 The Courtyard of the Grille and The Courtyard of Lindaraja

These two courtyards were laid out when alterations were made in 1526 to accommodate King Charles I on his state visit to Granada. The new royal apartments, containing beautiful Flemish coffered ceilings, were in fact hardly used because one of Granada's frequent earth tremors scared the king's new bride, Isabel of Portugal, into retiring to the Monastery of St. Jerome in the city below. In 1828 Washington Irving wrote in these rooms one of the first and most important works of American literature, **"Tales of the Alhambra"**.

The Courtyard of the Grille. The large, wrought-iron grille along the balcony, which gave the courtyard its name, can be clearly seen in the photograph.

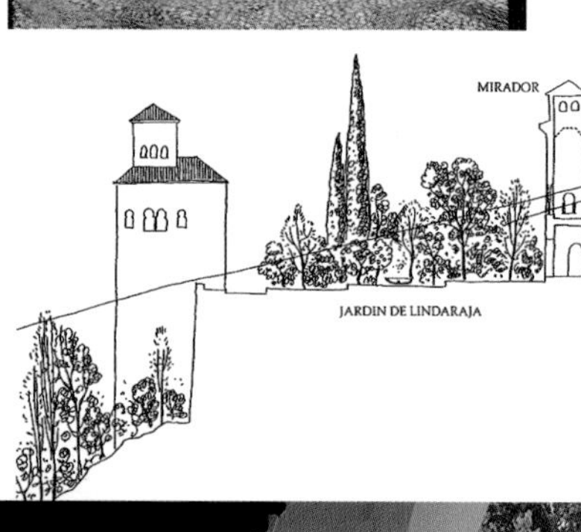

From this drawing by Francisco Prieto Moreno it is obvious that before the Christians added their own structures the most intimate rooms of the Harem were clearly visible from outside.

The Courtyard of Lindaraja. The magnificent fountain like the one in the centre of the Mexuar Courtyard, is a copy of the original.

Baño

The Bath-House

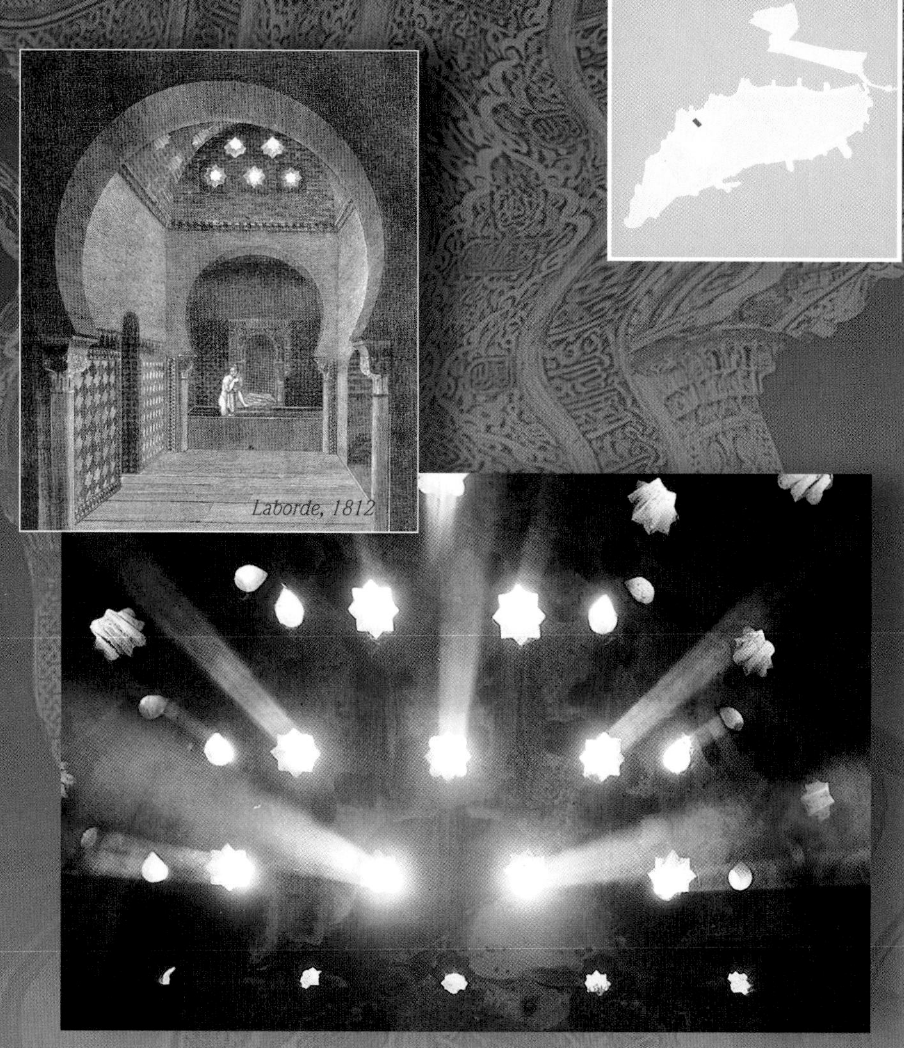
Laborde, 1812

The bath-house of the Comares Palace had a very specific function directly related to politics and diplomacy. The position of its door, the first on the left in the eastern wall of the Courtyard of the Myrtles, close to the entrance to the Hall of the Ambassadors, betrays its use: it was a comfortable place to conduct the friendly management of official business.

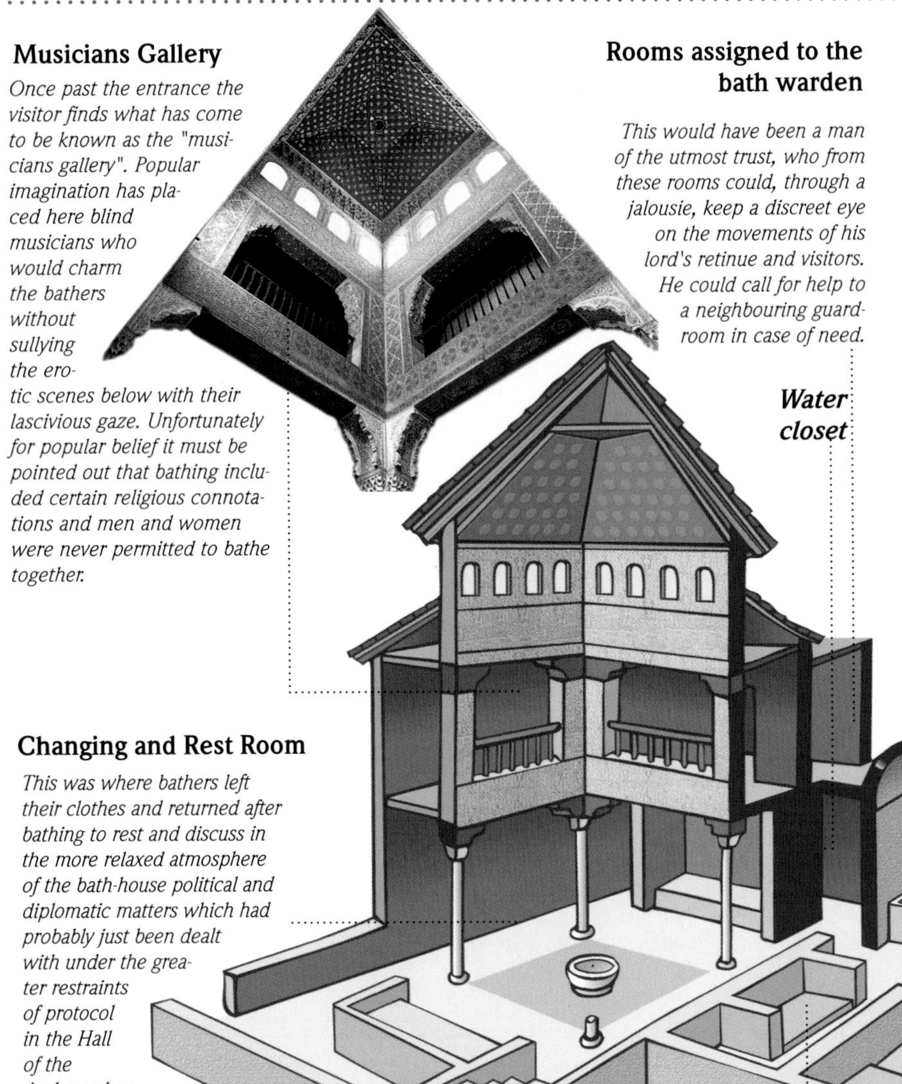

Musicians Gallery

Once past the entrance the visitor finds what has come to be known as the "musicians gallery". Popular imagination has placed here blind musicians who would charm the bathers without sullying the erotic scenes below with their lascivious gaze. Unfortunately for popular belief it must be pointed out that bathing included certain religious connotations and men and women were never permitted to bathe together.

Rooms assigned to the bath warden

This would have been a man of the utmost trust, who from these rooms could, through a jalousie, keep a discreet eye on the movements of his lord's retinue and visitors. He could call for help to a neighbouring guardroom in case of need.

Changing and Rest Room

This was where bathers left their clothes and returned after bathing to rest and discuss in the more relaxed atmosphere of the bath-house political and diplomatic matters which had probably just been dealt with under the greater restraints of protocol in the Hall of the Ambassadors.

Cool Room

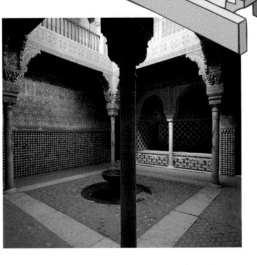

This vestibule must have served as a massage room and for general acclimatisation before entering or leaving the baths themselves. The small basin (right) was for personal ablution. The religious aspect of bathing generally required this ritual. The Moorish ceramics on the basin surround are an abstract design representing the reflection of water.

Warm Room

Water ran through a small central channel while heat circulated from the furnace through underground conduits, finally escaping up chimneys hidden within the walls. On contact with the marble, heated from below, the water turned into steam, which softened the skin and opened the pores, cleansing them of impurities and preparing the body for bathing. Seated or lying on daïses behind the pillars the bathers were rubbed down by servants who until then had remained in the room where the bathing equipment was kept. These bath attendants were highly regarded for their skills and enjoyed a social importance second only to the cup-bearers, young servants entrusted with serving wine to the household. All those who had to walk around the various rooms of the baths protected their feet with sandals with thick wooden soles.

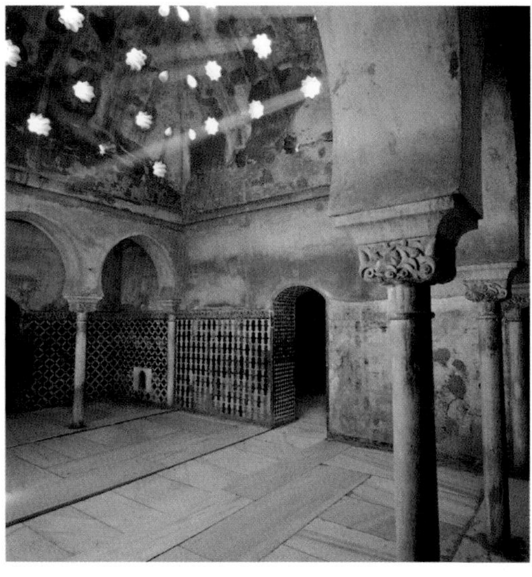

According to the verse surrounding the marble niche, the ***King's Bath*** *had two spouts, one for hot and one for cold water. Charles V altered this bath to make it suitable for total immersion, a practice not observed by the Muslims.*

Cauldrons

There were three copper cauldrons for hot water, but these were sold some time ago to help pay for restoration work elsewhere in the palace.

Furnace

The furnace, was brick-built and wood-fired. It communicated with the hot and warm rooms via underground conduits.

Hot Room

Many small conduits criss-crossed back and forth beneath the floor of this chamber bringing hot air almost directly from the oven and thus, as might be imagined, the temperature was very hot indeed in this part of the baths.

This cistern was built alongside the furnace to ensure that the water coming from the cauldrons stayed hotter here than in the other deposits. This was the water that was thrown onto the tiling to produce steam.

*In the **cupolas** of the Hall of the Pillars and the Hall of the Cisterns there are lantern windows that can be opened and closed from outside to regulate the temperature of both rooms. For this reason the roof up to the cupolas is provided with a brick staircase. It seems that the panes of these lanterns were of red glass, thus giving an intense light, which, together with the ferruginous plaster rendering on the inside walls, would have contributed to the feeling of heat.*

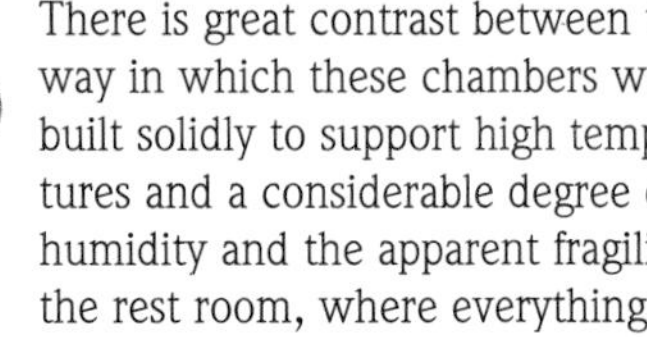

There is great contrast between the way in which these chambers were built solidly to support high temperatures and a considerable degree of humidity and the apparent fragility of the rest room, where everything is made of wood and stucco.

 The rest room

The reconstruction of this chamber was undertaken by Rafael Contreras between 1848 and 1866. The work has invited considerable criticism from some writers but what is certain is that the chamber came to his hands in a very sorry state. He preserved what he considered to be in acceptable condition: the pillars, the fountain and the XVI century tiles, taking away the initials PV (Plus Vltra) and putting in their place a design of alternating black and white, horned helices of very dubious taste.

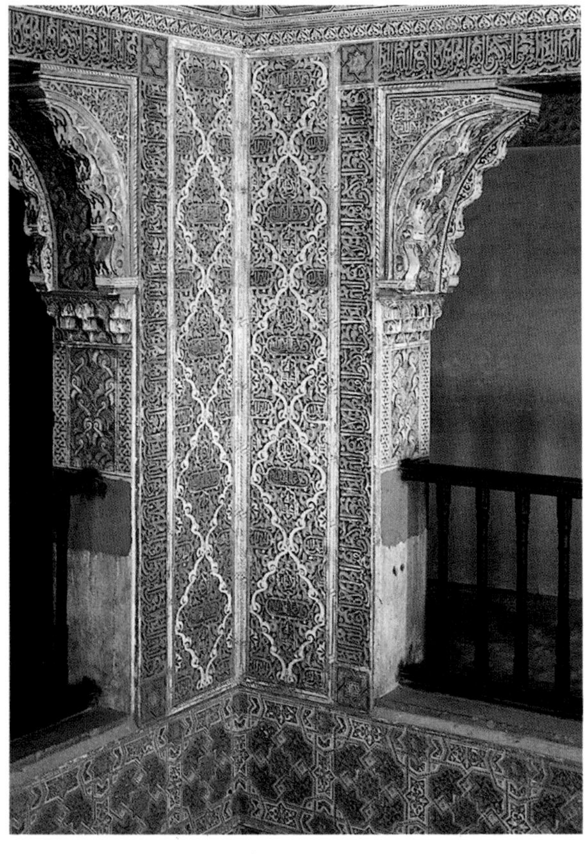

It is fair to say that Contreras committed two great errors: firstly, in replacing the original red-ochre of the polychroming with carmine, a colour unknown in Europe before the discovery of the New World; and secondly, without knowing any Arabic, in allowing himself to arrange the inscriptions, copied from the few originals he possessed, in an entirely arbitrary fashion with verses being thrown together meaninglessly. Today it is impossible to make out which of the inscriptions are the originals and this casts doubt upon whether it was Ismail, Yusuf I or Muhammad I who had the baths built.

The Arabs took the layout of their baths from the Roman thermae. From them they inherited the characteristic division into a cool room (frigidarium)), warm room (tepidarium)) and hot room (calidarium), and adapted the concept to their own taste and architectural styles.

Longitudinal section of the baths by Owen Jones (1842)

The firewood for the furnace arrived from the woods along a track called the Callejón de Leñadores *(woodcutters track), which led from the gate to the woods up to entrance to the oven, which is now the west gallery of the Courtyard of Lindaraja. The neighbouring Hall of Secrets would have been simply a wood store.*

The Alhambra, a palatine city with a population of between 1,500 and 2,000 inhabitants, would have had a dozen or so bath-houses for the use of its lords and their families, its soldiers and the artisans who worked in the different industries in the service of the crown. Of these bath-houses two or three at least were public.

1. Alcazaba bath-house
2. Comares bath-house
3. Bath-house of the Palace of Yusuf III
4. Polinario bath-house
5. Bath-house of the Palace of the Abencerrages
6. Bath-house beside the Palace of the Abencerrages
7. Bath-house belonging to the Palace upon which the Fanciscan friary was built
8. "El Secano" bath-house

Cool Room

Apart from his obligatory ritual ablutions, bathing has a very important place in the life of a Muslim; he usually washes both before and after meals, whenever he touches a dirty object, after using the lavatory, before touching the Koran, and on other occasions. Throughout the history of Islam, the public bath has been second only to the mosque as a focal point of social life and had the same influence on mediaeval urban activity equivalent to the town square in the west or the agora in ancient Greece.

Partal

Lewis, 1835

The open portico of the Torre de las Damas (Tower of the Ladies) overlooking a small esplanade containing a pool is called a *partal* in Arabic and today this name has been extended to include the whole area beside the Palace of the Lions. Small, stepped terraces, well adapted to the uneven lie of the land, form veritable hanging gardens of flower beds. Also included in the Partal are the small houses adjacent to the Tower of the Ladies, a mosque and various ruined dwellings, palaces, streets, stairways and cisterns, all long since vanished. In its day this whole area was one of elegant houses and mansions surrounded by beautiful gardens.

The Tower of the Ladies

The Tower of the Ladies is a huge mirador from which one can see the Albaicín beyond the river Darro, the orchards of the Generalife and of course the gardens just in front, surrounding the pool in which it is reflected.

Three XIV century ***Muslim houses*** *from the reign of Yusuf I have survived. In one of them there are some interesting, albeit deteriorated paintings.*

Gardens

Torres Balbás recreated these gardens so expertly that no serious criticism has ever been voiced against his restoration work

The Tower of the False Cemetery

Exit from the Partal to the Palace of Charles V (round tour). This is one of the alternatives to finishing the tour of the Nasrid palaces, either to leave towards the Alcazaba via the Royal Road or to return down to Granada.

The path along the walls

The citadel of the Alhambra was closed to the north by the ramparts and defensive towers, which served above all to separate the royal city of the Alhambra from the city below (the Granada of today). The path around the walls passes below towers and palaces to appear here as a walkway from which the ramparts could be guarded. Beside it there runs another, deeper, wider track, designed to be patrolled on horseback.

Gardens

Nowadays the path through the gardens bordering the towers provides a delightful stroll from the Partal on the northern side eastwards to the Generalife.

The Palace of Yusuf III

's is one of seven palaces that existed hin the walls of the citadel. Little of it ıains today except these few ruins, ıfficient really to make out its original pe and appearance.

The Tower of the Ladies

This tower beside its pool is the only surviving element of the building work carried out in this area by **Muhammad III** between 1302 and 1309, making it earlier therefore than the other palaces.

This oil painting by David Roberts (1838) shows a view of the palace when it was being used as a dwelling.

In extremely bad shape in the XIX century, it was restored by Torres Balbás with square pillars (right). F. Prieto Moreno replaced these in the XX century with the pillars we see today.

View from inside the mirador towards the Albaicín

Its structure is based upon the idea of a secluded space yet open to all four winds: intimacy protected by landscape rather than by walls, where the view was as important as the viewpoint itself. The jalousies, now lost, hid anyone sitting inside down to floor level.

The western eye tends to visualise everything in a horizontal and sequential plane, whereas the oriental mind views from the corners and admires the whole in all directions at once.

*The **cupola** of the tower was adorned with one of the most beautiful Nasrid coffered ceilings, the original of which is in the Islamisches Museum in Berlin. Above, the coffered ceiling of the portico.*

The Partal Oratory

Given its similarity to other constructions of the time this oratory probably dates from the beginning of the XIV century, during the reign of Yusuf I. It is a small mosque with side windows alone, which is not surprising if we imagine how distracting to prayer a view behind the mihrab might be.

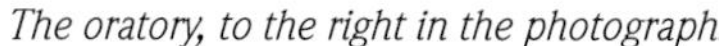

The oratory, to the right in the photograph.

Above, the interior, and below, a window in the oratory

*Most of its exterior decoration has been lost, but inside the oratory the exquisite detail of its tracery and ornaments can still be seen, particularly the coffered ceiling and the delicacy of the **mihrab**, with its stilted horse-shoe arch. Until recently the oratory had a ceramic-tiled dado*

The Gardens

The Tower of the False Cemetery

The small brick tower joined to the south of the Courtyard of the Lions is known thus because it was thought to have been the cemetery of the sultans of the Alhambra. Nowadays it is known that the royal tombs were in some nearby ruins. It was believed that Boabdil, the last Nasrid sultan, had taken all his ancestors' remains to be reburied in the village of Mondújar to the south of Granada, but then in 1999 other human remains began to appear in the rauda. Legend has it that Boabdil's father, Muley-Hassan, was buried on the highest peak of the Sierra Nevada, and hence its name today, Mulhacén.

This pool full of water lilies crowns the stairway in the Partal gardens at a crossing of the ways.

Earthenware pots of flowers, no longer here, once formed an important and vivid part of the ornaments in the gardens.

 The Palace of Yusuf III

This palace was the residence of the governors of the Alhambra until 1718, when it was abandoned and demolished. Built by Yusuf III (reigned 1408 -1417) during the height of Nasrid culture, it repeats the general scheme of a central pool surrounded by pavillions.

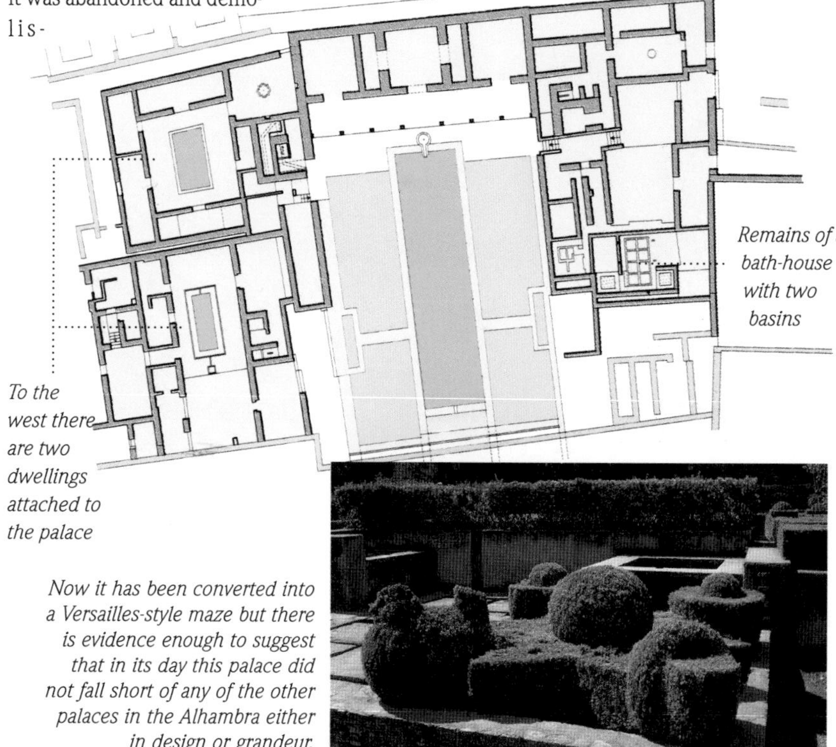

Remains of a bath-house with two basins

To the west there are two dwellings attached to the palace

Now it has been converted into a Versailles-style maze but there is evidence enough to suggest that in its day this palace did not fall short of any of the other palaces in the Alhambra either in design or grandeur.

 Paseo de la Muralla

Leading from the gardens is a path that follows the line of the battlements along the north side of the citadel until the entrance to the Generalife.

Along the way the path passes the Spiked Tower (right), Tower of the Princesses and Tower of the Captive Princess (see the following chapters concerning the various towers). In the background is the Generalife with the Castle of St. Helen's above it.

Elms, birches and cypresses compete in height with the spire of the **church of St. Mary** of the Alhambra, built by the Christians on the site of the Moslem mosque

Torres

The Towers

Of the thirty or more towers which originally fortified the ramparts surrounding the Alhambra twenty-two still exist. The outer walls were built at the beginning of the XIII century, before the palaces themselves, and their role was clearly defensive. Each of the towers, gates and miradors has its own name. Some of these are obviously based on mundane usage and are thus probably contemporary with Muslim and early Christian habitation (the Arms Tower, the Outskirts Tower, the Wine Gate, the Iron Gate, to mention a few). Others are slightly later interpretations from linguistic evidence, which may be based on fact (the Justice Gate, from an inscription found inside it) or completely erroneous. The Mirador of Lindaraja falis into this category. From the Arabic *ain dar aixa*, meaning "The eyes of the house of Aixa (Mulhacén's wife), uninformed commentators invented the figure of a mysterious princess "Lindaraja", and the name has stuck. Later names such as the Tower of the Princesses and the Tower of the Captive Princess, among others, are based on romantic tales concerning their occupants and are entirely apocryphal. Other names are "nicknames" given to towers by the inhabitants of the Alhambra, such as el Cubo, or "the Tub", because

of its round, squat shape and la Torre de los Picos, "the Spiked Tower". The interpretation of this latter name is interesting in that it may refer to the pointed merlons around the ramparts (i.e. spikes) or equally to the masonry corbels that jut out from the corners below the battlements (resembling bird beaks). The word for both "spike" and "beak" in Spanish is "pico", thus the name couid well be interpreted as "the Beaked Tower".

The Spiked Tower

This tower is easily distinguishable by the masonry corbets jutting out from it, which once supported machicolations, and above all by the spikey, pyramid- ***shaped merlons*** *on its battlements, both of which may have given the towe its name. Laborde, 1812*

The Outskirts Gate

This was the northernmost entrance to the city and the gate that the sultans and their families normally used to come and go between the Alhambra and the Generalife

The Justice Gate

Built in 1348 by Yusuf I, this was always one of the main entrances into the Alhambra. It is a masterpiece of military engineering and contrasts in its massive solidity and austere grandeur with the fragility of the Royal House (Engraving by Laborde, 1812).

The Wagon Gate

This gate is angled slantwise through the wall and was opened up after the conquest to allow easy access to the wagons which brought the materials for the construction of Charles V Palace in the XVI century. Nowadays it is still the gate used by wheeled traffic to get into the citadel.

The Tower of the Judge

The Tower of the Captive Princess

The names "the Captive Princess" and "the Princesses" were coined in the XVII and XVIII centuries according to apochryphal stories woven around the supposed inhabitants of these towers.

The Tower of the Princesses

The Tower at the End of the Way

The Water Tower

Apart from its defensive function, this tower played the very important role of protecting the aqueduct to the royal waterway, which carried water to the whole city. The Arabs rarely constructed aqueducts unless for strategic motives, as was the case here.

The Tower of Juan de Arce

The Tower of Baltasar de la Cruz

The Tower and Gate of Seven Floors

This is the tower that suffered most damage when Napoleon's troops blew up some of the ramparts on their withdrawal in 1812. Fortunately its structure had been well recorded in earlier engravings and its appearance today is much as it was before its destruction. Tradition has it that Boabdil left through this gate as he abandoned the Alhambra for the last time and through his express petition the gate thenceforth remained closed "porta castri granatensis semper clausa" *(Bucknall Escourt, 1827).*

The Tower of the Captain

The T. of the Witch

The Tower of the Heads

The Tower of the Abencerrages

Secano (dry area)

This avenue of cypresses climbs gently from the square opposite the parador (the national hotel in what was once the Franciscan friary) to the entrance to the Generalife, providing a general view of the towers along the south wall of the Alhambra on the way.

The Outskirts Gate and The Spiked Tower

This complex was obviously heavily defensive. Originally there was only a gate with a pointed horse-shoe arch and the Tower of the Spikes. It wasn't until the XV century that the outer bastion was constructed along with a courtyard surrounded by stables. This second precinct, with a double elbow, severely restricted access past the gate in either direction, overlooked as it was by the Spiked Tower.

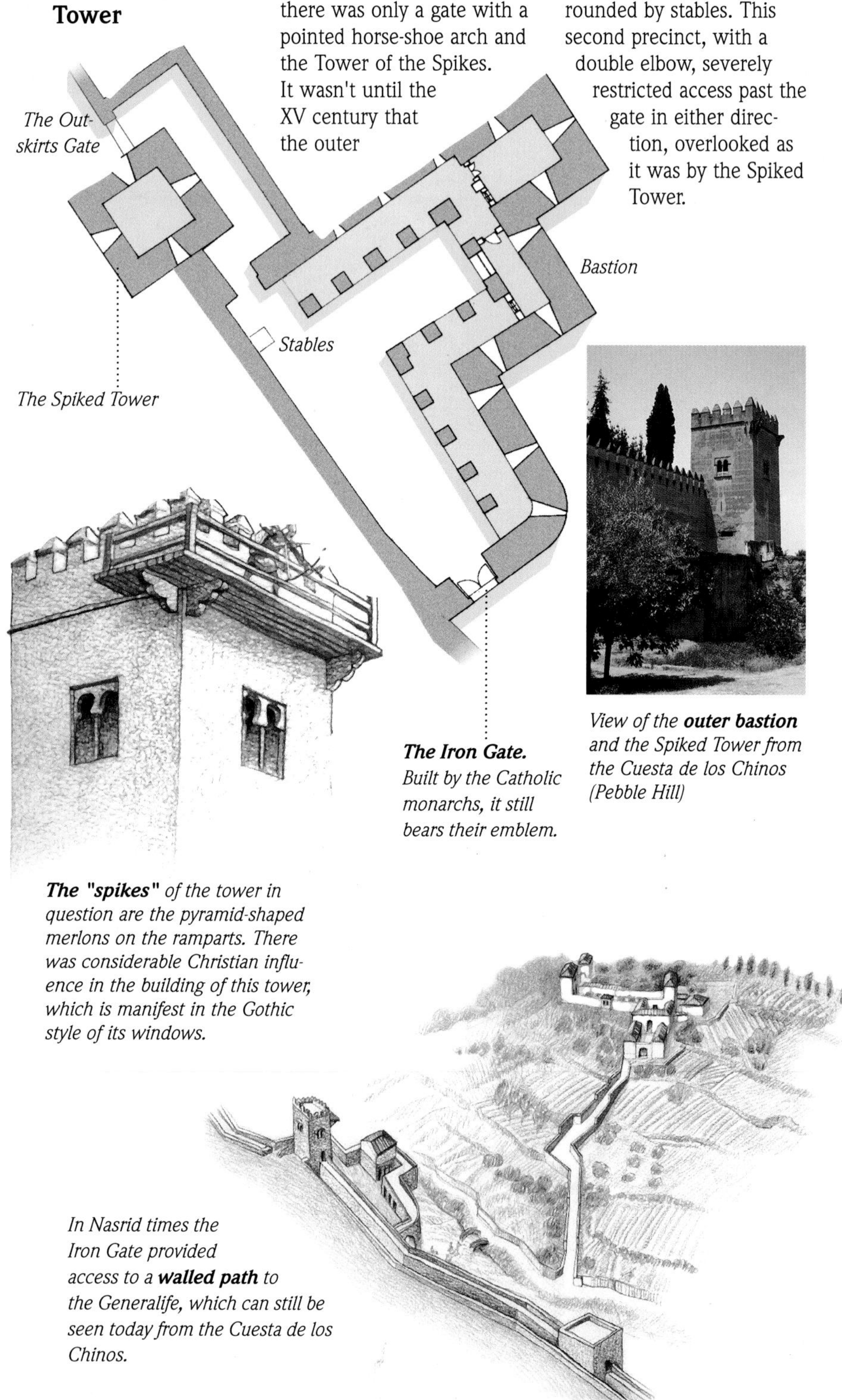

The Iron Gate. *Built by the Catholic monarchs, it still bears their emblem.*

View of the ***outer bastion*** *and the Spiked Tower from the Cuesta de los Chinos (Pebble Hill)*

The "spikes" *of the tower in question are the pyramid-shaped merlons on the ramparts. There was considerable Christian influence in the building of this tower, which is manifest in the Gothic style of its windows.*

In Nasrid times the Iron Gate provided access to a ***walled path*** *to the Generalife, which can still be seen today from the Cuesta de los Chinos.*

The Tower of the Captive Princess

This tower and that of the Princesses are in fact two small palaces with the mere appearance of fortresses, standing astride the walkway along the battlements.

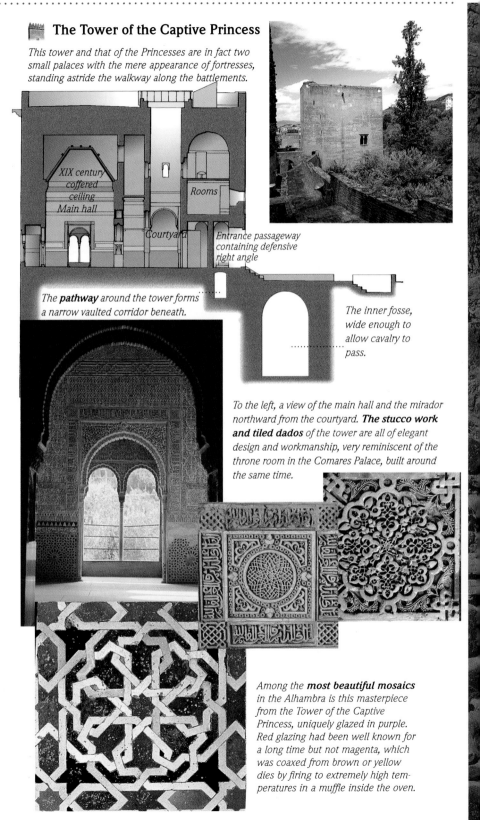

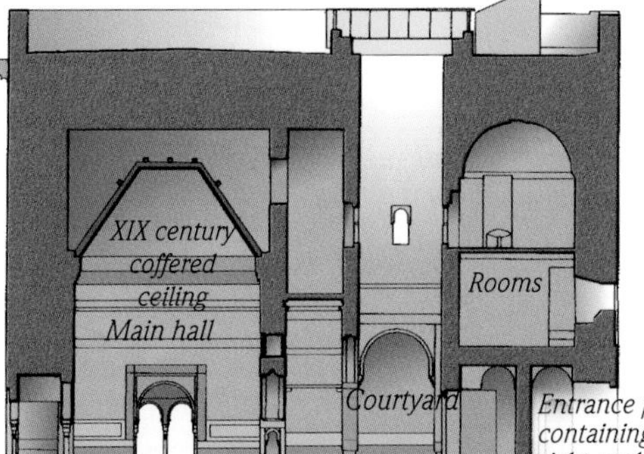

Entrance passageway containing defensive right angle

*The **pathway** around the tower forms a narrow vaulted corridor beneath.*

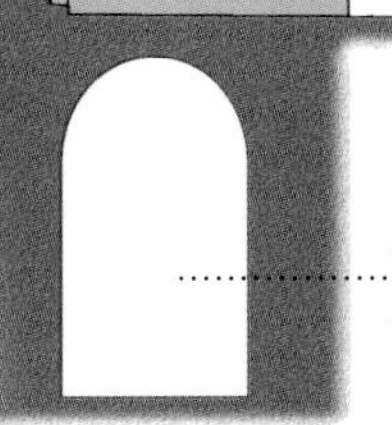

The inner fosse, wide enough to allow cavalry to pass.

*To the left, a view of the main hall and the mirador northward from the courtyard. **The stucco work and tiled dados** of the tower are all of elegant design and workmanship, very reminiscent of the throne room in the Comares Palace, built around the same time.*

*Among the **most beautiful mosaics** in the Alhambra is this masterpiece from the Tower of the Captive Princess, uniquely glazed in purple. Red glazing had been well known for a long time but not magenta, which was coaxed from brown or yellow dies by firing to extremely high temperatures in a muffle inside the oven.*

The Tower of the Princesses

This tower was built in the XV century, somewhat later than the Tower of the Captive Princess. Its ornamentation shows a certain decline in Nasrid art, a lack of originality and variety in the stucco work and mosaic tiling.

The entrance passageway does however hold a pleasant surprise in store: this groined vault with large mocárabes, more reminiscent of the Asiatic steppes or Egypt than Nasrid design. Each element is composed of three polyhedrons fitted into each other.

After a double-elbowed corridor the entrance leads into a small square courtyard roofed by an octagonal lantern, which was erected in the XIX century to replace a vault of mocárabes that had been demolished by an earthquake. The singular charm of this courtyard made it a favourite spot for romantic illustrators such as J.F.Lewis, who drew it in 1835 (below).

Generalife

Laborde, 1812.

Of the many private granges and pleasure gardens that once existed on the Hill of the Sun this is the only one remaining. The Generalife was a retreat where the Granadan monarchs could relax, away from the daily toil and bustle of the court. Nevertheless, its proximity to the Alhambra meant that the sultan could still be close enough to palace affairs to attend to any urgent matter which might arise, whilst at the same time be far enough away to enjoy the intimacy of the countryside.

The Cypress Courtyard

Romantic Mirador

The Water Stairway

Lower, or New Gardens

Planted in 1931 on the site of older orchards

North Pavilion

The Water Garden Courtyard

After a fire in 1958 the original design of this courtyard was discovered and reconstructed. It is the focal point of the whole residence and a perfect example of a Spanish-Muslim garden.

The Dismounting Yard (Patio Polo)

Orchards

The land around the Generalife was always cultivated; it took pride of place among many such outlying farmsteads owned by the sultan. Fortunately its orchard terraces have survived relatively unchanged to this day.

According to most scholars the name Generalife derives from the Arab words djennat, meaning "garden", "orchard" or "paradise" (all similar concepts to desert nomads), and al-arif, meaning "architect" or"master bulider". Thus the name could be translated as, "The Garden of the Architect". Neverthe-less, other commentators believe they have found evidence in contemporary Arab and Christian writings to translate it as, "Principal orchard" or "The most noble and highest of all orchards".

Open-air Concert Arena

In 1952 this amphitheatre was built upon the ruins of old agricultural outbuildings. The sunken arena provides an ideal setting for ballet and dance, particularly during the annual Festival of Music and Dance, and many famous ballerinas, such as Margot Fonteyn among others, have performed here.

The Cypress Walk

Cypress trees have always been associated with cemeteries, particularly since the Romantic period, for the good reason that their roots grow straight and deep and don't break into the tombs. Muslim architects favoured the cypress for the same reason: it seeks water at depth and can be planted closely to form a dense evergreen screen.

Access to the Alhambra

This bridge was constructed quite recently to allow direct access between the Generalife and the Alhambra. In former times the aqueduct alone existed, watched over by the Water Tower.

Entrance

Ticket office

The Lower Gardens

Outside the buildings all that remains of the original gardens are the cultivated, orchard terraces. These terraced gardens climbed to the very top of the hill, and looking from above, a single garden seemed to stretch endlessly all the way down, a garden of an infinite variety of colours, carefully planned by the skilful planting of mixtures of ornamental and fruit trees on every terrace.

The planting of the present-day gardens was begun in 1931 and finished in 1951 under the care of the architect Francisco Prieto Moreno, and although they may not closely resemble those of the middle ages they undoubtedly lend beauty and dignity to an area that was in a seriously neglected state.

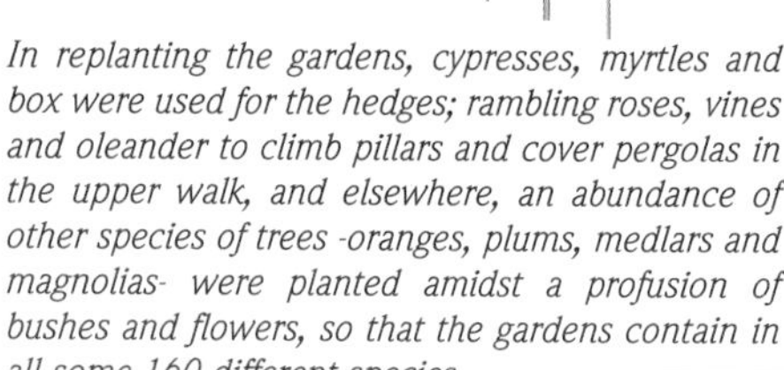

In replanting the gardens, cypresses, myrtles and box were used for the hedges; rambling roses, vines and oleander to climb pillars and cover pergolas in the upper walk, and elsewhere, an abundance of other species of trees -oranges, plums, medlars and magnolias- were planted amidst a profusion of bushes and flowers, so that the gardens contain in all some 160 different species.

The **walks** are paved in traditional Granadan style: a mosaic of small pebbles, white ones from the river Darro and black from the river Genil. Paving of this sort is still laid in courtyards and squares throughout the city.

The **central pools** *(right), in the shape of a cross, are typical of many Muslim gardens.*

The role of the Generalife, recaptured in these new gardens, was the same as that of the houses known as carmens in the city of Granada, which were used as Autumn retreats. Autumn is the most beautiful season in this city; the temperature is mild, with neither the suffocating heat of summer nor the dry cold of winter; flowers still linger in the gardens, there is no persistent rain and the sky is blue almost every day.

The Carmen

"It is generally accepted that the word carmen *derives from a term meaning "vine" or "vineyard" and thus by analogy has come to be applied to smallholdings situated in the city comprising a dwelling and a small area devoted to the cultivation of flowers and vegetables and adorned with both ornamental and fruit trees. Their situation on hillsides or slopes within the urban area, allowing them only limited space, affords these houses a combination of virtues in which the idiosyncrasies of their design reflect perfectly their very human scale. Their limited space does not, however, result in their losing any of their agricultural essence, as they are always cultivated, albeit more for aesthetic than productive purposes."*
(Francisco Prieto Moreno, in *Jardines de Granada*).

The ***carmen*** derives from the traditional Andalusian house with a courtyard, which in the Albaicín becomes an orchard *cum* garden. After the conquest many of these properties passed into the hands of Christians, who incorporated their own architecture into the buildings whilst preserving the quasi-natural character of the cultivated areas.

"All around there are so many Morisco houses, which although often hidden between the trees in their gardens, gathered all together would constitute another city such as Granada; it is true they are small but they all have water and roses, eglantine and myrtle, and are very peaceful."
(Pedro Mártir de Anglería, XVI century)

In all of the ***Albaicín*** *(above)* carmens *can be seen intermingled with more modest dwellings, mixed higgledy-piggledy at the mercy of the twists and turns of the old streets. On the right, a typical house and the* Carmen de los Chapiteles.

The Spanish-Muslim Garden

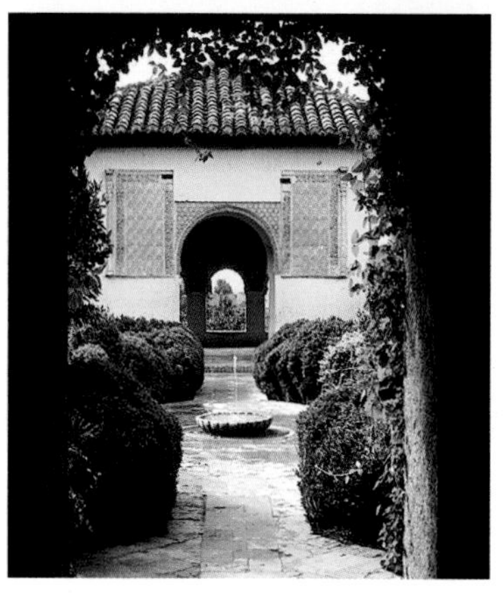

To situate a house within a garden you should select a rise in the ground to make it easier to guard. The building should be at the entrance to the property and orientated towards midday, and the well or irrigation tank should be sited at the highest point of all. Better still than a well is a channel, which should run in the shade of the plants and trees. Plant clumps of all sorts of evergreens close to the channel to delight the eye, and, a little farther away, as wide a variety of flowers and evergreen trees as possible. Let a vineyard surround the garden and in the middle climbing vines provide shade for the paths between the flower beds. At the very centre erect an open pavilion for the hours of rest, surrounded by climbing roses, myrtles and other varieties of flower to beautify the view. The garden should be longer than it is wide so as not to tire the eyes in contemplation. A room should be built at the lower end for guests. Make a pool hidden between the trees so that it might not be seen from a distance. It is also useful to build a dovecote and a habitable tower. The house itself should have two doors so as to be more easily protected and the owner feel secure.

Ibn Luyun, *Treatise on Agriculture and Gardening*

In the words of Professor Manzano, the Generalife was at one and the same time a *djennat*, or paradise, and a working grange which supplied the Royal House with provisions.

"An orchard is only a fragment of nature, carefully walled off from a dry or desert exterior, which is always hostile to man. The space inside the walls, irrigated and brought to life with water, is geometrically laid out and planted with trees and carefully selected bushes and flowers to make it into a domestic environment, leafy and fragrantly perfumed,

a true image of djennat, *or paradise on earth". "It does not attain the dimensions of the great hunting reserves of the Omeyan princes, which certainly also existed in Granada, attached to palaces built farther outside the city beyond the hill upon which the Generalife is built. This type of royal garden existed as a contrast to the urban palace in all the courts of emirs, caliphs and minor taifa kings throughout the history of Islamic Spain".*

The Muslim garden was to be enjoyed with all the senses: the sight and smell of the flowers, the sound of water and the feel and taste of fruit as they were picked from the trees while walking beneath them.

The Dismounting Yard

Following the traditional path from the Alhambra to the Generalife through the Puerta del Arrabal and then along and up the steep, walled alley outside the city walls, a visitor first arrived at a huge door beneath a pointed arch, opening onto the Dismounting Yard. Nowadays, walking up through the New Gardens, it is the first courtyard of the tour of the Generalife.

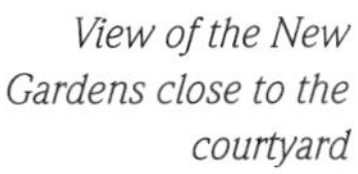

View of the New Gardens close to the courtyard

Entrance

*The **symbolic key** of the Alhambra above the ogive arch serves as a sign of a royal residence.*

*The name **Dismounting Yard** comes from the supposition that it was here that riders left their horses. It certainly has the appearance of a rustic corral in its simplicity, shaded by vines and climbing roses. It has a drinking trough, a stone bench and an outbuilding with twin arches (the old stables)*

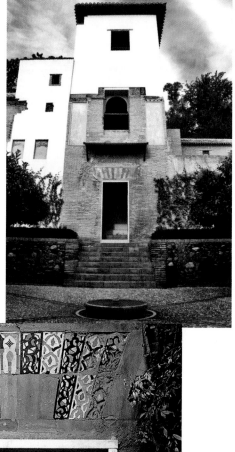

*The **next courtyard** seems to be a second anteroom, with orange trees growing around a central fountain. Through the door opposite there is a lobby with benches for the guards. The servants' quarters seem to have been located here. A narrow stairway with steep steps and the usual sharp corner half-way up leads to the Courtyard of the Water Garden.*

*The entrance is far from grand but the **door lintel** is decorated with a fine mosaic ataurique design in simple hues of black, green and blue on a white background.*

 The Water-Garden

Despite being the oldest of the palaces and having undergone substantial alterations, this is possibly the area of the Alhambra which best preserves the style of the mediaeval garden in al-Andalus. In its original conception it relied upon the normal plan of an elongated courtyard with a pool to reflect the surrounding façades. The later addition of water spouts has broken up the surface of the mirror. The west wall would have had no openings save the small mirador, following the tradition of "a closed paradise", invisible from outside and turned in upon itself, a tradition which dominated Andalusian architectural design.

The original concept was that water trickling into the pool from the two fountains at either end would make a gentle murmur, like soothing music - the most pleasant of sounds apart from silence to encourage meditative thought. The rationalists of the eighteenth-century age of reason, however, and above all the romantics of the following century, imposed their own vision and taste, replacing the sonorous silence and gentle, natural flow of water with artificial splashing. During the latest restoration some jets were put in, which, at the last resort, might be said to imitate the music of rain falling.

Kurt Peterkarfeld
(foto 1930)

The ground plan *shows what the original shape of the courtyard may have been (in red) towards the beginning of the XIV century, and the elements added either by successive Nasrid rulers or during the Christian era. The north pavilion was lower until another floor was built on top of it. (Adapted from A. Orihuela,* Casas y Palacios Nazaríes)

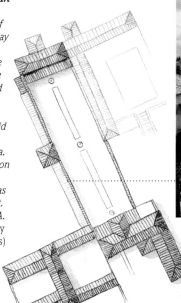

*The **west wall** was lowered during the reign of the Catholic monarchs and converted into a gallery. Arches were opened in the wall to allow a view of the countryside around from the courtyard, contrary to the intimate and introspective nature of the Muslim courtyard. Originally the outside could only have been seen from the **central mirador** (left), the walls of which are decorated in the style of the time of Ismael I, although superimposed on earlier decoration.*

The present layout of the buildings can be seen in this elevation by F. Prieto Moreno.

*The **north end**, which appears here in a drawing by Asselineau (1844), is the best preserved of the pavilions. The façade has three round arches supported upon pillars with mocarábe capitals, the arch in the middle being higher than those on either side.*

*A **poem** written on a lapis-lazuli background (below) runs above the arches. It is dedicated to the sultan Abu l-Walid Ismail and the reference to the year of "the great triumph for religion" dates the decorative work to the year 1319.*

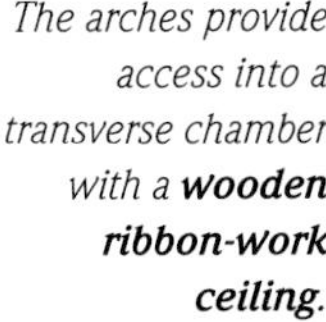

*The arches provide access into a transverse chamber with a **wooden ribbon-work ceiling**.*

*The position of this room at the far end of the courtyard and the presence of **niches** for ritual jugs of water (left) suggest that this was the sultan's reception room.*

*The chamber finishes in a **mirador** added during the reign of Ismail I (1319), slightly angled to the right compared to the central axis of the pool, as can be seen in the photograph. In fact the whole pavilion is a few degrees out of line with the courtyard.*

It is quite difficult to comprehend how in the hottest months the north mirador always catches a breeze to alleviate the suffocating heat of midday. Doubtless there is a combination of factors to explain this phenomenon, the secrets of which the master builder knew well: the situation, the height, the orientation, so perfect throughout the Alhambra, and here in this mirador, just slightly slant-

ed off-centre to achieve that breath of air which surprises us so much today. It provi-des an object lesson for architects of the twenty-first century, who are striving to integrate nature into their buildings and create microclimates, even within closed spaces, to relieve the weight of concrete and the visual aggression of cement.

The Cypress Courtyard

The original layout and appearance of this courtyard is not completely clear. The U-shaped pool is not Nasrid, as in 1526 the Venetian ambassador Andrea Navaggiero described this court as being, "like a meadow with trees", which was irrigated regularly by some ingenious system that brought the water as though from nowhere. It is also known as the Courtyard of the Sultana, because of the legend of the sultana who arranged her trysts here with one of the Abencerrages, an affair which led to the massacre of all the men of that family.

*A magnificent **wisteria** overhangs the path down from the romantic mirador (left).*

The Upper Gardens

This delightful example of a romantic garden was laid out here over the abandoned remains of the original gardens.

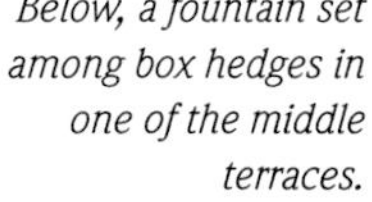

Below, a fountain set among box hedges in one of the middle terraces.

The Water Stairway

This is one of the few genuine Nasrid features to be preserved in this part of the gardens. The Muslim obsession with water led them to the extreme of creating a liquid hand rail.

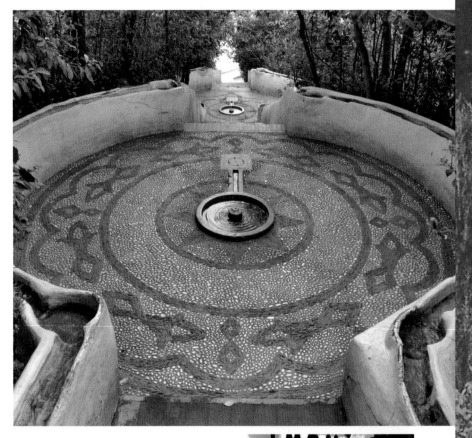

The Romantic Mirador

A nineteenth-century folly built over pre-existing walls, of unknown origin, although their orientation would suggest that there may have been an oratory here. The water enters into the Generalife beside this Mirador and thence down the water stairway. Curiously enough, however, despite Navaggiero's observations, this water is not that which irrigates the rest of the Generalife, which enters directly into the Cypress Courtyard lower down. This higher channel is destined for the Alhambra, sufficient water for the stairway being drawn off through sluice gates.

The Hydraulic system in the Alhambra and Generalife

Any of the views from the Alhambra are enough to explain why its founders chose to build their palaces on this hillside. All they needed was water to achieve perfection. When he began to build his palatial city, Ibn al-Ahmar first constructed a watercourse, the Royal Waterway, which took its water from the river Darro some six kilometers upstream and entered the Alhambra via the Generalife.

*The **Valley of the Darro.** Upstream, near to a farmstead called Jesus del Valle, the watercourse crossed the river via an aqueduct after turning the wheel of a now-abandoned flour mill.*

Beginning of the watercourse

Old mill

Jesus del Valle farmstead

The northern face of the Hill of the Sun, where vestiges of the original watercourse can still be seen.

Plain of the Partridge

River Darro

Acequia Real

*At a later date the **watercourse** was diverted here to provide water to irrigate the upper acres of farmland and orchards belonging to the Generalife.*

At a later stage, when palaces such as Dar al-Arusa and Alixares were built higher up the hill, water was collected in various new ways, such as sluices on the royal waterway at the highest point of the hill, cisterns to capture rainwater, and a new system of irrigation channels, of which unfortunately little trace remains today.

Cistern of Rainwater

Dar al-Arusa

Generalife

Alhambra

Granada

Rainwater cistern

Before the watercourse was branched higher up, in order to irrigate the upper reaches of the Generalife a huge cistern, gallery and wells had been built and water was lifted by a wheel from the original watercourse lower down. When the second branch of the watercourse was dug this cistern was left as a reservoir and water distribution centre. In our own times both Torres Balbás and Prieto Moreno had other cisterns built alongside the first (right).

Water wheel

Cistern

Deposit 1

Deposit 2

Deposit 3

Royal waterway

Subterranean gallery

Adapted from D. Pedro Salmerón Escobar and María Cullel

The watercourse of the Alhambra forks to descend the ***Water Stairway****.*

The ***upper irrigation channel*** *ran from the cistern to water the nearby orchards and branched again farther down, its lower branch joining that of the Generalife. Together they crossed the* ***aqueduct*** *to enter into the Alhambra. The watercourse then followed more or less the line of the* ***Royal Street****, ending up at the Alcazaba.*

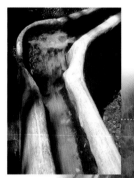

Albercones

Emplazamiento antigua noria

a Carmen de los Mártires y S. Cecilio

GENERALIFE

Acueducto

Torre del Agua

ALHAMBRA

Parador Nacional

Río Darro

Palacios Nazaríes

Calle Real de la Alhambra

Palacio Carlos V

Plaza de los Aljibes

Alcazaba

The ***aqueduct*** *via which the watercourse entered the Alhambra, crossing the gully of the Cuesta de los Chinos. The* ***Water Tower*** *is known as such because it was designed to guard this strategic point in the Alhambra's defences.*

Water in al-Andalus

Agriculture, the garden and the myth of earthly paradise were all born in the East, idealised in oriental tradition and transmitted by the oldest human cultures. Both the Arabs and the Berbers were heirs to this tradition and they knew more than anyone about the physical laws governing the principles of irrigation. As thirsty nomads, water was always their first concern and it was this of course which determined the site of settlement in the first place.

*The **acequia**, or irrigation channel, is the heart of any watering system. Captured initially from a river by means of an **azud**, or small retaining dam, the **principal water course** allows the water to be kept higher than the original river bed and thus gain potential energy. Secondary channels are then used to draw off water from the main watercourse. **Albercas**, large pools or cisterns, serve as reservoirs and distribution points. Gravity combined with a judicious **terracing** of the land allows the water to be directed to any area of land to be irrigated and finally to return to its original course.*

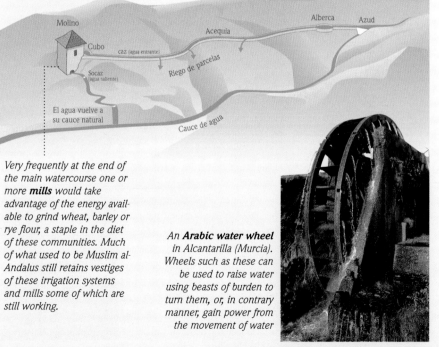

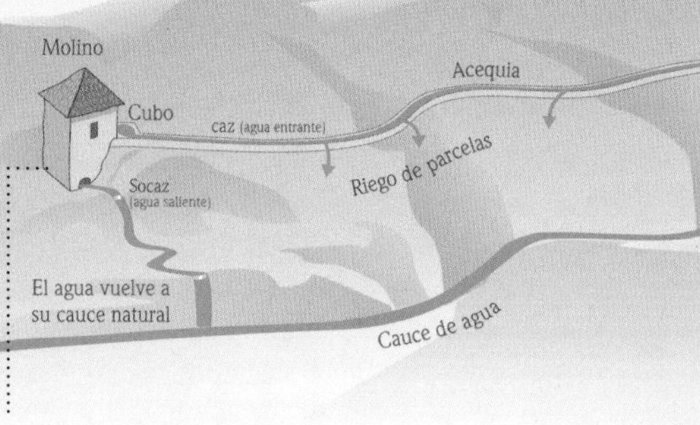

*Very frequently at the end of the main watercourse one or more **mills** would take advantage of the energy available to grind wheat, barley or rye flour, a staple in the diet of these communities. Much of what used to be Muslim al-Andalus still retains vestiges of these irrigation systems and mills some of which are still working.*

*An **Arabic water wheel** in Alcantarilla (Murcia). Wheels such as these can be used to raise water using beasts of burden to turn them, or, in contrary manner, gain power from the movement of water*

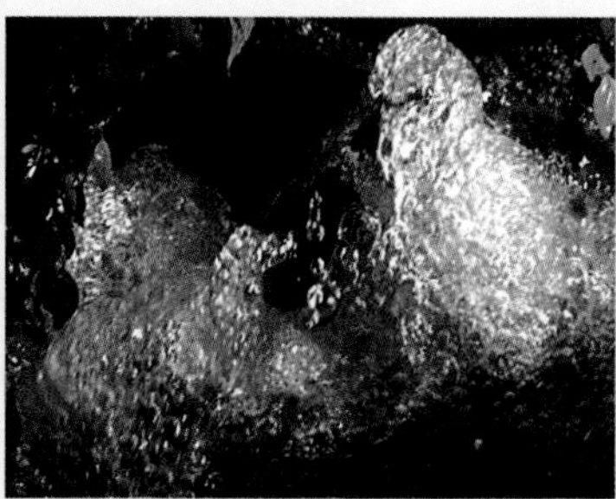

It was in the cities, however, that Andalusians were most concerned about water. It is well known that for reasons both of hygiene and religion the Muslims had a much closer relationship with water than did their Christian counterparts of the time. Whether for drinking, bathing or ritual ablution it was essential that all the inhabitants of the city should have access to this priceless resource, and rulers were quick to create the necessary infrastructure to put this into practice.

Water came from springs, and to a lesser extent from rivers and wells, and it was this of course which determined the site of settlements in the first place.

Sometimes it was necessary to bring it from some distance away via ***watercourses****, such as that of* Aynadamar*, which supplied the Albaicín, and springs from the* ***Fuente Grande*** *at the village of Alfacar (left).*

Occasionally the Arabs reconstructed complex distribution networks from the remains of abandoned Roman systems. Water channels and underground galleries wove throughout the town, emerging in ***public fountains****, cisterns and reservoirs. Part of the system supplying the Albaicín can be seen here: more than twenty cisterns covered the needs of the population of this part of Granada.*

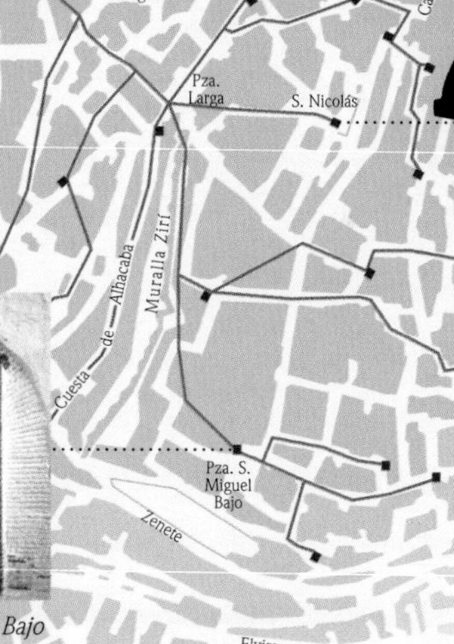

St. Nicolas's cistern

Aljibe de S. Miguel Bajo
St. Michael's Cistern

Many houses had their own conduits made of ***atanores****, or pipes of baked clay and many collected their own rain water in private cisterns. The less well-off went to the public fountain or cistern for their water and the courtyards of their houses always contained a great half-buried, earthenware pot to keep it in.*

Sewage tended to be emptied straight into the river if it was nearby, or carried there in conduits. City regulations established strict controls on the subject of public hygiene, the norms applicable to itinerant water sellers and the quantities assigned to each area and to individual buildings.

The flowers

Acanthus
Acanthus spinosus

Spirea
Spirea cantonensis

Horse chestnut
Aesculus hippocastanum

Japanese anemone
Anemone japonica

Pagoda tree
Sophora imperium

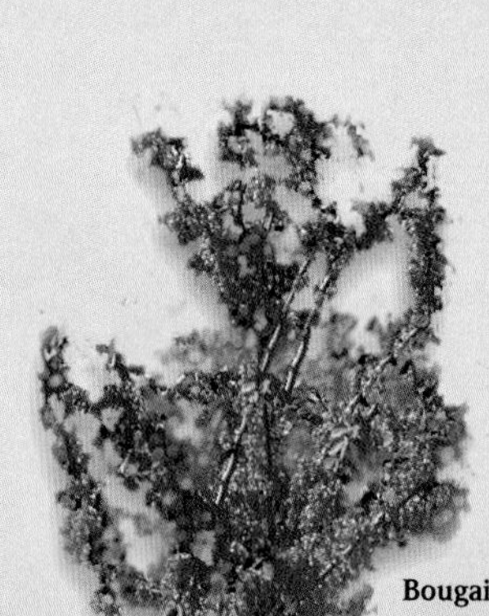

Bougainvillea
Bougainvillea glabra

Pagoda flower, glory flower
Clerodendrum bugei

Day lily and Crape myrtle (Pride of India)
Hemerocallis dumortiere and Lagestroemia indica

Barberton or Transvaal daisy
Gebera jamesoni

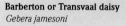

Cockscomb
Celosia cristata

Weigela
Weigelia Dierrilla florida

Cidonia
Cydonia japonica

Rosemary
Rosmarinus officinalis

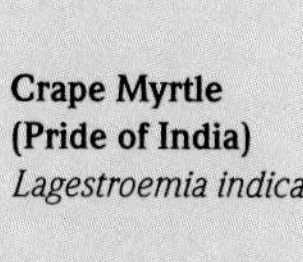

Crape Myrtle (Pride of India)
Lagestroemia indica

Lady Banks' rose
Rosa banksiae

Seville orange
Citrus auranteum ver. Amara

Tamarisk
Tamarix parviflora

Soucer Magnolia
Magnolia soulangeana

Magnolia grandiflora
Magnolia grandiflora

Italian cypress and kaki
Cupressus sempervirens, Dyospyros Kaki

Scented waterlily
Nymphaea ordorata

Candytuft
Iberis sempervirens

Ampelosis
Ampelosis tricuspidata

Scarlet sage
Salvia splendens

Scotch marigold and Dandelion
Calendula officinales &
Taraxacum afficinalis

Globe amarant
Gromphrena globosa

Wintersweet
Chimonanthus praecox

Snowball
Vibumum opulus

View of an ornamental flowerbed in the Partal gardens

Golden-rain tree
Koelreuteria paniculata

African lily
Agapanthus
Agapanthus africanus

Hybrid rose
Rosa hybrida

Canna lily
Canna indica

Rockcress
Arabis alpina

Statice, Everlasting flowers
Statice fruticans

Scorpion senna, Crown vetch
Coronilla glauca

Blanket flower, Firewheel
Gaillardia pulchella

Petunia
Petunia hybrida

Delphinium, Kark spur
Delphinium hybr.

Golden rod
Solidago canadensis

Blanket flower
Gaillaria aristata

Wisteria
Wisteria sinensis

Honeysuckle
Lonicera sempervirens

The Generalife was entrusted by the Catholic monarchs into the care of the Knight Commander Fray Juan de la Hinestrosa. After a series of inheritances and marriages the tenancy of the grange passed into the hands of the Granada Venegas family and finally the Marqueses of Compotéjar, who were related to the Grimaldi-Palavicinis of Milan

Left, The west gallery of the Courtyard of the Water Garden. Below, the rectangular chamber which precedes the mirador.

After a long legal wrangle in which the Spanish state claimed ownership of the Generalife, the case was settled in favour of the defendants, the private owners. Having won their case they ceded ownership of the Generalife to the Spanish government free of charge in 1921, for which King Alfonso XIII created for the family the Marquessate of the Generalife to reward their generosity

The relentless ***power of the weather.*** *Anyone comparing this photograph of 1999 with those on pages 156 and 160 will immediately miss the handsome cedars and cypresses to the left, which were uprooted in a storm during the winter of 1998.*

The upper Alhambra

Alhambra alta (Secano)

Nicolás Chapuy, 1844

The *Secano* is a part of the Alhambra which has almost completely disappeared: the southern and eastern areas of the city, which today comprise no more than a few remains and odd vestiges of what in Nasrid times was the densely populated site of the *medina*. It was a complete city within a city, palaces, administrative buildings, soldiers' quarters and the houses of courtiers packed together cheek by jowl. Workshops, baths and markets were all woven into a rich and varied fabric around the mosque.

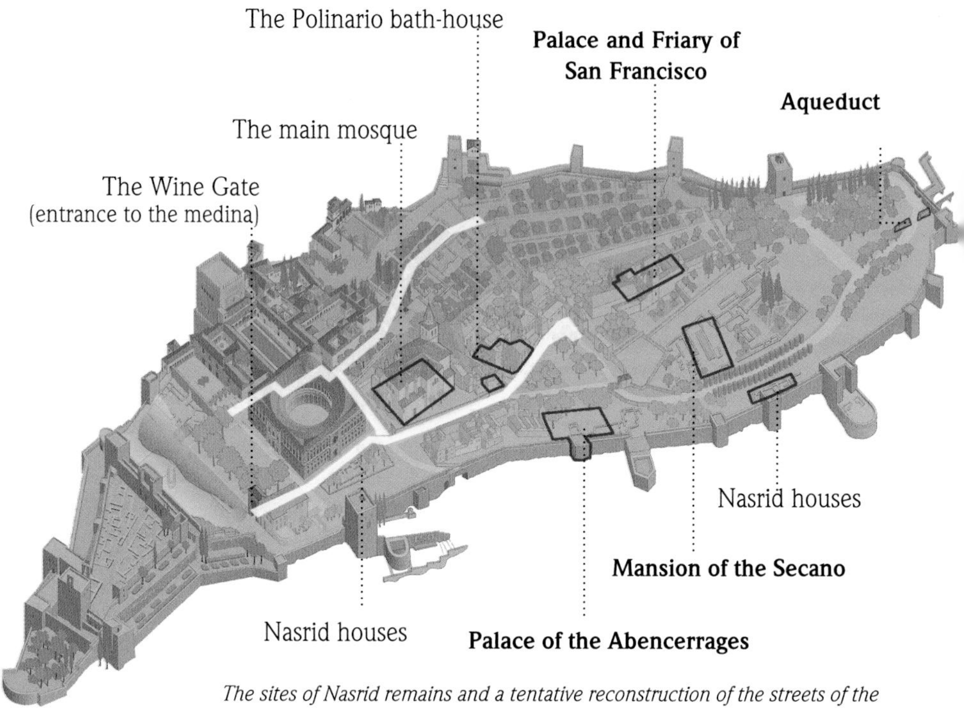

The Polinario bath-house

Palace and Friary of San Francisco

Aqueduct

The main mosque

The Wine Gate
(entrance to the medina)

Nasrid houses

Mansion of the Secano

Nasrid houses

Palace of the Abencerrages

The sites of Nasrid remains and a tentative reconstruction of the streets of the medina. *The dotted lines indicate sites to which some doubt is still attached*

 The Royal Street. The streets of the *medina*

Most of the present-day Royal Street follows the same line as the old Upper Royal Street, although it was modified slightly near to the Franciscan friary when the square was laid out. In Nasrid times it began at the Wine Gate. The Royal Waterway ran beneath it, and alongside it were dwellings and baths such as the Palace of the Abencerrages and the Polinario bath-house, the latter of which survives to this day.

The church of St. Mary of the Alhambra, built on the site of the mosque.

A Palace and the Friary of San Francisco

The first known construction on this site was a Nasrid palace, built at the beginning of the XIV century either by Muhammad III or Yusuf I. In 1495 a Franciscan friary was built on its ruins and it was here that Queen Isabel was first entombed before her body was removed to the Royal Chapel in Granada. After the expulsion of the Franciscans in 1835 it was left to fall into ruins until in 1929 the Granadan architect Leopoldo Torres Balbás restored it and converted it into a residence for landscape painters. Since 1942 it has been a Parador de Turismo (a state-run hotel).

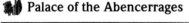

Only the principal hall of the original palace remains, incorporated today into the modern building. It has a mocárabe ceiling and a mirador overlooking the Partal.

Mirador
Baño
Qubba
Patio
Alberca/Acequia
Patio Convento
Torre Convento

Hypothetical ground-plan of the Nasrid palace superimposed upon the present-day building (pink), according to A. Orihuela. The palace pool must have been part of the Royal Waterway itself, which afterwards would have continued its course under the Royal Street.

Palace of the Abencerrages

This palace abutted onto the city wall at the point now known as the Tower of the Abencerrages, which in fact formed an intrinsic part of the palace, containing as it did the qubba, or main hall of the dwelling. It is believed to have been built either at the end of the XIII or beginning of the XIV century and must have belonged to the family of that name.

Hypothetical reconstruction according to A. Orihuela. The tower interrupts its longitudinal symmetry, thus putting more emphasis on the transverse axis. The scheme of a courtyard followed by a long room before arriving at the main hall predates the similar lay-out of the Comares Palace. The walkway along the parapet formed a narrow passageway as it crossed the lower part of the tower.

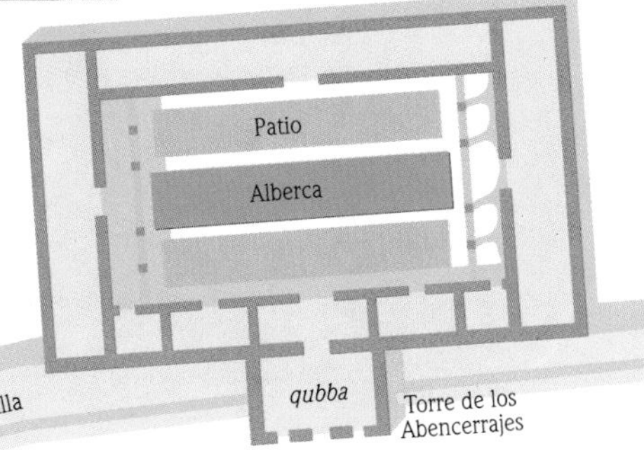

The Cypress Walk

There is now a walk along the secano, *bordered by cypress hedges, which was laid out by Leopoldo Torres Balbás to mark where a mediaeval street used to connect the Nasrid palaces to the Generalife outside the Partal. On both sides the visitor can see the footings of walls belonging to Nasrid and later buildings.*

 Archaeological remains in the Secano

The archaeological remains in this area of the Alhambra are very diverse, including as they do houses from Nasrid times, a bath-house and dyeing workshops, together with more modern elements.

The most important edifice would seem to have been a palace or mansion, the pool and some wall footings of which are all that remain (below). These can clearly be seen from the cypress walk.

 The Royal Waterway

The Royal Waterway was built by al-Ahmar, the founder of the Nasrid dynasty. It enters into the confines of the Alhambra at its southernmost point, alongside the Water Tower (left), where the remains of the aqueduct that carried it across the gully of the Cuesta de los Chinos can still be seen. It then turned towards what today is a national *parador*, in front of which a large cistern served to control the flow. As this is the highest area in the Alhambra the water only needed to follow the contours downhill to reach everywhere in the royal city.

Carlos V

The Palace of Charles V

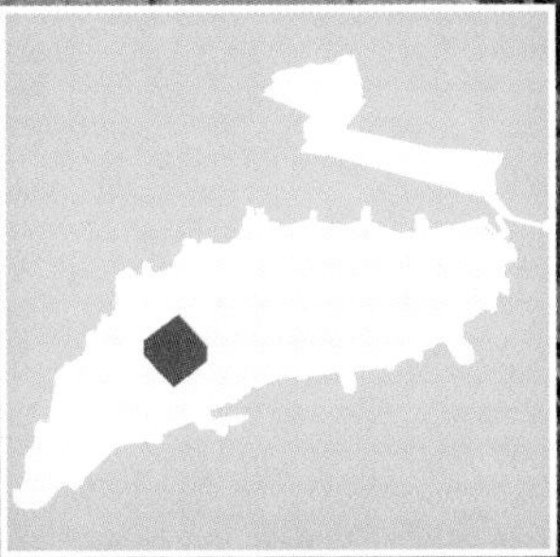

Lewis Meunier, 1668

If any one monument can be so controversial and misunderstood, and yet so often referred to as outstanding, it is the Palace of Charles V. Romantic clichés vilified it as an attempt by authoritarian Spanish monarchs to erase the Muslim past but a more dispassionate look at history will reveal the contrary to be true. The Spanish monarchy invested the conquest of Granada, with enormous symbolic value. Their political intention was to reinforce Granada's role as a capital city, which it had enjoyed for so many centuries, by building great new monuments without destroying the old, complementing rather than detracting from the past.

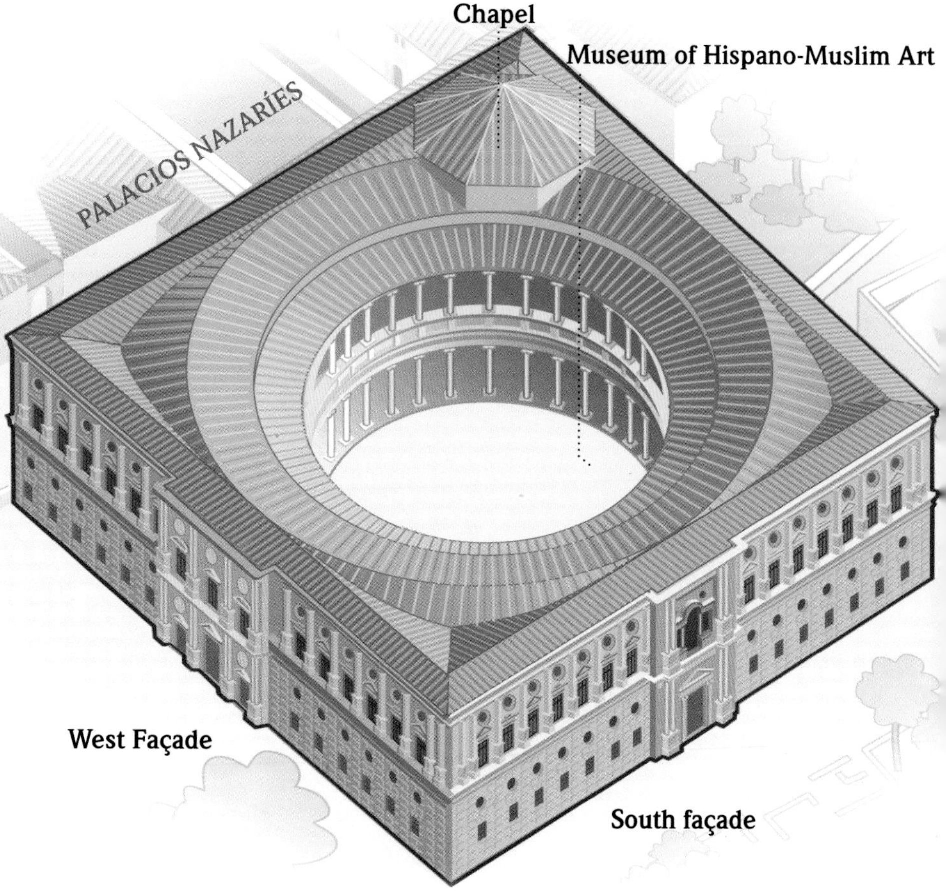

Chapel

Museum of Hispano-Muslim Art

PALACIOS NAZARÍES

West Façade

South façade

The Palace of Charles V

The palace was built upon an old Christian quarter, a lower annex to the Nasrid city. An error in geometry meant that its design would encroach very slightly upon the Alhambra itself. Within this context, however, it might be worth trying to understand the reasons behind such a new and radical project. It is also probably thanks to the Palace of Charles V that the Alhambra came to be included in the patrimony of the Spanish Royal Palaces instead of being reduced to an archaeological remnant of a defeated culture.

The Catholic monarchs had already built a funerary chapel in Granada, the Royal Chapel. The Emperor Charles V was enthusiastic about ennobling the city and took personal interest in the project. During his state visit to Granada, which coincided with his honeymoon with Isabel of Portugal in 1526, Charles visited the Alhambra and stayed in a suite of rooms which henceforth were known as "the lodgings of Charles V". Proof of his appreciation of the old Nasrid city was his desire to add to it and make it suitable for the needs of a modern court. Thus he entrusted the building of a palace to the Marquis of Mondéjar, governor of the Alhambra. The emperor left no specific orders as to the design or to the way the work should be carried out; he delegated responsibility to men of trust. Thus we cannot really speak about a "Charles V style"; the palace reflected the renaissance style in vogue at the time in Italy. Nevertheless, it will always be the symbol of a reign that began with so much zest for projects which in the end would never be entirely accomplished. It should be remembered for example that the roof over the second floor of this palace is of modern construction. From his seat in Toledo, the Marquis of Mondéjar, scion of the noble family of Mendoza, had contributed towards spreading an appreciation of the new Renaissance art throughout Spain

Probable portrait of Charles V

Below, roof structure remained uncovered until 1960

Pedro Machuca, who was to be entrusted with the building work, had had a solid apprenticeship in Rome, working with both Michael Angelo and Rafael. Thanks to this training he would have known in theory about the most elaborate creations of the Renaissance. Proof of this lies in his choice of the very singular design of a round courtyard within a square building, which had been the basis of the highest aspirations of ideal design since the days of Alberti.

*Precedents for this palace can probably be found in **San Pietro in Montorio** in Rome (above), which must have been surrounded by a circular courtyard, according to the ground plan published by Serlio (above right), in the round courtyard of the **Villa Madama** (below) by Rafael and in the drawings of Leonardo da Vinci.*

When Machuca died in 1550 he was succeeded by his son Luis and later by Juan de Orea, who worked under the supervision of Juan de Herrera as far as the design of the stairs and the upper part of the main doorway were concerned. This building phase finished under the direction of Minjares.

All the sculptures, the work of Niccolao da Corte, Juan de Orea and Antonio de Leval imbue the emperor with a clearly majestic mien (He is seen here potrayed as Caesar).

Hercules *as a mythological reference to the emperor*

The battle of Pavia, *by the Italian sculptor Niccolao da Corte.*

Rectangular windows *are surmounted by round windows on both floors, thus returning to the interplay of line, a theme with which the Renaissance was enthralled.*

Ionic pilasters *upon pedestals adorned with different reliefs counterpoise the weight of the bosses with their vertical lightness.*

Doric columns *on the first floor*

Ionic pilasters *upon pedestals adorned with different reliefs counterpoise the weight of the bosses with their vertical lightness*

Fame, Victory *and* ***Fecundity*** *are the three feminine personages depicted on the south façade.*

La Victoria.

The palace is arranged into large halls around the side, except in the north-west curvature, where the chapel and the crypt are housed (cf. page 76).

The chapel was in fact the most important detail of the palace as far as Charles was concerned. On receiving the projected design, he wrote on 30 November 1527, *"I only want to ask that the hall at the front be large and that there be a chapel in it to say and hear mass.."* But in this original plan the new Royal House could already be seen as a theatrical aggrandisement of the older dwellings of the Nasrid city.

This shield of Phillip II takes pride of place on the main façade.

***Bas relief** on the pedestal of a pillar.*

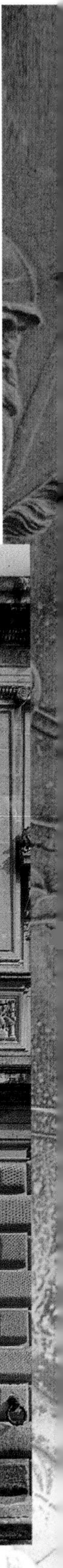

The interior, is characterised by its completely sober austerity: two floors with Doric and Tuscan lintels and a great stairway which joins the magnificent annular barrel vault over the vestibule.

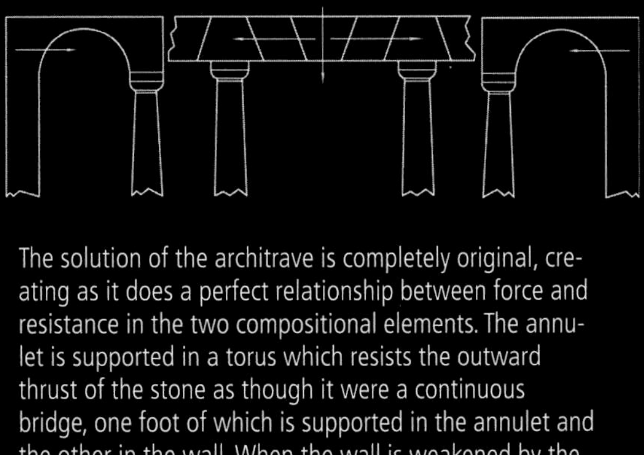

The solution of the architrave is completely original, creating as it does a perfect relationship between force and resistance in the two compositional elements. The annulet is supported in a torus which resists the outward thrust of the stone as though it were a continuous bridge, one foot of which is supported in the annulet and the other in the wall. When the wall is weakened by the presence of a door, as it is in the west wall, the strength of the outer wall is augmented by a depressed vault or with buttresses of some other kind.

The original project envisaged the west and south façades preceded by squares surrounded by pillared galleries but these were left unmade. The palace was never finished and never occupied by Charles. Today it houses the Alhambra Museum and is used during the Festival Of Music and Dance to stage concerts.

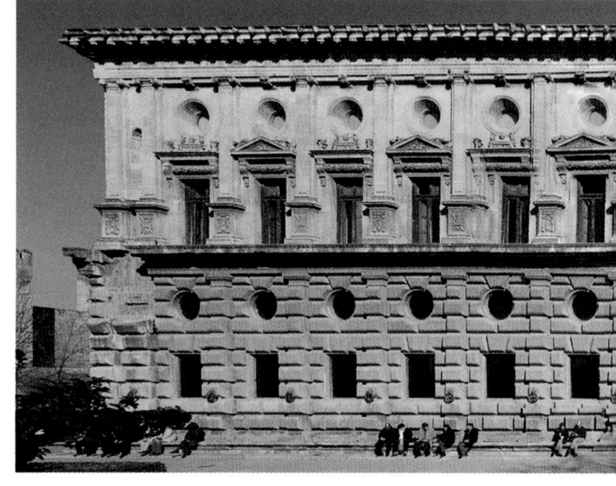

The Alhambra Museum

In the closing years of the twentieth century the collected pieces belonging to the Spanish-Muslim Museum were transferred to the ground floor of the Palace of Charles V to constitute the new Alhambra Museum. Among its exhibits are the famous Gazelle Jar, the original door to the Hall of the Two Sisters, various coffered ceilings, ceramics, capitals, tombstones and a comprehensive collection of other more mundane pieces which help to enlighten us about everyday life in Madinat al-Hambra. *Entrance is free and a visit is highly recommended (closed on Mondays). On the first floor of the palace is the Museum of Fine Arts, which houses many works that came to light with the disentailment of the church in 1835, such as "el Cardo" by Sánchez Cotán, works by Siloë and many other paintings of the Granadan school.*

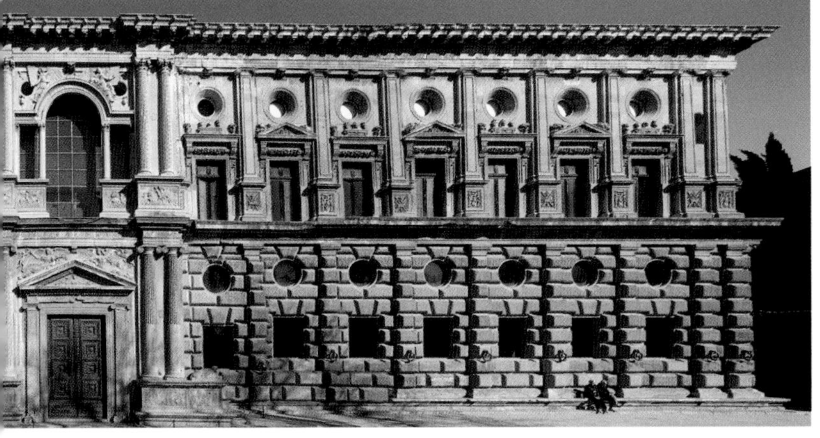

Bibliographie

AZNAR, F. *Al-Ándalus.* Madrid 1992, Anaya.

Bermúdez Pareja, Jesús. *La Casa Real Vieja.* Albaicín/Sadea. Granada.

BORRÁS, Gonzalo M. Anaya. *La Alhambra.* Madrid 1989.

BURKHARD, Titus. La Civilización Hispanoárabe. Alianza. Madrid, 1985.

CABANELAS RODRÍGUEZ, D. *El techo del Salón de Comares.* Granada, 1988. Patronato de la Alhambra y el Generalife. Granada 1982.

GRABAR, O. *La Alhambra: iconografía formas y valores.* Madrid, 1980. Alianza Editorial, S.A.

MANZANO, Rafael. *La Alhambra,* Anaya. Madrid. 1992.

ORIHUELA UZAL, A; VÍLCHEZ VÍLCHEZ, C. *Aljibes Públicos de la Granada islámica.* Granada, 1991. Ayuntamiento de Granada. 1991.

ORIHUELA UZAL, A. *Casas y Palacios Nazaríes. Siglos XIII-XV.* Barcelona, 1996.

PUERTA VILCHEZ J.M.: *La aventura del Cálamo.* Edilux, Granada, 2007.

PRIETO MORENO, F. *Los jardines de Granada.* Madrid 1983, Patronato Nacional de Museos.

SALMERÓN ESCOBAR, PEDRO, *La Alhambra, Estructura y Paisaje.* C. G. de Ahorros de Granada. Ayuntamientto de Granada, 2000.

SECO DE LUCENA, LUIS, *La Alhambra, como fue y como es.* Granada 1935.

VARIOS AUTORES. *El enigma del agua en al-Ándalus.* Barcelona, 1994.

VARIOS AUTORES. *La casa hispanomusulmana. Aportaciones de la arqueología.* Granada, 1990. Publicaciones del Patronato de la Alhambra y el Generalife.

VARIOS AUTORES. *La imagen romántica del Legado Andalusí.* Barcelona, 1995.

VARIOS AUTORES. *Plan Especial de protección y reforma interior de la Alhambra y Alijares.* Granada, 1986. Consejería de Cultura, Junta de Andalucía; Ayuntamiento de Granada; Patronato de la Alhambra y Generalife.

Overleft, engravings based on photographies by Clifford around 1860.

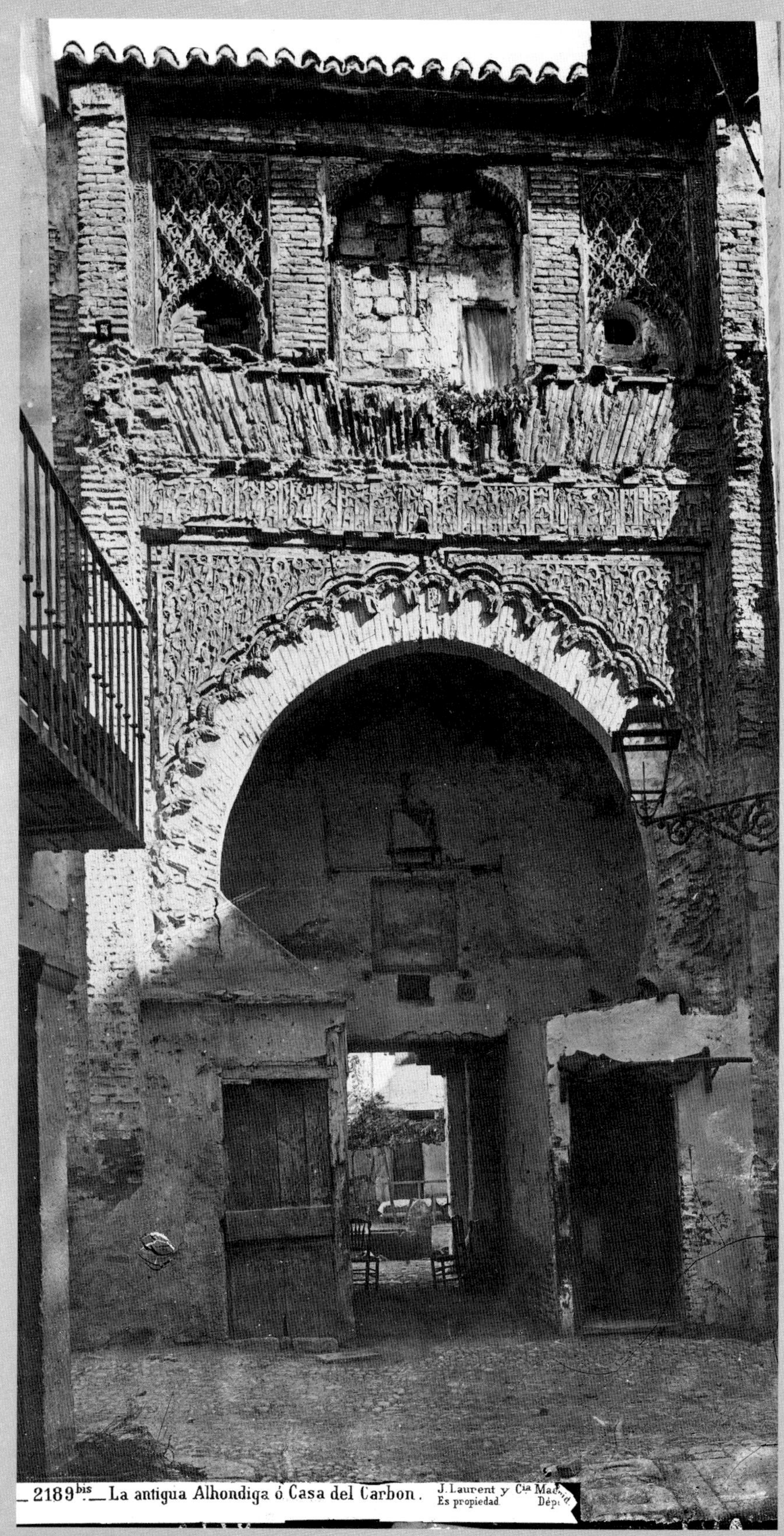

Fotography by Laurent (1880). Archivo Ruiz Vernacci IPHE, Madrid.

Christian Granada

by Arturo Gutiérrez Castillo.

English version by Jon Trout.

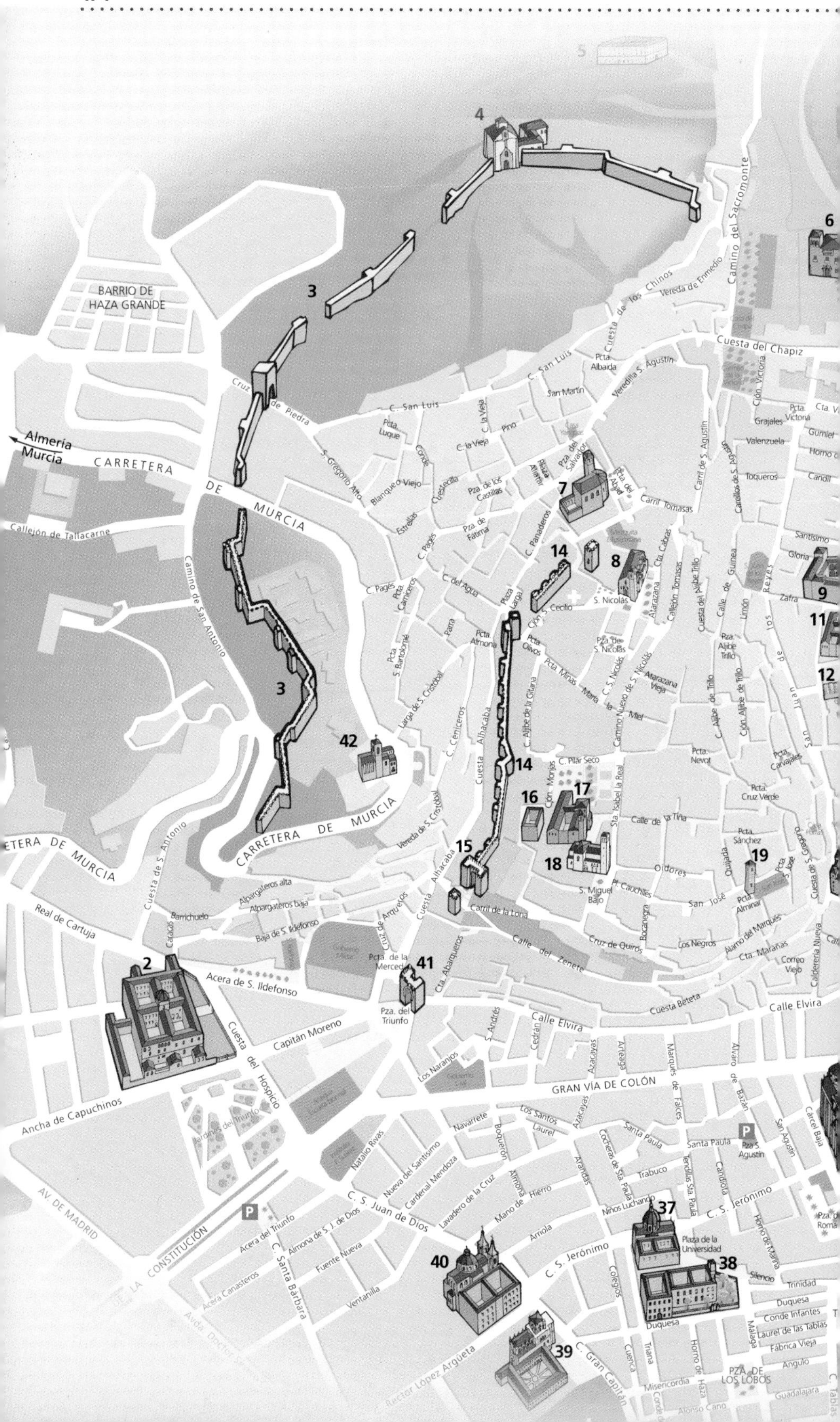
BARRIO DE HAZA GRANDE
Almería
Murcia
CARRETERA DE MURCIA
Callejón de Tallacarne
Camino de San Antonio
Cruz de Piedra
C. San Luis
Cuesta de los Chinos
Vereda de Enmedio
Camino del Sacromonte
Cuesta del Chapiz
Pcta. Albaida
Veredilla S. Agustín
San Martín
Pcta. Luque
S. Gregorio Alto
Blanqueo Viejo
Estrellas
C. Pagés
Pza. de los Castillas
Pza. de Fátima
Pza. del Salvador
Carril Tomasas
Carril de S. Agustín
Grajales
Pcta. Victoria
Valenzuela
Toqueros
Gumiel
Candil
Santísimo
Gloria
Zafra
C. del Agua
Plaza Larga
Pcta. Almona
Pcta. Olivos
Cjón. S. Cecilio
S. Nicolás
Pza. de S. Nicolás
Atarazana Vieja
Cta. Cabras
Callejón Tomasas
Cuesta del Aljibe Trillo
Calle de Guinea
Pza. Aljibe Trillo
Limón
Pcta. S. Bartolomé
Larga de S. Cristóbal
C. Ceniceros
Cuesta Alhacaba
C. Aljibe de la Gitana
Pcta. Minas
María la Miel
Camino Nuevo de S. Nicolás
C. Pilar Seco
Cjón. Monjas
Sta. Isabel la Real
Pcta. Nevot
Pcta. Carvajales
Pcta. Cruz Verde
Calle de la Tina
Pcta. Sánchez
Oidores
Pl. Cauchiles
S. Miguel Bajo
San José
Pcta. Alminar
Álamo del Marqués
Cta. Marañas
Correo Viejo
Calderería Nueva
Vereda de S. Cristóbal
Carril de la Lona
Calle del Zenete
Cruz de Quirós
Bocanegra
Los Negros
CARRETERA DE MURCIA
Cuesta de S. Antonio
Alpargateros alta
Alpargateros baja
Barrichuelo
Baja de S. Ildefonso
Real de Cartuja
Cruz de Arqueros
Pcta. de la Merced
Cta. Abarqueros
Acera de S. Ildefonso
Pza. del Triunfo
Capitán Moreno
Cuesta del Hospicio
Calle Elvira
Cuesta Beteta
S. Andrés
Cedrán
Azacayas
Arteaga
Marqués de Falces
Álvaro de Bazán
Los Naranjos
GRAN VÍA DE COLÓN
Ancha de Capuchinos
Jardines del Triunfo
Natalio Rivas
Nueva del Santísimo
Navarrete
Boquerón
Los Santos
Laurel
Santa Paula
Pza S. Agustín
San Agustín
Cárcel Baja
Cardenal Mendoza
Lavadero de la Cruz
Almona
Mano de Hierro
Arandas
Cocheros de Sta Paula
Tendillas Sta Paula
Trabuco
Niños Luchando
Plaza de la Universidad
C. S. Jerónimo
AV. DE MADRID
AV. DE LA CONSTITUCIÓN
Acera del Triunfo
C. Santa Bárbara
Almona de S. J. de Dios
C. S. Juan de Dios
Fuente Nueva
Ventanilla
Acera Canasteros
Arriola
Colegios
Silencio
Trinidad
Duquesa
Conde Infantes
Laurel de las Tablas
Fábrica Vieja
Angulo
Guadalajara
Málaga
Cuenca
Triana
Horno de Haza
PZA. DE LOS LOBOS
Misericordia
C. Gran Capitán
Rector López Argüeta
2
3
4
5
6
7
8
9
11
12
14
15
16
17
18
19
37
38
39
40
41
42

1. Monasterio de la Cartuja (S. XVI-XVIII)
2. Hospital Real (s. XVI-XVII)
3. Muralla Nazarí (s. XIV-XV)
4. Ermita de S. Miguel Alto
5. Abadía del Sacromonte (s. XVII)
6. Palacio de los Córdova
7. Iglesia del Salvador (antigua Mezquita)
8. Iglesia de S. Nicolás (s. XVI)
9. Casa de Castril. Museo Arqueológico
10. Iglesia de S. Pedro (s. XVI)
11. Convento Sta. Catalina (s. XVI)
12. Baño árabe del Bañuelo (s. XI)
13. Puente del Cadí (s. XIII)
14. Muralla Zirí (s. XI)
15. Puerta de Monaita (s. XI)
16. Palacio de Dar-al-Horra (s. XV)
17. Convento de Sta. Isabel la Real (s. XVI)
18. Iglesia de S. Miguel Bajo (s. XVI)
19. Minarete de S. José (s. X)
20. Iglesia de Sta. Ana (s. XVI)
21. Real Chancillería (s. XVI)
22. Puerta de las Granadas (s. XVI)
23. Torres Bermejas (s. XII-XV)
24. Casa de los Tiros (s. XVI)
25. Casa árabe de los Girones (s.XIII)
26. Iglesia de S. Matías (s. XVI)
27. Iglesia de Sto. Domingo (s. XVII)
28. Iglesia Comendadoras de Santiago
29. Iglesia de S. Cecilio (s. XVI)
30. Carmen de los Mártires (s. XIX)
31. Basílica. de las Angustias (s. XVII)
32. Corral del Carbón (alhóndiga s. XIV)
33. Alcaicería (s. XIV-XIX)
34. Madrasa (escuela coránica) (s. XIV-XVI)
35. Palacio de la Curia
36. Catedral, Capilla Real, Iglesia del Sagrario (s. XVI-XVIII)
37. Iglesia de S. Justo y Pastor (s. XVII)
38. Universidad Vieja (s. XVII), Jardín Botánico
39. Monasterio de S. Jerónimo (s. XVI)
40. Igl. y Hospital S. Juan de Dios (s. XVI-XVIII)
41. Puerta de Elvira (s. XI)

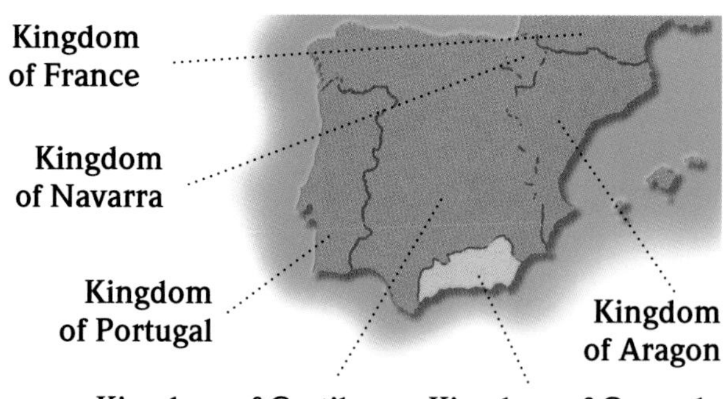

CHRISTIAN GRANADA

For more than two and a half centuries, from 1238 to 1492, the city of Granada, capital of the last Muslim kingdom in Spain, was a tempting prize for the kingdom of Castile. Even for the rest of the western world this exotic city nestling in its southernmost extreme quickly became seen as a nagging, deeply embedded cyst, testimony to the growing menace of Islam towards Europe. Nevertheless, internal strife and difficulties in the Christian kingdoms not only of Spain but the rest of the western world did not allow Christian worries about Islamic power to work to their advantage. It was not until the second half of the XV century that a series of favourable circumstances eventually allowed Castile to undertake the responsibility of settling the historic commitment to reconquer the kingdom of Granada. The XV century was enormously important for the kingdom of Castile. It was during this time that the scene was set for the great dawning that allowed the advent of modernity in Spain and the rise of the Castilian crown to that of a major power. A rapidly expanding economy and social demand for a strong and authoritarian monarchy helped to overcome the internal crises and heralded the way towards a new model for the management of political power.

Ferdinand and Isabel were married in 1469 and the dynasties of Castile and Aragon were joined together in 1479, when Ferdinand succeeded to the throne of Aragon. At this juncture the Catholic Monarchs, as they came to be known, set their sights on the centuries-old desire to finish off the process of reconquest by incorporating the Muslim kingdom of Granada into their own. This they achieved after a systematic and methodical campaign that employed many modern techniques of warfare. After a decade of clashes and skirmishes the end of the kingdom of Granada was sealed, coinciding with the beginning of an almost magical year: 1492. Nearly forty years had transpired before Christendom could repay Islam for the sacking of Constantinople. This quest came to be seen as the last European crusade and perhaps for this reason Granada soon became a symbol for the whole western world: the new Jerusalem; the western Jerusalem; a focus of spirituality strengthened and promoted by the church itself and by the generosity of the crown in establishing religious foundations and public and political administrative institutions. Under the aegis of such a favourable religious and political climate it was not long before Granada became the focal point of Renaissance culture and art in Spain, and also the ideal setting to give expression to the new concepts of religious harmony encouraged by humanistic ideals.

This spiritualistic fervour was accompanied by an urgent need to furnish Granada, a city with almost no Christian heritage, or at least a very distant one, with the most elementary ecclesiastical and cultural resources in order to evangelize and Christianize its mainly Muslim population. The surprising and spectacular fruits of these new times still survive in a multitude of monuments and other testimonies to be found throughout the town and its province. The intention of this short book is to give the reader some idea of what these historical landmarks meant in their own time and what they represent today.

Capilla Real

The cenotaphs housed in the nave of the Royal Chapel together with the coffins kept below them in the crypt bear witness to the desire that Granada should be the final resting place for the mortal remains of the Spanish royal family. The Catholic Monarchs, whose mausoleum is to be seen in the foreground of the photograph, were finally laid to rest here in 1521, together with Prince Michael, their first grandson. Their son-in-law, Phillip the Fair, was brought here in 1525 and his wife Joan in 1574, both of whom lie sculpted in marble on the cenotaph in the background. The remains of the Empress Isabel of Portugal, wife of Charles V, were laid in the chapel crypt in 1539. She was later taken to the Royal Pantheon at the Escorial Palace.

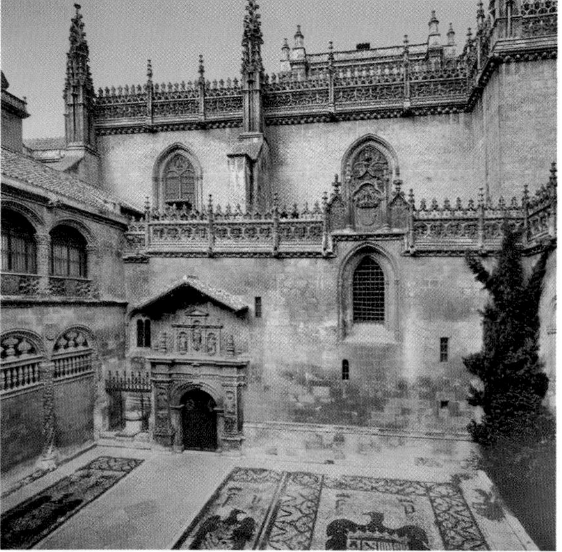

Top: view of the outside of the Royal Chapel, and below it the old mercantile exchange.

As far as Isabel and Ferdinand were concerned, they could have chosen with all justification, in consonance with their ancestors, one of many other places for their royal mausoleum, such as Miraflores, Toledo, Sevilla or Poblet. But Granada was one of the most precious symbols of their kingdom and they deemed it fitting that Granada, which had covered them in glory during their lives, should cover them with its

earth for their eternal rest. In fact the final aspect of the Royal Chapel as we know it today is the result of a fortunate disobedience towards the personal wishes of Queen Isabel, which she set out in her will shortly before her death in October 1504. In the end little respect was shown for her desires as to its situation and Franciscan simplicity. So today we can enjoy a funeral chapel that exceeds by far anything that tradition had established for such a monument.

The Royal Chapel was not only endowed with numerous works of art but also with important objects that had formed part of the daily life of Queen Isabel: a hand mirror, converted into a monstrance in the XVIII century; a beautiful silver-gilt jewellery box and a missal illustrated with exquisite borders showing royal shields and emblems, letters with figures of saints and a miniature of the crucifixion in mid-relief.

Queen Isabel's missal.

The building of the Royal Chapel did not take long. The work was begun in 1506 under the supervision of master builder Enrique Egas and, according to the inscription around the wall in the chapel, was finished in 1517, although there is good reason to believe that some work continued until 1521. The result was a building in the Isabelline style, a variation of traditional Gothic that incorporated new, flamboyant decorative motifs. In this way both the exterior and interior of the building display a striking contrast between the simple lines of their basic architecture and the extravagance of the ornamentation. As far as its structure is concerned, the plan of the chapel is that of a church with a single nave, four side chapels (although only two are used as such) and very shallow transepts, followed by steps leading to a raised presbytery and finally elegant ribbed vaulting.

The crown and sceptre of Queen Isabel and the ceremonial sword of King Ferdinand: three symbols which, despite their innate simplicity, forcefully evoke the spirit of the most powerful European monarchy of the age.

The altar-piece is another undeniable example of the triumph of artistic expression. It was wrought between 1520 and 1521 by Felipe de Vigarny, but also owes much to other distinguished artists of the day such as Berruguete and Jacobo Florentino, together with a whole team of wood carvers, carpenters, moulders, painters and assemblers. As a whole the altar-piece offers us a complex iconographic and iconological argument on both the religious and political levels.

Constructed upon the steps of the presbytery the altar-piece appears as an enormous backcloth gathering together all the spirituality and symbolism contained in the Royal Chapel. Its structure reflects the rules that should be observed for these iconographic spaces, consisting as it does of two basement stages followed by three upper tiers divided into five vertical sections, all surmounted by a pediment. Outstanding within its imagery are the repeated allusions to the patrons saints of the Catholic King and Queen, St. John the Baptist and St. John the Evangelist (above), scenes relating to the conquest of Granada and the subsequent baptism of the "Moriscos" (right) and a possible tribute to the Emperor Charles V in the figure of one of the Three Kings (immediate right) in the Adoration of the Magi within the lowest tier of the screen.

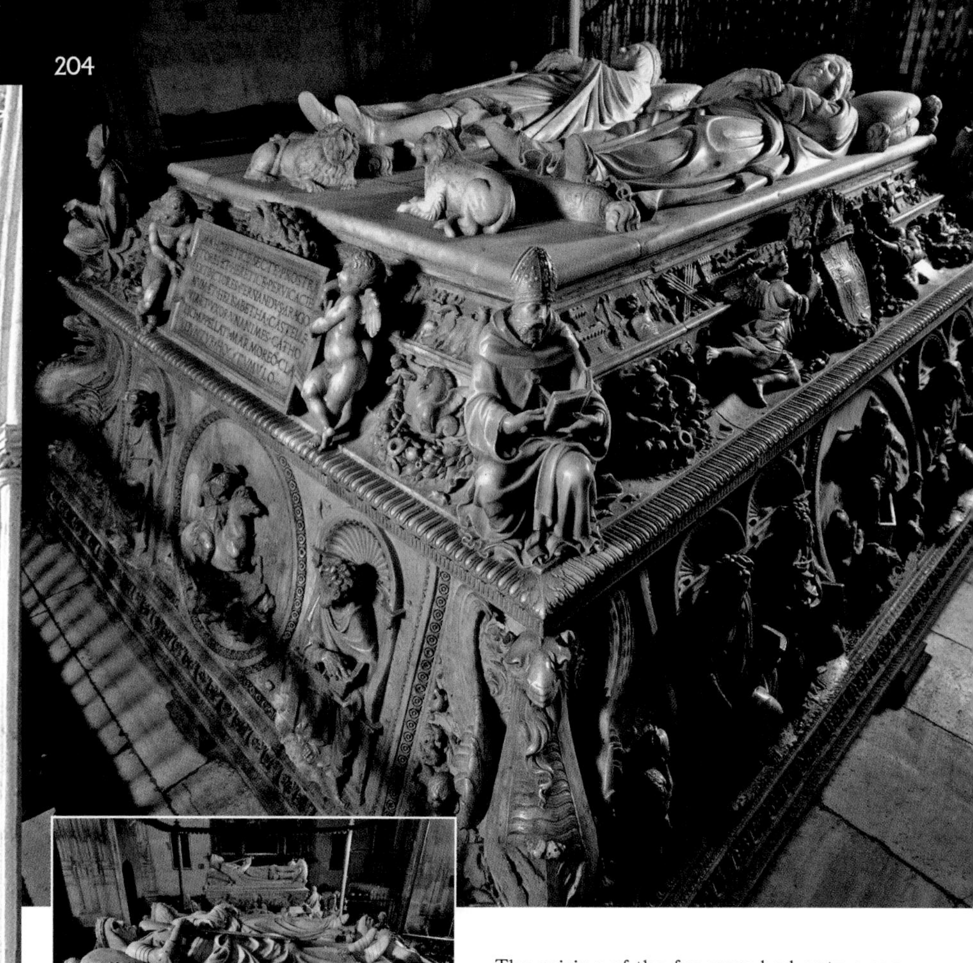

Fortunately the wishes for simplicity and poverty that the queen had expressed for her final resting place were not respected. Her husband, Ferdinand, preferred a magnificent marble mausoleum to share with his wife in their eminence and glory. The Italian Domenico Fancelli sculpted their cenotaph in Carrara marble between 1514 and 1517. The shape of the cenotaph was highly innovative compared to traditional Spanish funerary sculpture of the period, sculpted in the form of a truncated pyramid, on top of which lie the figures of the king and queen.*

The raising of the funerary bed onto a second level, the importance of the edges with griffons acting as guardians against malevolence and sin and the inclusion of a complex iconographic programme that brings together mythology and Christianity are some of the most original of its features. The gentle delicacy typical of Florentine sculpture can be seen in most of the sculpted forms, whether carved in relief or as separate individual figures. But where experts on the subject are in general agreement is in the sculptor's skill in shaping the head of King Ferdinand. It transmits a feeling of such naturalness and physical beauty that it is believed to be one of the most realistic likenesses of the king ever achieved. The figure of the queen, on the other hand, seems to conform to more stereotypic values rather than being a true likeness of her physical features. The intention to exalt royal power is clearly present everywhere: the king's armour, crowns, a pair of lions and a proliferation of monarchic shields.

The cenotaph of Juana la Loca (Joan the Mad), daughter of Isabel and Ferdinand, and that of her husband Felipe el Hermoso (Phillip the Fair) is the work of Bartolomé Ordoñez, a sculpture from Burgos in the north of Spain. His death in 1520 led to the intervention of other, less-skilled hands until the mausoleum was finished in 1526, but the merit of the design and shaping of the cenotaph live up to Ordóñez's original conception. Its most striking novelty lies in the vertical base, the added height of the sepulchre, the placing of the recumbent figures upon a sarcophagus and the substitution of the angular griffons with nymphs and satyrs in daring poses. All in all, this cenotaph is much more dynamic compared to the balance and serenity of that of the Catholic King and Queen. This is due in part to the presence of satyrs who reflect with startling reality the tortuous twisting of Laocoön and the counterpoint of a serene St. Andrew, particularly reminiscent of Michael Angelo.

Possibly one of the most beautiful effects is contained in the reliefs of the medallions (tondi) on all four sides of this monument. What is remarkable about these is the sculptor's spatial conception of his compositions, showing an almost pictorial approach, in which it is easy to appreciate how he achieves the aerial perspective by skilfully superimposing plane surfaces and sfumata.

Below: four examples of the sculptures on the royal cenotaphs in the Royal Chapel. The first represents St. Augustine and forms part of the sepulchre of King Ferdinand and Queen Isabel. The three figures of St. Andrew, St. John the Evangelist and St. John the Baptist, all carved upon the sepulchre of Phillip and his wife Joan, contrast strongly with the studied balance and composure of St. Augustine. St. Andrew and St. John the Baptist to play a nicely defined contrapuntal role, whilst St. John the Evangelist, although less well sculpted, is more static and thoughtful.

In the photographs above and below the differing concepts of the surrounding borders of the two cenotaphs can be clearly appreciated. Above: a young boy (putto) with a nymph, designed by Ordoñez. Below: a griffin on Fancelli's cenotaph.

To the left and right: polychrome wooden sculptures of the Catholic King and Queen at prayer, attributed to Felipe de Bigarny because of stylistic similarities to some of the carvings in the main altar-piece, at the foot of which they must have knelt until they were replaced by those of Diego de Siloé, which remain there today. Bigarny's original wooden sculptures are now in the Royal Chapel museum, one on each side of the triptych of the Passion (next page, below).

Prayer in the Garden of Gethsemane *by Boticelli.*
*Below: a triptych of*Christ's Passion *by Dierick Bouts incorporated within the altar-piece made by Jacobo Florentino.*

Boticelli's paintings have always been appreciated for their poetic sensitivity, for the idyllic tone of their themes and the strong lines of the drawing. The most surprising aspect of this Prayer in the Garden, however, is the skill with which the artist uses composition to draw the viewer into the painting. He moves Christ back from the foreground as though he were relinquishing his usual hierarchic position in favour of the three apostles asleep on the ground before him. The disciple in the middle of the three, duly foreshortened, invites the viewer to enter into the garden through the gap in the fence. From there, a short curved path leads to the height of the rocky promontory where the message of Christ's prayer appears: the acceptance of the sacrificial cup.

This panel contains a complete inventory of the most outstanding characteristics of the early Flemish school of painters. Thus, what is most immediately noticeable are the well balanced composition, the use of background landscape and architecture to give perspective and, above all, the highly detailed treatment of the texture of the materials and clothes: the infant Jesus lies upon a cloth of white linen and the Virgin is richly clothed in a dark blue dress, gold brocade mantle and a red cloak; and beneath her feet to complement her dress, a multicoloured carpet and a black-and-gold brocade cushion.

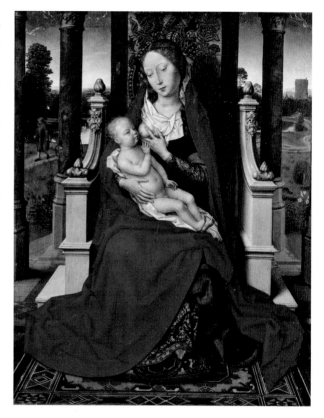

Madonna and Child enthroned *by Hans Memling.*

In this panel, drama, form and colour are further clear features of the Flemish school. The hands encircling the grieving Virgin and the body of the dead Christ provide a frame and a focus for the profound sentiment of the scene. In addition, a precise attention to draughtsmanship together with a great purity of colour results in a remarkable definition in the outlines of the figures.

The Descent from the Cross *by Rogier van der* Weyden.

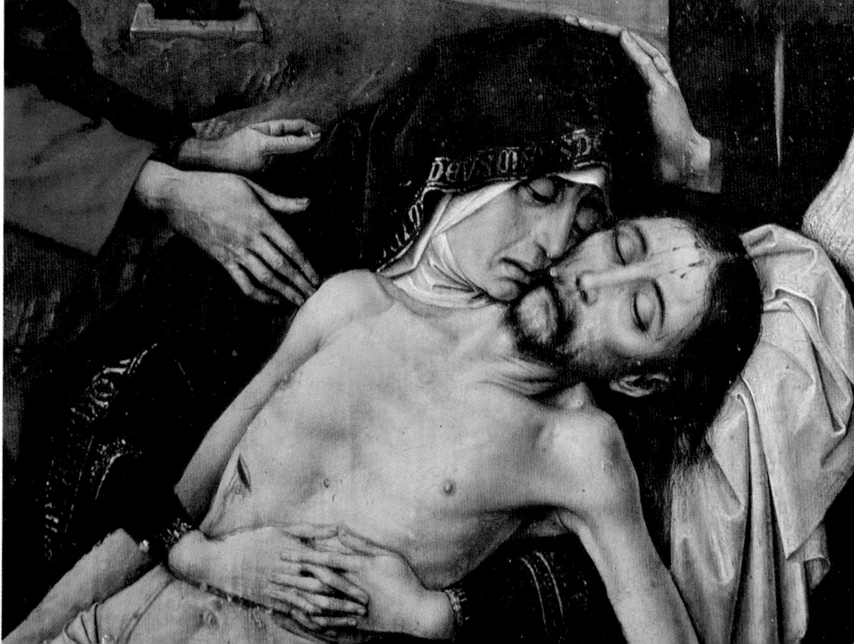

Above: Pietà *by Hans Memling.*

Memling emphasises the dramatic quality of the scene by drawing attention to the most striking details of Christ's Passion: his own wounds, one of which is framed by his fingers, and, in the background, the most important people and instruments involved in the event. The geometry and rigidity of the folds of Jesus' loincloth accentuate the feeling of grief that emanates from the painting.

Below: Head of Christ by an unknown sculptor, who must, however, have been closely involved with the school of Dierick Bouts. This painting has undergone several unfortunate, rejected attempts at preservation. Nevertheless, it remains a good example of an iconographic style that was widely used amongst the so-called Flemish primitives.

RENAISSANCE PAINTING

It is not easy to analyse the features of such a prolific and ever-changing form of artistic expression as was Renaissance painting. It can hardly be denied that from Giotto onwards the production of pictorial art became so widespread and developed to such an extent that every painter, artist, creator and innovator, both within Italy and abroad, established his own Renaissance style. Nevertheless, it is possible to define certain aspects and features of their work that might be looked upon as common reference points to what we generally call Renaissance painting.

As far as techniques were concerned, most Renaissance artists painted with tempera al fresco on walls and used oils on panels and canvas. They were singularly prepossessed with the layout and ordering, that is the overall composition, of the individual elements that went into their work. Similarly they were concerned with perspective, depth and the creation of three-dimensions within what was essentially a two-dimensional plane. To this end they used geometrical vanishing points to achieve linear perspective. Later these Renaissance artists realised that there was also some other element that came between their figures as they retreated into the distance: air. From whence they derived a new technique, that of sfumato, by which the figures became more hazy and blended into one another, thus putting the finishing touch to the depiction of perspective.

Apart from their techniques, Renaissance painters can also be recognised by the subjects and arguments dealt with in their work. In this regard, religious paintings predominate over the secular, in perfect consonance with the power that the Catholic Church wielded in all spheres of life. Thus the repertoire of biblical, evangelical and hagiographical subjects is practically endless, whilst secular subjects are reduced to historical, mythological and allegorical scenes. But more importantly, we witness the appearance of the portrait in response to a desire for personal prominence which characterised the newly emerging bourgeois spirit of these times.

During the Renaissance both shape and colour enjoy special importance with regard to the evolution of painting itself: whereas the quattrocento was devoted to precisely drawn outlines, the cinquecento tended to favour colour at the expense of draughtsmanship. At the same time, Renaissance painters pursued relentlessly the concepts of naturalism, realism and idealism in an attempt to achieve perfection, and even improve on it, as had the classical artists of the ancient world. Thus the study and understanding of the human body and an appreciation of its artistic possibilities were always present in their art. The same was true of light, another element of nature that inevitably formed part of their work, but with different possibilities according to the interpretation of the artistic mode of the time. At the beginning of the Renaissance light resided in the mind and the palette of the painter alone, an idea, a concept, one more element of his composition, which he employed according to his own whim, but after a time it acquired the role that it really plays in nature, depending upon its origin and the surfaces that it illuminates.

THE FLEMISH PAINTERS

From the XV century onwards art in the north of Europe underwent a renovation, just as it did in Italy. This is often referred to as the Northern Renaissance but is also recognised as being the result of a new contribution by brilliant local artists, who became known as the Flemish Primitives. Great attention has traditionally been paid to the new techniques involving the use of oils that the early Flemish painters introduced into European art. This may well be true but it is not the only side to the story. The use of oil in painting had been known for some considerable time and even in the XIV century some artists had experimented with this approach. Nevertheless, a full understanding of its possibilities combined with the difficulties involved in its correct application meant that at first it was not readily accepted as the medium of choice. When painters did begin to recognise the advantages of oil their work was enriched in many different ways: they were able to superimpose successive coats of translucent colour to produce effects of roundness and depth and nuances of light and shade that related more closely to reality; the fluidity of the medium allowed them to define clearer outlines; and they could correct their mistakes because the paint dried relatively slowly.

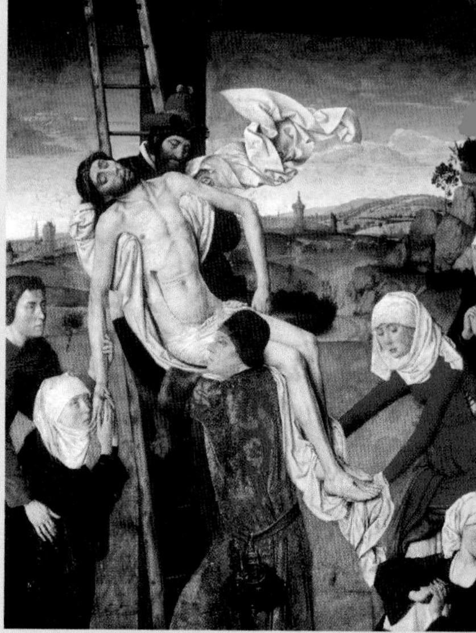

Above: The Descent from the Cross *by Dierick Bouts. Below:* Lamentation of the Holy Women *by Hans Memling.*

Initially the Flemish painters chose to depict religious scenes, very often in an every-day, domestic context. A lot of these scenes were framed within typical merchant-class houses in Flanders, which more often than not were portrayed as having numerous wide windows and porticos through which the artist could construct studied linear perspectives. To make their environment even more convincing, and without doubt more profitable, they also included real, perfectly recognisable people into their surroundings. We are dealing once again then with the triumph of bourgeois individualism, the desire to stand out in a society defined more and more by emulation and competition. The great beneficiary of this social behaviour was the painted portrait; objective representation became the norm and everything that defined an individual, whether it be a physical characteristic or his clothing, was focused upon in the portrait as a distinguishing characteristic.

Sometimes such a degree of realism may lead to the impression that these paintings were eminently materialist but it should be stressed that the reiteration of such details as these did nothing to detract from the overall meaning of the painting, which may be imbued at times with considerable levels of concealed symbology.

One final aspect of this Flemish school of painting that cannot fail to draw our attention is their constant reliance upon drapes and elegant materials and the exquisite detail of their quality, all of which may be expected in the context of the thriving textile industry which existed in Flanders at the time.

Catedral

The view of façade of Granada Cathedral is confined by a narrow square that hinders any proper view of its real majesty and obscures the fact that many experts consider it to be unique amongst XVII century church façades. One of its greatest virtues is that, despite being firmly wedded to the Baroque, it is able to communicate outwards the feeling of the internal structure of a Renaissance church, including the symbolism of the architectural rhythms inside the cathedral: the idea of victory emphasised by the systematic use of the triumphal arch as an integral part of the structure. It was no coincidence that the cathedral was built upon the site of the Great Mosque of the Muslim city and that the theme of triumph should be repeated in the cartouche above the Door of Forgiveness: "After six hundred years of Muslim dominance, these peoples give both Faith and Charity to the Catholic Monarchs.". The façade was constructed according to the design of Alonso Cano, which he completed shortly before his death in 1667.

Almost a quarter of a century after the conquest of Granada the city could still not boast of a new cathedral to laud the great triumph of Christianity. The reasons were many and each was sufficient to justify the delay. The building of the Royal Chapel, which took priority due to the death of Queen Isabel, was still underway and funds were scarce after the long siege of the city. On top of this, new political enterprises such as the wars in Italy and other parts of the Roman Empire were diverting the attention and

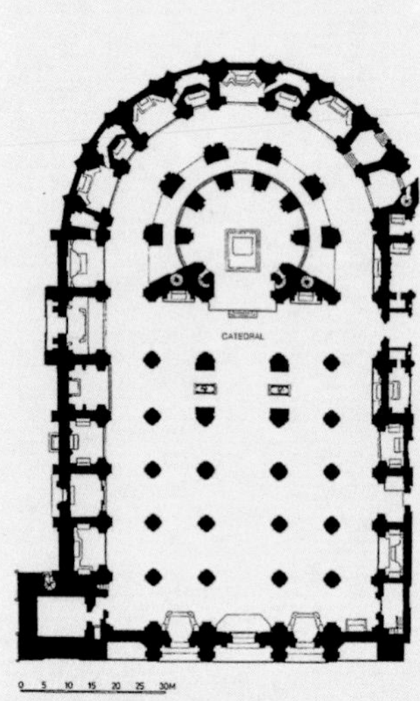

The ground plan of Granada Cathedral reveals a new concept of space joined to the ideological expression of the times. The central position of the main chapel must be viewed in the context of the Church of the Holy Sepulchre in Jerusalem and also of course the wishes of the emperor to make it the site of the royal pantheon. The layout of the basilica itself is closely related to the Roman pattern, a world which Charles V was eager to recreate in order to fulfil his grand desire for "Universitas Christiana".

finances of Spain's rulers away from domestic building projects. It should also be remembered that during the years

Immediately after the conquest the Christian population of Granada had not grown sufficiently to warrant such an enormous enterprise as a cathedral and neither did the sloth of the Muslims in their conversion to Christianity make the project more urgent. And finally, from the first moment of the conquest, a papal bull of May 1492 had made it clear that the foundation of this religious institution was to be authorised in Granada. From this moment until the new basilica itself was built the episcopal church was obliged to occupy various establishments. The first of these was the Royal Mosque in the Alhambra, then the neighbouring Franciscan monastery, followed by another Franciscan monastery in the Realejo district, and finally

Cathedral precinct

Royal Chapel

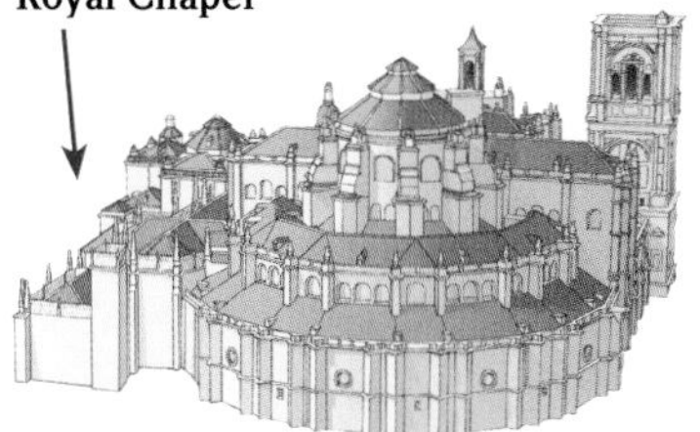

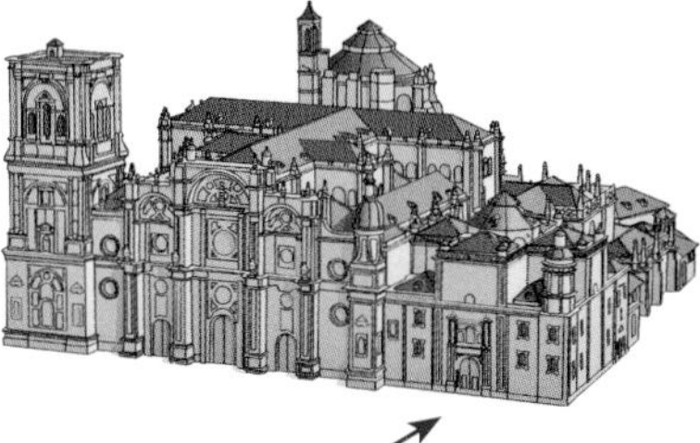

Church of the Sagrario on the site of the old Great Mosque

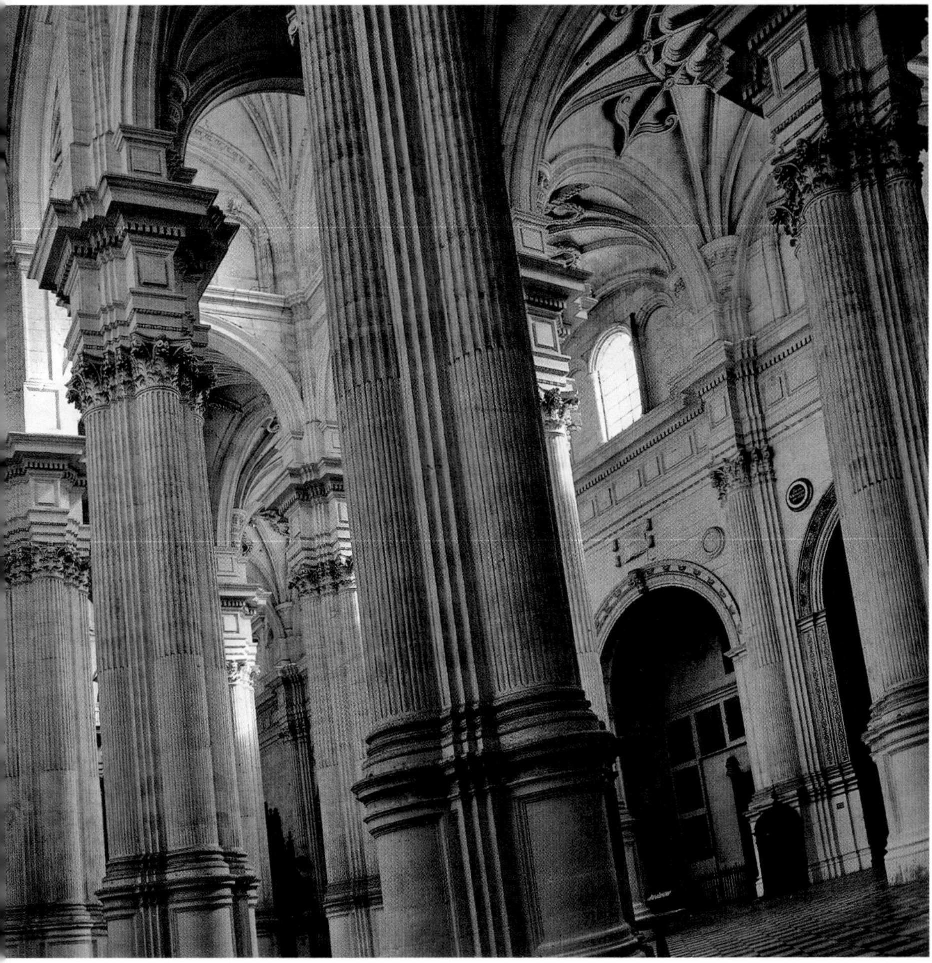

the Great Mosque in the centre of Granada, reconsecrated as the church of St. Mary of O. And so it went on until 25 March 1523, thirty-one years after the conquest. From that date until 1704, when the work was finally deemed to be finished, 181 years were to pass, almost two centuries, more than enough time for the history of the building to undergo numerous alterations. Of these the most controversial was its metamorphosis from a Gothic ground-plan to a Renaissance elevation. Professor Rosenthal, the

Above: an interesting photograph, which shows the startling but somewhat incomprehensible contrast between the Renaissance elevation of the pillars and the Gothic ribbed vaults. The puzzle is easily resolved, however, when we realise that de Siloé had intended the naves to be covered by ribbed vaults, although in the Roman style, just as can be seen in the chapels in the apse and in the seven arches that join the ambulatory to the central rotunda, but that his successors had ignored his plan and settled for the Gothic style that they were more comfortable with.

architectural scholar who best understands the history of the cathedral, assures us that Diego de Siloé rejected the work already carried out until 1528 by the designer and master mason Enrique Egas and his surveyor, Sebastián de Alcántara, both of whom were firmly entrenched in the precepts of Gothic architectural style. In other words, de Siloé designed a new plan on the basis of the emerging triumphant Renaissance style.

At first sight the inside of the cathedral offers an exciting variety of features. The photograph on pages 212 and 213 serves to show the overwhelming effect that the brilliance of the whitewash has on the interior of the cathedral. The walls are known to have been whitewashed in 1703 but it is not certain why. It has been suggested that the reason was to cover up inconsistencies and flaws in the stone and brickwork or that it was used to prepare pillars and other facings for covering with gold leaf. It may even be argued that the whiteness of the walls formed part of the original scheme to achieve the spatial luminosity that Diego de Siloé intended, because this white scheme was certainly in keeping with Renaissance church precepts.

Below: a tapered vault in which the coffers have also had to be tapered, but this apparent distortion fits perfectly within the canons of Classic architecture.

The great architect and designer Diego de Siloé was in charge of the work until his death in 1563. He was followed by seventeen successive master builders, none of whom, with the exception of Alonso Cano, could match his expertise; one of them was even thrown into jail for his incompetence. It is not to be wondered at therefore that with the intervention of so many new architects the work on the cathedral underwent the most disparate changes of direction and styles.

To the left on the facing page: inside the Monastery of St. Peter of Rhodes (XI century) on the medieaeval road to Rome, a building which de Siloé must have known.

This perspective, apart from its undeniable aesthetic attraction, leads us to see new aspects of the many artistic innovations of the cathedral. The piers, for example, which are reminiscent of those in the cathedral of Pienza in Italy, designed by Bernardo Rosellino in 1460, are surprising in their elegance and the impression of lightness that they convey, although they are some four metres in diameter. This, together with the distance between them, gives the building a feeling of such lightness and spaciousness that the concept of a single space triumphs over the unfolding pathway traditional to Roman and Gothic architecture. In contrast to the older longitudinal vision that pushed the worshiper firmly towards the main altar, he is now invited to look around in all directions. In this way Diego de Siloé is following in the footsteps of Brunelleschi, who in the first half of the fifteenth century was already trying out similar ideas of rotundity of space and vision in the churches of San Lorenzo (St. Laurence) and Santo Spirito (the Holy Ghost) in Florence.

We mentioned above the luminous effect that the whitewash lends to the inside of the cathedral. This contribution to the limpid clarity of the interior becomes even more obvious when we bear in mind that a great deal of light was lost when later architects decided to block up a considerable number of the windows originally planned by de Siloé, as can be seen in the photograph. In fact, de Siloé's predecessors closed off half of the 150 windows that he had counted upon. If they had followed de Siloé's plan the symbolism of divine light bathing everything in its glow would have reached its highest expression on earth in this cathedral. To a certain extent this behaviour represented a continuity of the spiritual ideas expressed by the earlier Gothic architecture. The church was no longer just a place of meditation and fearful penitence; now there was room for joy and hope thanks to a new religious spirit that spoke much more of God as a loving father than as an implacable judge.

Finally, it is worth mentioning that Diego de Siloé was clearly a faithful interpreter of the assumptions made by Renaissance architecture through such renowned exponents of its cause as Alberti. The picture here allows us to appreciate the pervasive presence of concepts such as number, proportion, geometry and harmony. The whole idea in the end was to recover the essence of the Roman style in such a way that architecture could be its own protagonist on the sole basis of the disposition of its own elements wisely and appropriately ordained.

DE SILOÉ'S NEW DESIGN

Possibly Diego de Siloé's greatest talent lay in his capacity to harmonise all the architectural knowledge of the time in one building. The following pages offer a small sample of this ability. Firstly, we have to consider how he solved the problem of harmonising the cathedral's great height with the proportions laid down by Classic architecture. According to these rules the correct height of pillars and columns was determined by their diameters. As far as Granada Cathedral was concerned, obedience to this principle would have meant the incorporation of a giant order, which would in turn have gone against the other great premise of Renaissance architecture, that of airy spaciousness. The plan on the left clearly shows the solution to this problem that de Siloé arrived at. He adopted the model of a Roman temple for the pillars: plinth, base, shaft, capital and entablature. Each of these elements is enriched with decorative details such as moulding, fluting, very pronounced borders and daringly projecting cornices. To fill the distance between the entablature and the base of the vaults he introduced a new element, a further tier, composed once more of a base and pilaster. It has been suggested that the source of de Siloé's inspirational solution to the problem of height in Granada Cathedral may well have come from the similar additional tier of arches in the Great Mosque at Córdoba. The diagram shown below reveals the felicitous combination of the drive of the new Renaissance style and the persistence of the Gothic tradition. On the one hand, de Siloé moves the cupola from its traditional place above the crossing to the apse. There may have been two motives for this decision: that the royal pantheon was not after all to be installed in the sacrarium of this cathedral, or more probably that the main altar should receive daylight directly from outside. Whatever the reason, the outcome was the same.

Opposite page: a view of the second tier with a new plinth and pilasters..

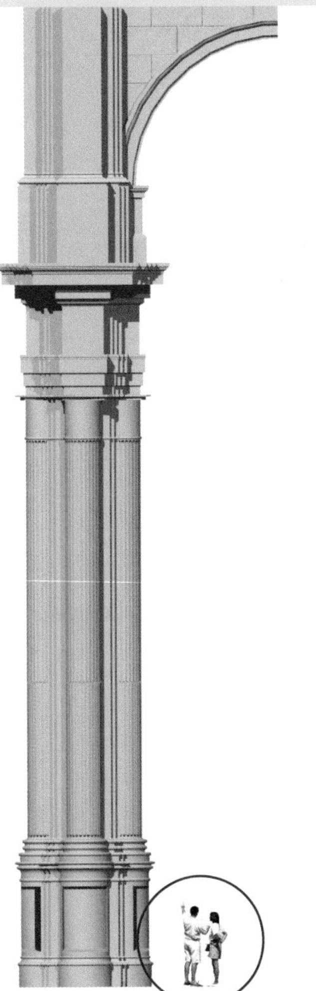

Human scale

The most important part of the church was bathed in light flooding through stained-glass windows. On the other hand, the same plan equally reveals de Siloé's recourse to the mediaeval techniques of buttressing. He was aware that the farther the lateral thrusts were transmitted the more stable the central body would be, and he achieved this by the judicious use of traditional buttresses and flying buttresses. To ensure the union between these two types of buttress he used the pinnacle, which played the role, both symbolic and dynamic of a nail. As can be seen in the diagram, the staggering of the buttresses guaranteed the absorption of the thrust generated by the colossal cylinder surrounding the main chapel.

According to the norms of Gothic architecture, the main altar forms the natural conclusion to the central aisle. During the Renaissance, however, whilst this scheme sometimes survived it was also common to find a central raised altar or else the juxtaposition of both schemes. As we have already seen, de Siloé also dared to use the two schemes, basilical and central, in the same church, but in a different way. He moved the central elevation to the end of the nave in such a way that the final layout was not one of a juxtaposition of elevations but rather one of addition. This design implied the difficulty of providing harmonious communication between both areas of the church without disrupting the feeling of unity within the building. To do this he made an opening in the cylinder where it joined the central nave, thus depriving the cupola of a large part of its support, and to solve this considerable difficulty he came up with quite a remarkable idea. He designed an enormous arch (see page 218), which, in order to adapt it to the base of the cupola, had to be warped somewhat and attenuated towards the middle. This deformation is impossible to see from floor level in the central nave (see page 219). Nevertheless, the outcome of the idea was that the arch in question had to support a third of the weight of the dome above it, despite the narrowing that it had to undergo towards the keystone. This toral arch is framed by two smaller ones on each side, where the two side aisles end. The tripartite rhythm created here, which is repeated throughout the cathedral, turns the crossing into a veritable triumphal arch into which it was possible to incorporate all the symbolism that this represented.

This scheme shows the vertical section of the rotunda, in which the great size of the buttresses is apparent; it is these buttresses that receive the direct lateral thrust of the cylinder and the cupola. The bulk of the structure is lightened by passages and corridors, which were to have been used for the tombs of the royal family.

Here, the typical system of Gothic flying buttresses has been replaced by the roofs of the ambulatory and the surrounding chapels.

The photograph on the right reveals the warping and attenuation of the soffit of the main arch and the point where it joins with the base of the cupola. But above all, the most impressive and significant aspect of the overall view is the perfect harmony between the basilical and central areas in the church.

View of the main arch from the central aisle

The photograph on the right is taken straight upwards from the floor. Apart from capturing the same view as that of a person standing beneath the cupola, it allows us to appreciate the perfection of the toral arch, together with the vivid contrast between the Classic structure of the rotunda and the archaic style of the estrellada vaults.

S. GREGORIVS
S. AMBROSIV
S. HIERONIMVS

The Door of Forgiveness

This door into the cathedral is that which embodies the greatest artistic and symbolic merits of all. Diego de Siloé himself worked on it, showing once more his capacities as a man of the Renaissance: architect, sculptor and carpenter, which was quite normal in a master builder of the time. On this occasion he also left us his signature "S" in a cartouche below one of the niches in the lower stage of the door. It was during the Renaissance that such "masters" as de Siloé and others of his creative talent began to change their status of "artisan" to that of "artist", which must be recognised as one more facet of the new Renaissance cult of individualism.

This door belongs to the north transept of the main crossing, the other, in the south transept, being that which opens into the Royal Chapel, within the cathedral itself. To maintain this union that the cathedral has with the Royal Chapel an axis, a relationship, a kind of dialogue was established via the transept between the royal mausoleum and the Door of Forgiveness. This is the reason why above the central arch there is an inscription alluding to the conquest of Granada by the Catholic Monarchs (see page 211) and for like reason an eagle with the royal shield appears upon the left-hand pier. But at the same time, the cathedral is the great project of the Holy Roman Emperor Charles V and the future pantheon of the royal family; consequently it was necessary to add one further element to embody the marriage between the empire and the Catholic religion, of which Charles was a staunch supporter. The response to this demand lies in the double-headed eagle of the Hapsburg dynasty sculpted on the right-hand pier.

At the same time, the doorway betrays the crisis of the Renaissance and the so-called "exhaustion of styles". The stylistic differences between the lower stage, designed and worked on by de Siloé, and the upper one, overseen by Ambrosio de Vico after de Siloé's death, speak for themselves. From a structural point of view the Door of Forgiveness complements the scheme of the triumphal arch that presides over the whole cathedral. It underpins an iconographic programme that was never completely fulfilled. The many empty niches suggest that the intention was to fill them with statues of a symbolic nature designed to combine the religious effect of the doorway with the message of power exhibited in the central cartouche. Diego de Siloé worked on this doorway from 1535 to 1538. The result was a magnificent sculptural work in which the elegance of the modelling of the allegories of Faith and Justice are interwoven with the fine, delicate carvings of the flora and fauna of the grutecos?. The decoration takes up all the space available, including the jambs and intrados of the arch. De Siloé also intended that the upper stages of the doorway should be decorated in a similar way but his successors did not follow his design in its entirety. Thus, in 1610 Ambrosio de Vico preserved the same architectural structure as that of de Siloés first stage but refrained from copying the exuberance of the original ornamentation. This paucity of decoration is emphasised even more by the lack of the relief of the Incarnation that was originally intended to have occupied the central encasamiento below the tympanum of the arch. Neither does the sculpting of the statues of the Eternal Father in the middle or of David and Isaiah on the enjutas possess the power and fluency of de Siloé's work. Finally, the rounding off of this second stage, with its split pediment and roleos heralds the imminent arrival of the Baroque.

These two beautiful busts on the jambs of the toral arch of the cathedral represent the heads of Adam and Eve. They are Alonso Cano's last sculptural contribution to the cathedral, with which he perhaps intended to initiate the iconographic programme of the Royal Chapel starting from the creation of man. Their gaze, apart from obeying the formal requisite of avoiding direct eye contact, invites the viewer to look towards the most spiritual place in the cathedral: the tabernacle.

STAINED-GLASS WINDOWS

Even a brief description of the stained-glass windows in the main chapel could not avoid the complexity of ideas that they arouse. The first point to be addressed would have to be their value as examples of an art that was very scarcely represented in Granada during the Renaissance. Apart from a few examples in the church of St. Jerome, these in the cathedral are the only true reference point for this style of window in Granada. Furthermore, apart from their being complementary to the architecture of the building, all twenty-four of them have their own artistic merit. One of the main stylistic features of these windows is their pictorial quality, like great paintings on glass instead of canvas. Colour, composition perspective and light all contribute to giving them a fluidity and vividness unknown in similar stained-glass windows of the time. They also explain the question about the space they occupy within the general scheme of the cathedral. There is no doubt that de Siloé himself decided that the main chapel should be enriched by the addition of stained-glass windows, which he himself sketched. He must have had some three reasons for this decision. Firstly,

Above: two fragments of the **Coming of the Holy Ghost.** *Some commentators have suggested a likeness in the face of the apostle to that of the Emperor Charles V. Left:* **"The Arrest" and "The Flagellation".**

the weight of tradition, which dictated that stained glass should be incorporated as an architectural element to create coloured light. Secondly, he needed to illuminate the main chapel, the focal point of the whole cathedral, the Sancta Santorum and place of the tabernacle, but with a different light from the daylight outside. This would almost certainly explain why the windows in the aisles are glazed with simple transparent panes, to establish a clear difference between their light and that in the main chapel. Finally, he would have also needed some way of supporting the development of the iconography in the chapel. As far as this is concerned, it must not be forgotten that the traditional ways of informing the faithful had suffered considerable setbacks in past years: frescoes and murals had disappeared quite early on, followed by the elimination of all the profusion of figures and scenes that in the past had covered archivolts and tympani in the doorways. Thus it was the altar-piece itself that inherited the tradition of informing and instructing via visual images. The splendid stained-glass windows that surrounded the main chapel fulfilled this mission admirably. The retable of the main altar would be the most logical place to concentrate all the power of religious imagery. But, with the main chapel being in a central position there was no possibility of erecting a traditional altar-piece behind it and so it was the windows that conveyed this imagery to the worshipers

Another equally important feature is that of the symbolism of the main chapel. Specialists on this subject have expressed various views. The fact that the iconographic subjects are devoted to the life, passion and death of Jesus Christ has lead some experts to relate the light entering through the stained-glass windows with the evangelical message, "I am the light of the world". According to others, it is the idea of the triumph over death which prevails and thus would be connected to the intended use of this point as the royal pantheon. Notwithstanding the possible validity of these theories, it is also worth bearing in mind that sometimes simple answers may

Below the stained-glass windows, between the light and the shadows, hangs a series of canvases considered to be "unique in the history of Spanish painting", painted by Alonso Cano to celebrate the life of the Virgin Mary. We are dealing here with a new iconographic programme sharing the same space and symbology as the stained-glass windows. There are numerous reasons to justify this reference to Marian faith within the main chapel of the cathedral. Firstly, it would seem that de Siloé had already decided to devote this part of the church to scenes of the life of Mary, but using sculpture rather than paint as his medium. The depth of the arches suggests his intention to place groups of statues or reliefs in them rather than paintings. Another explanation for this series of paintings referring to the life of the Virgin might lie in the dedication of the church itself to the Incarnation; it is obviously not coincidental that the central canvas is devoted to this mystery. On the other hand, the strong current of support for the Immaculate Conception that had held sway in Granada since the conquest must also be taken into account. Joined to this is the belief that the life, passion and death of Christ make no sense without the presence of his Mother. Even after death She mediates between her Son and humanity. Perhaps for this reason the paintings are situated between the triumph of Christ at the highest point of the rotunda and the earthly church at the bottom. From 1562, during the last years of his life, the genius of Alonso Cano was responsible for imbuing the cathedral with the presence of the Virgin Mary. Steeped in classicism, Cano combined monumentality, emotion and religion in each of his seven canvases (left: the Immaculate Conception). With equal mastery and devotion he produced the unequalled carving of the sacristy (left). Here the message of the Virgin Child, the Immaculate Conception and Virgin Mother are transmitted in a delicate and reverential language that manages to be both mystical and human at the same time.

serve best to answer apparently complicated problems.

The last reference is to the authors of these splendid works. They were two Flemish artists whose names were quickly translated into Spanish as Teodoro de Holanda and Juan del Campo. The former crafted the whole series of panes in the double windows and the latter was put in charge of the upper windows. Although stylistic differences can be perceived in the work of both artists they are not very evident at such a distance and both sets of stained-glass panes are very similar both in the unity of their subject matter and the fluency with which they treat it.

THE FAÇADE

This façade does not correspond to the general idea of the Barroque, particularly when we remind ourselves that it was designed in 1667, a time at which both Bernini and Borronini had established the new canons of the emerging style: artifice, spatial illusion, curves, countercurves and much movement in general. Once more, however, Alonso Cano's marked sympathy for the Classic style becomes evident in his approach to the façade of Granada cathedral. Instead of designing a façade completely alien to the church it was meant for, as other builders had often done before with their so-called "curtain façades", he tried to imbue it with the same stylistic characteristics as the rest of the cathedral. Thus the triple arch, a veritable triumphal arch, reflects the interior structure of the building and ushers the faithful into the three main aisles of the cathedral. In view of the final result, it might be asked what, apart from the time of its building, are the elements that most identify this work with the Barroque. To answer this it is only necessary to look at the circular oeil-de-beuf window in the centre, finished off with zig-zag teardrops que crearán escuela; the use of ornamentation based upon plaques and cartouches and the violento pronunciado of the cornices to counter the verticality of the three stages of the neighbouring tower. Experts usually add the chiaroscuro of the deeply inset arches to this list of Barroque references, but all in all the façade betrays the deeply rooted style of the Mediaeval and Classic traditions and cannot thus lay claim to any great novelty.

The image to the right shows what may well have been Diego de Siloé's original design for the façade of the cathedral. As can be seen, Alonso Cano showed sufficient respect towards his predecessors plan and did not stray very much from this first design. Only the unfinished tower to the left and its twin to the right, which was never even begun, detract to any great extent from the present-day façade compared to that designed by de Siloé.

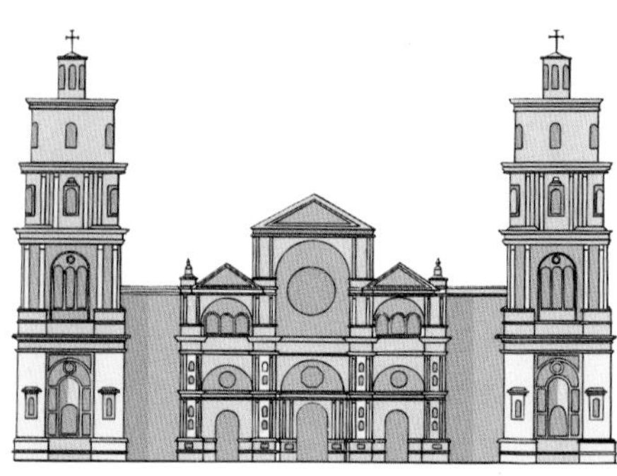

Granada

In the photograph the city of Granada appears to be dominated by the massive peaks of the Sierra Nevada and by the no less majestic size of its Moorish palace, the Alhambra. And this seems to have been Granada's lot throughout its recent history. Even today something similar might be said of the view visitors have of the city. It is as though nature, prodigal and generous to a fault with this land conspires with the exotic character of the Nasrid palaces to leave all its other many monuments, works of art and places of interest in the shade. So the intention of the next few pages of this book is to restore the balance mention a few of the other delights that Granada has to offer, taking the visitor on a trip from the city centre to the more outlying districts and then on into the countryside and the mountains.

This series of photographs shows how the Islamic tradition spread its influence much more widely than the mere confines of the Alhambra. The panorama above is of the many huddles of houses that once upon a time made up the Muslim quarters surrounding the hill of the Alhambra, with such resonant names as "Almanzora" and "Mauror".

Also visible are the lower slopes of the Albaicín quarter, face to face with the Nasrid citadel across the river Darro. Then we have two views of the Alcaicería, the old silk market in Granada, which was famous throughout the Muslim world. It had to be rebuilt after it burnt down in the XIX century

.

Lastly, the cupola of the oratory in the Madraza, the old Muslim university founded by Yusuf 1 at the beginning of the XIV century. Its presence within the old city centre adds one more touch to the richness of Granada's cultural heritage.

Top: a view from the rooftops of Plaza Nueva.
Below that: The Alcaicería
Above:Cupola in the Madraza, founded by Yusuf 1 in the XIV century, in which the remains of its oratory have been restored.

A WALK THROUGH THE OLD CENTRE OF GRANADA

Bibarrambla Square (to the right) is that central meeting point that typifies all cities. Bibarrambla means the Rambla, or Riverbank, Gate. It is the point of arrival and departure of a network of streets and alleyways. In recent centuries it has been watched over by its inseparable companion the cathedral tower, but long before that it was the open space where people gathered to witness and take part in a wide variety of social activities. History and tradition compete in recalling epic events that have taken place in this square: courtly tournaments and jousts between legendary Islamic families (the Abencerrages and Zegríes), cruel executions ordered by the Inquisition, bonfires of "subversive" books, bull fights, flower-bedecked alters during the religious celebrations of Corpus Christi; in all, a wide and extensive esplanade of human correction and amusement. As one illustrious son of Granada commented, "Bibarrambla represents the whole history of Granada, but all that remains of this is the sky that looks down upon it". Nevertheless the Arabic name of one of the gates in the city wall still remains: the Rambla Gate.

A short distance from Bibarrambla, across Reyes Católicos street, there is an interesting building known as the Corral del Carbón (to the right and below). This was in Muslim times a "fondak", or lodging house, where visiting merchants stayed while they sold their wares in the city. It dates to the XIV century, the early part of the Nasrid dynasty, and is the finest example and best preserved of its kind still extant in Spain. From Christian times onward it suffered numerous vicissitudes, becoming a charcoal store (from whence the name Corral del Carbón derives), a playhouse and a tenement for the poor, which nearly resulted in its entire ruin. At the beginning of the XX century, however, it was rescued by the city council and thoroughly restored to something like its original condition.

Bibarrambla Square: in the background, the archbishop's palace and the cathedral tower.

Below: Corral del Carbon, a lodginghouse in the XIV century.

Plaza Isabel la Católica (Isabel la Católica Square), where Reyes Católicos street crosses the end of the Gran Vía de Colón. In the background, two magnificent examples of early XX century architecture. In the centre, a monument to the treaty of capitulation agreed to by the Catholic Monarchs upon the surrender of Granada (sculpted by Benlliure in 1892).

Below: a partial view of Plaza Nueva (New Square) with the church of St. Anne to the left and the watchtower of the Alhambra on the hill above. Below that, the superb façade of the Royal Chancellery, the finest example of the Granadan Mannerist style.

The Darro Walk

This narrow street gives the impression that it has changed little in appearance throughout its history and this may well be true of the last few hundred years. But this was not as it would have been perceived by those who stayed on immediately after the Christian conquest. The left bank of the river underwent the greatest changes at this time, taking on the appearance that romantic visitors of the XIX century recorded in their writings and engravings, an image that it retained until the XX century: wooden eaves jutting out over the street, numerous orchards and gardens, wide Castilian-style projecting windows, a few Mudejar houses... Walking down the street, after a number of noble mansions there is a splendid example of an Arab bathhouse (El Bañuelo). Opposite this are the remains of an important Muslim bridge between the Albaicin and the Alhambra, El Puente del Cadí (Magistrate's Bridge). Farther along the street is the Zafra convent with a small Moorish-style house inside it, then the house of Castril, now the archaeological museum, and the church of St. Peter. And so it continues until it widens into the Paseo de los Tristes (The Walk of the Bereaved), so called because it was along here that funeral processions used to make their way to the cemetery of St. Joseph just above the Alhambra. The street finally turns left upwards to the Albaicin and the Sacromonte.

Below: la Carrera del Darro (The Darro Walk) with la Casa de Zafra and the church of St. Peter.

Below: the Darro Walk with the Zafra convent and the church of St. Peter.

Below: La Casa de los Tiros (The House of the Shots) is one of the many old houses in Granada's Realejo district. Its name refers to the muskets that protrude from just below the roof. The façade itself is adorned with a curious rebus consisting of the word THE followed by a sword piercing a heart below it and then the word RULES, which may be interpreted as, "The sword rules the heart" Even more enigmatic are a trio of square, triangular and octagonal escutcheons fastened to the wall by hearts, which form the rebus, "IT (heart) RULES. MEN OF WAR BEAR ARMS. THE (heart) BREAKS WHEN MADE A KNOCKER CALLING US TO BATTLE. BLOWS ARE WHAT GOD GIVES AND WHAT ARE SUFFERED BY THE (heart)."

The Realejo quarter is one of the districts in Granada that still retains all the flavour of its original identity. In Muslim times it was where royal (real) families had their orchards and gardens and hence the name Realejo. It also contained the Jewish enclave in the city, which survived as such until their expulsion in 1492. In more recent times it was the centre of a prosperous artistic weaving industry, of which little remains today. The hub of the district is el Campo de Principe (Prince's Square) (above), an attractive square situated at the foot of the hill leading up to the Alhambra. It is named in memory of the marriage of Prince John, son of the Catholic Monarchs, to Margaret of Austria in 1497, the year of his death. The square is watched over by a XVII century stone statue of Christ (Christ of the Favours).

It is no more than a few minutes stroll though the backstreets of the Realejo to the town centre, or else downwards to the river Genil and the Walks of the Salón (below) and the Bomba, where the people of Granada go to relax and enjoy themselves away from the bustle of the city centre.

Casa de los Tiros

Following on from the Paseo Walk runs the Carrera de la Virgen (Avenue of the Virgin), the focal point of Granada's religious ceremonies. The church of La Virgen de las Angustias (The Virgin of Anguish) is where all Granadans go to pay homage to their patron saint. Farther up this avenue is Puerta Real (The Royal Gate), the true centre of Granada, marked by the symbol of the city, a pomegranate tree. From this central point within a few minutes' walk in any direction a visitor can savour the old city by visiting such monuments as the monastery of San Jeronimo (St. Jerome), the first Christian university in Bibrambla Square, the XVIII century university (once the seat of the Jesuits and today the Faculty of Law), the Ansoti Palace (pictured to the right) and many others.

Apart from the mediaeval city there is a new Granada with a very different face, which offers an attractive, modern cultural diversity. This is the most recent expression of a city that intends to add the hope of a promising future to its past glories.

Below: one example of this vibrant new Granada is its sports stadium, equipped with the most up-to-date technology of the time. It is not only used for sporting events but has also staged a wide variety of cultural performances and a view of one of the auditoriums of the Conference and Exhibition Hall, which brings meetings and congresses of all kinds, both national and international, to Granada.

Below: the Science Park, the first of its kind in Andalucía. It was opened in 1995 and since then, apart from its permanent exhibits, has attracted both young and old alike with a series of fascinating scientific and natural exhibitions.

THE ALBAICÍN

The sketch map on the right reveals the dominant position of the Alhambra over the Albaicín quarter. It also clearly shows the twisting and turning labyrinth of its streets and back-alleys. And finally, the wealth of important buildings bears witness to its key role in the past as Granada's most important civil neighbourhood.

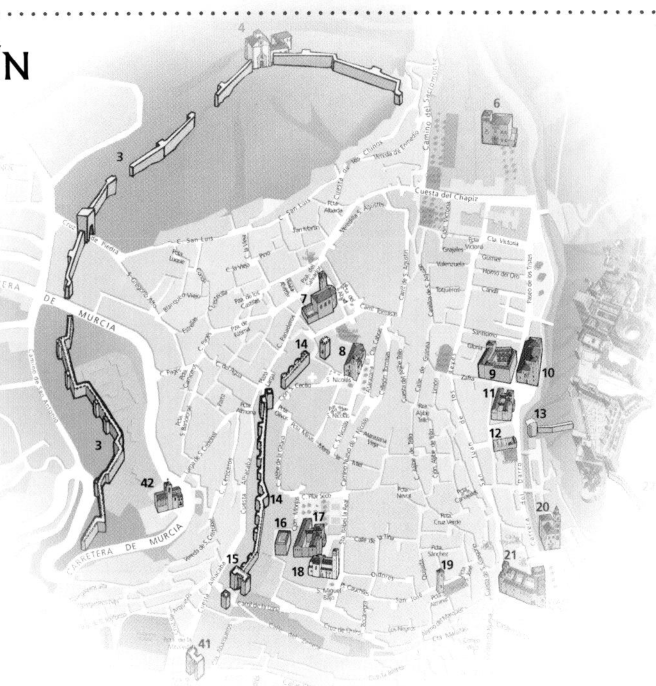

The **Albaicín** is a place of magic, a backwater where the essence of centuries of history is pooled and can be felt gently stirring. This is as it should be: the endless legacy of ancient civilisations, the ege-old witness that has watched over innumerable changes, and a sentimental refuge for all those of nostalgic and romantic bent. But it may well be that a definition of this sort bears little relationship to the Albaicín that waits to be discovered by a visitor to Granada. This is the great risk that words entail because as carefully as one might choose them they often do not end up being as precise and meaningful as one would have liked. Above all when one´s intention is to explain the inexplicable.

This brief allusion to the limits that language imposes is no more than an apology for writing of the Albaicín in the traditional descriptive way, a way which best tallies with the ideas of those who have not yet visited the place. Writing of the seductive charms that made it famous as the most suggestive and exotic district of Granada. For example, it houses piled on top of each other like swallows´nest; the anarchic twist and turns of its narrow streets; the exuberant vegetation that tumbles promiscuosly over the tops of orchard walls; the wide open panoramas across the plain and towards the Alhambra and the Sierra Nevada behind it; the hidden corners that the privileged walker comes across from time to time with pleasant surprise...And for those who want something more, because they are not content with the plasure of the senses alone, there is history and art.

Hidden between these houses and sometimes incorporated into them there are still some important vestiges of the earliest settlers and cultures on this hill, which are often relegated into second place by the later presence of the Mulslims. It seems to be the fate of this dictrict to be always reminded of the times that gave it its greatest splendour. When, at the beginning of the VIII century, Asad ibn Abderraman al Saybani built a fortress in what is today San Nicholas´ Square, the Qasabat Garnata of Muslim chonicles, no one could have imagined the splendours of the future that awaited it.

In the XI century it was already the palatine residence of the first Islamic dynasty to govern the area, the Zirids. From this beginning the Alcazaba Cadima grew up, and in its shadow and under its protection numerous smaller quarters until they occupied the whole of the hill. Neither did the decision by Muhammad ibn Nasir al-Hamar in the XIII century to transfer the royal court to the opposite hill, the Sabika, where he would start to build the new palatine citadel of the

Alhambra alter the fortunes of the Albaicín. It continued to grow until it bacame a veritable city within the city of Granada. In the XIV century it had its own administrative system, judges and militia. The wealthy Nastid aristocracy built sumptuous mansions there; it had some thirty mosques, including the Great Mosque, which was more beautiful than that of Granada itself; a cleverly built and complicated network of waterways fed a similar number underground cisterns the clacking of its looms bere witness to an extensive cotagge industry making cloths of the finest quality; in like mode, other wares made of leather, pottery, enamel, glass, copper, wrought iron and marquetry left small workshops in thousands of different shapes and sizes, expressing the inexhaustible imagination and limitless industry of the Albaicín.
That was the Albaicín in its times of glory: admired and at the same time feared because its population was both numerous and difficult to govern. That was the legendary Albaicín, which, against all logic, we want to find an our way. Of that Albaicín little remains today except atavistic vestiges, relics, even rubbish from the past that has survived the takeover of the new Castilian powers quite by chance. But there is no room for regret because history´s designs are irregutable when it comes to putting each of us in our place. We cannot complain if history turned its back upon this district, bacause nature has done its best to compensate the loss. Thus the Albaicín of today is bathed in spring-time aromas from closed gardens, the radiant hues of plants climbing over walls, counterpoints of light and shade in the bachgroun like patterns on a chequer board and the panormic views that always appear round many a different corner. From time to time the severity of a monastery wall, the elegance of a palatial mansion, the loftiness of a campanile, or the squabbling of sparrows in the branches, a dog barking in the distance, all speak of closer, more mundane Albaicín.
Every visit to the Albaicín should be made with no previous route in mind. It is far better to improvise and lose oneself in the general idea, for example, of heading upwards through the twisting alleyways to a high vantage point and then wandering back down again in another direction to the foot of the hill. But one should not attempt to swim entirely against the current and ignore the places that attract most popular acclaim. Thus we must recognise the enchantment of such places as the mirador of San Nicolás, Plaza de San Miguel Bajo and Plaza Larga, the mirador of San Cristobal, carril de la Lona, Caldererías, Zenete, Plaza de los Carvajales and the paseo de los Tristes, because, although it might mean following in the footsteps of the multitude, the Albaicín is always wo 0rth it.

Above: the square in front of the church of St. Nicholas; one of the most famous views in Europe, across the river Darro to the Alhambra, which must be seen by any visitor to Granada, especially at dusk, when the last rays of the sun linger for a few last moments on the towers of the Moorish palace.

To the right is the marvellous view from the mirador of St. Christopher. In the foreground is part of the Zirid wall (XI century), just behind which are the monastery buildings of Santa Isabel la Real together with a length of wall belonging to the palace Dar al Horra, built by Muley Hacen for his banished wife Aixa. .

Above on the facing page: Placeta de Nevot (Nevot Square) with the Carmen of the Crescent Moon (right) and the Carmen of the Angustias (centre).
To the left: patio in the Albaicín woth its typical grapevine.

Below: Plaza Larga (Long Square), bedecked with crosses and flowers for the Day of the Cross on 3 May.

Granada is the city of "carmens", which means a rural house and its surrounding garden and orchard transported figuratively into the urban scene; an anarchy of bushes, trees and flowers planted on a grand scale, sprouting and spreading wantonly; an exuberance of climbing plants escaping into the street over the tops of the surrounding walls; peaceful nooks in which to delight and forget about the present; and above all, water... the constant presence of water flowing from a spring or trickling into a pool.

The patio of a typical house in the Albaicín, generally referred to as "morisca" or "mudejar", meaning that the architectural design follows the new Christian trends but that the decorative elements remain essentially Moorish.

Below: the Monaita gate, one of the entrances to the city in its surrounding wall. The church of St. Christopher can be seen in the background.

Above: of all the mosques to be found in Granada before the reconquest, some thirty or so in the Albaicín itself, all that is left is this courtyard, which today belongs to the church of the Saviour.

Left: a street market in Plaza Larga (Long Square). For the local residents this square is like the patio of a large house, where in the mornings they can catch up on local news and gossip and have a coffee in one of the little cafés nearby.

A short distance above the Albaicín lies the Sacromonte, an old traditional gypsy quarter where many of the inhabitants live in caves. Photographs from 1956 and 2008

With the passage of time the Carmen (from the Arabic "karm", meaning a grape vine) has lost its original identity of a piece of land used to grow fruit and vegetables and has come to mean a grand, luxurious town house used only for pleasure.

The entrance to the Carmen de la Media Luna (the Carmen of the Half Moon).

The houses of the Albaicin maintain their traditional structure and lay-out, always with an inside patio decorated with potted plants and household tools and equipment. In the hot summer months these patios become an important room in the house and are filled with bustle and comings and goings. Below: a patio in the Albaicín, and to the left: the façade adorned with flower pots of a house on the way to the Sacromonte.

THE MONASTERY OF St. JEROME

The photograph above shows the special beauty of the interplay of the shapes of the cloister, the convalescents' gallery and the south face of the church, together with the contrasts of light and shade that they produce. All this is presided over by the tower, which had to be rebuilt after being demolished by the French in order to rob the stone to build a bridge over the river Genil.

The main cloister (below) is very spacious and it is not difficult to visualise the original, almost pastoral setting that contemporary chronicles describe. It is Gothic in design and divided into two stories: the lower one with semicircular arches and leafy capitals and the upper with depressed arches supported by shorter columns and a stone balustrade. The cloister can be entered through several beautiful doorways, seven of which were designed, and possibly made, by Diego de Siloé himself.

This is one of the several religious foundations ordained by the Catholic King and Queen just after their conquest of Granada. In this case it was the earliest of these foundations because it was first ordained in the siege town of Santa Fé in the year leading up to their possession of the city. Work on the monastery in Granada began in 1504 and by 1521 it was already being used and lived in by the monks. The church attached to the monastery was begun in 1513 but was not finished until the end of the XVI century. During their lifetime both the monastery and church have suffered severe vicissitudes: because of the French occupation in 1810, the disentailment of religious property in 1836, their later use as a military garrison and finally their complete abandonment. Such was their state of neglect that at the end of the XIX century it was considered advisable to pull them down. Nevertheless, at the beginning of the XX century a magnificent effort was made to restore the monuments, which left them in the superb condition in which we find them today.

Two crucial events occurred

during the building of the monastery of St. Jerome: the first was the initiative of the Duchess of Sesa to have her husband, el Gran Capitán, the hero of the reconquest, buried there; and the second was the arrival of the renowned architect Diego de Siloé to take charge of the building work in 1528. From this combination of interests arose the main chapel, in which the architecture and sculpture combine with exquisite perfection. Diego de Siloé had to undertake the vaulting of the choir and the crossing of the church. For the choir he proposed a vault with three cascos preceded by a barrel vault, all filled with an abundance of imagery together with fanciful medallions and large ceiling roses. The vaults of the short arms of the cross are dealt with in a similar way. De Siloé's brilliance is expressed above all in the dome above the transept, which had not been built to carry such weight. Thus he designed a structure that was simple and safe but at the same time a work of genius. From four conchoidal pendentives he stretched four tapered arches to support a tercelete ogive vault. In this way the outward pressure was reduced to a minimum, stability was guaranteed and the aesthetic result was worthy of the church.

THE CARTHUSIAN MONASTERY

The Carthusian monastery was built in Granada in response to a plan by the monastic order to extend the presence of its monks throughout the Castilian domains. After a few failed attempts their aspirations were realised when Gonzalo Fernández de Córdoba (the Catholic Monarchs' "Great Captain" of the reconquest) lent his help to the Carthusians by deciding to have his mortal remains interred in the church of the proposed monastery. At a later date disagreements between the monks and don Gonzalo led to his abandoning the idea but they continued to build their monastery anyway. Work was begun in 1517 but would not be finished until halfway through the XVIII century and it is this delay in completion that confers upon the monastery some of its singular attraction: a complete evolution of architectural styles from the Gothic to the Neoclassic.

Left: a figure of St. Bruno, in which the sculptor, José de Mora, attempts to represent the idea of spirituality rather than a particular person. Below: a general view of the monastery and a view of the sacristy with the amazing explosion of light provided by its stucco ornamentation.

It is surprising that a simple sacristy should acquire the status of a church within a church, as this one does. As can be seen, it is structured in four stages via a type of fajones arches supported by pilasters that separate the stages and regulate the eye's progress down the room. These are followed immediately by the crossing with its cupola, and finally the altar. The sheer size of the nave, the exuberant treatment of the walls and the design of the floor tiles all go to accentuate the sense of convergence, inviting the visitor to move towards the end as though in a church. The emptiness of the centre of the aisle enhances its horizontal lines; the constant rhythm of the decoration on the walls encourages movement, and finally the tiles, rhomboid instead of square, cover the floor with arrows pointing towards the altar.

Perhaps the greatest impression that a visitor receives in the sacristy is one of light, and more than light, brilliant whiteness. A harmonious combination of both produces an agreeable feeling of transparency and weightlessness, thus avoiding any sense of heaviness or pressure.

Neither can we ignore the splendid chests of drawers lining the walls. Apart from their utilitarian function as the repository of the holy vestments and the quality of their wood and carvings, they are perfectly integrated into the architectural structure of the nave itself in such a way that the drawers appear to be more important as continuations of the marble skirting than mere storage spaces for clothes.

Perhaps the greatest impression that a visitor receives in the sacristy is one of light, and more than light, brilliant whiteness. A harmonious combination of both produces an agreeable feeling of transparency and weightlessness, thus avoiding any sense of heaviness or pressute.

The artistic expression of the Baroque is also allowed to flower in all its limitless fantasy in the tabernacle of the monastery. Its building was entrusted to the Córdoban architect Hurtado Izquierdo during the early decades of the XVIII century. Once more the Baroque scenography creates an area charged with aesthetic and symbolic ideals. A small square floor supports a whirlwind of centrifugal energy, soaring upwards with the sole intention of exalting the tabernacle, in which lies the body of Christ. The centrifugal movement derives from the central baldachin and the pairs of columns at the corners that advance and project outwards to the centre of the room. So that no doubt might remain as to where the centre of attraction and worship resides, two figures painted upon each of the door jambs, David and Melchisedech, show the path to follow.

The upward movement is created by the pyramidal structure of the badalchin (below) together with the helical twist of the Salomonic columns that support its first level. The sculpted figure of Faith, which crowns the whole ensemble seems to connect it to the cupola, which represents heaven.

The rising shape of the baldachin leads the eye to the cupola, within which Antonio Palomino painted a series of images designed

The capacity of the Baroque to give scope within the same space to the most diverse elements is clearly seen in the sanctum sanctorum. Glass, marble, wood, materials treated with size, gold, painting, sculpture and architecture all go to create this amalgam of movement and convulsive energy with which the whole ensemble vibrates. And above all, to emphasise the reference to the Eucharist and the Holy Figure, which was always on display inside a silver tabernacle until General Sebastiani decided to steal it during the French occupation of Granada (interior of the tabernacle).

once again to exalt the Eucharist. Thus, the centre is occupied by the monstrance holding the Sacred Sacrament in the midst of a clear sky. From this central point the artist has created an imaginary vertical axis, which, through the earthly globe born by St. Bruno on his back and the figure of Faith, leads once more to the baldachin and the tabernacle. This is all designed to emphasise that the dialogue between earth and heaven can only be maintained through Christ and a perseverance of Faith. It is hardly surprising then that this virtue is depicted twice in an intentional continuity of religious imagery.

Virgin by Risueño.

Despite being Baroque in its outward form, the scene within the cupola owes an undeniable debt to some mediaeval depictions of the same idea. Possibly the symbolism in this cupola is most reminiscent of that in the van Eyck brothers' Adoration of the Lamb. As in the Dutch altar-piece, the protagonists in the cupola in the Carthusian monastery in Granada form groups of related figures, all in processional attitudes: angels, archangels, virgins, saints, prophets and patriarchs all share this adoration and reverence with the highest heavenly hierarchy: the Holy Trinity. From a technical point of view the painting is a splendid display both of the artist's command of the techniques of painting al fresco and his control of draughtsmanship, perspective and use of colour.

Within some of the chapels around the small cloister there are some splendid sculptures, such as Risueño's Madonna and Child (above) and the terra-cotta Ecce Homo by the García Risueño brothers (right).

THE SIERRA NEVADA

The Sierra Nevada is probably the clearest token of nature's generosity towards Granada. This mountain range is capped by the two highest peaks in the Iberian peninsula, Mulhacen and Veleta, both rising to more than 3,300 metres, whilst another fourteen peaks are higher than 3,000 metres. The range is covered by the southernmost snows in Europe and is home to such a wide variety of endemic flora and fauna that it has been designated a national park and protected biosphere reserve.

Several decades ago a small ski station was opened on the slopes of the Sierra Nevada, since when it has grown and improved its facilities to the extent that nowadays it is an important sporting and tourist resort, offering more than 70 kilometres of runs of all levels of difficulty. In 1996 Granada hosted the World Alpine Skiing Competition here.
In summer the mountains are a haven for walkers who want to escape along its innumerable tracks into the complete isolation and splendour of this reserve, magnificent for its views, its wildlife and its silence.

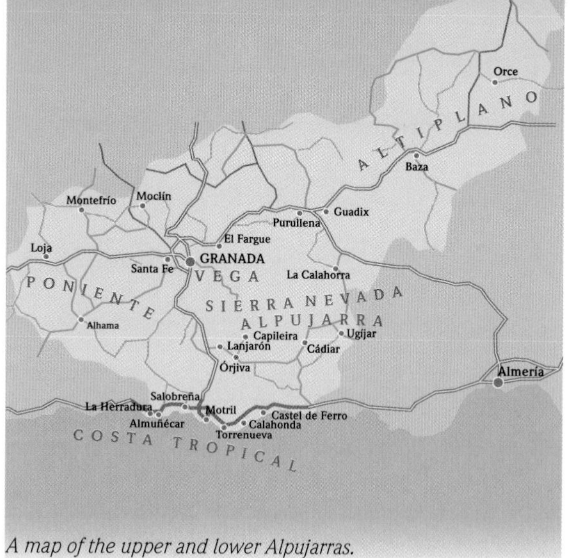

A map of the upper and lower Alpujarras.
Above: Trevélez, at 1,650 metres above sea level

THE PROVINCE

The orography and landscape of the province of Granada is extremely varied with very sharp contrasts ranging from the snow of the high mountains to its subtropical coastline. It is one of only three places in the world where you can ski and swim in the sea on the same day.

The province is comprised of seven districts: the Capital City, surrounded by mountains and the fertile plain to the west; Western Granada, with three importan towns: Montefrío, set in impressive rocky countryside interspersed with meadows and the towering Peña de los Gitanos, a stoney scarp containing some interesting prehistoric sites, Loja, known throughout history as "the Gateway to Granada" and Alhama de Granada, with its natural thermal springs and baths. Both these latter towns were important Moorish strongholds before and during the reconquest. The first to fall was Alhama and during a skirmish at Loja the last sultan of the Nasrid dynasty, Boabdil, was taken prisoner by the Christians. The medieval castles of both towns still overlook them from the heights of almost inaccessible crags. The thirth district is that of the Tropical Coast to the south, with seaside towns such as Almuñecar and Salobreña and Motril, where the only sugar cane in Europe is still grown. Other crops to grow

To the left: Salobreña, within whose castle more than one king of Granada has been imprisoned. Above: Montefrío, with its church balanced precariously above the ravine.

To the left: Castillo de Moclín, an erstwhile stronghold against the Christians on the frontier of the kingdom of Granada. Below: cave dwellings on the high ground around Guadix.

in this enviable subtropial climate are mangoes, avocados and custard apples. The Sierra nevada itself forms the fifth district of the province; almost all of it is a national park and nature reserve and is home to a large number of endemic species of planats and animals. It is also home to the southernmost ski resort in Europe.

The tow remaining districts lie in the north-east of the province and occupy the high Guadix-Baza plain arround the dip in the terrain known es the Hoya, which was in recent geological time an inland sea. Archaeologists have discovered here what may be evidence of the fisrt hominids in Europe and the area has certenly been inhabited countinuosty from earliest prehistoric times. Guadix and Baza were both importan Moorish strongholds and the ruins of their fortified Muslim citadels can still be seen today. One of their most curious attractions is the considerable troglodyte

population. The cave dwellings of the area can be quite luxurious and the constant, year-round temperture inside them of arround 18ªC is very much appreciated by their owners. On the southern slopes of the Sierra Nevada is the Alpujarra, a distric of mountain and villages, so special that it is worth a more detailed account in the following pages

Not far from Guadix, just beside the road to Almería, in the foothills of the Sierra Nevada, is the castle of La Calahorra (right and below), built in 1509 by a grandson of Cardenal Mendoza, using marble brought from Genoa, which would make it the first Renaissance building in Spain. It central courtyard (below) is one of the most beautiful and refines in the Italian XV centuriystyle in Spain.

THE ALPUJARRAS

Above, Bubión.
Below: Ugíjar

The Alpujarra region became tragically famous in the history of Spain because of the rebellion in 1568 of the Moriscos, the Muslims who had chosen to remain in Spain. Its tortuous orography together with the desperation of the rebels turned this revolt into a long and cruel war. Some place names, such as "the Valley of Blood", still bear witness to the ferocity of the skirmish. Nowadays the echoes of those tumultuous days have faded away and the Alpujarra is a very different place.

It is a remarkable region, lying between the Sierra Nevada to the north and the Mediterranean to the south. The river Guadalfeo divides it in two: the upper and lower Alpujarra to the north and the Contraviesa to the south. It is an area of dramatic contrasts, dropping as it does from the high mountains to the coast in a mere 35 kilometres as the crow flies, and within this descent it embraces a complete range of climates. It is rightly said that the Alpujarra has its head at the pole and its feet in the tropics. The ups and downs of its hills and valleys are tortuous in the extreme but this has never prevented people from exploring them and settling in their remotest corners. Valleys and hillsides well irrigated by the melting snows from the mountains and at the same time sheltered from extreme adversities of climate have allowed small villages and hamlets to thrive sometimes at more than 1,000 metres. Trevélez, at 1,600 metres, is the highest village in Spain.

The inhabitants of the Alpujarra have always relied on agriculture for their living and this has shaped the diverse fortunes of the region. When it was under Muslim rule the land

The colours of the countryside are always to the fore; the myriad hues of springtime green change during the autumn into inimaginable shades of red, yellow and orange, turning the whole of the Alpujarras into a sea of russet gold.

responded generously to their labours and produced a wide variety of different fruits and vegetables. After the expulsion of the Muslims, the new Christian landlords replaced the traditional crops with their own, based upon the trilogy of cereals, vines and olive trees. But as time went on these crops were once more complemented with other local produce such as fruit and vegetables and pasture for animals, which the land could support through its varied and benign climate. For brief periods the possibility of exploitation of its mineral deposits or its silk culture and weaving gave hopes of economic development but these were no more than ephemeral dreams which came to little. The natural conditions peculiar to the Alpujarra are responsible for the typical houses of the region. First and foremost they are designed to provide protection against the rigours of the winter and so whenever possible face south to capture the sun and the relative warmth of the sea breezes. These breezes also temper the heat of summer. Stone, as well as being the handiest building material, pro-

vides excellent insulation from both the cold of winter and the heat of the summer.

Only the ham-curing industry continues to thrive and enjoy a deserved international recognition.

Modern times have brought significant change to the Alpujarra; the general ageing of the population as a whole and the predominant agricultural structure of smallholdings in a context of global economic change have upset the traditional foundations of its economy. So nowadays the region is hoping to encourage visitors to enjoy its unrivalled potentials: wide horizons, total peace and tranquillity, walking and mountaineering for all tastes and capabilities and the delight of small villages each with their own traditional culinary specialities.

The photograph above shows a view of the village of Pampaneira, clinging to one of the higher slopes of the Alpujarra; further up is Bubión, overlooking the Poqueira ravine; and almost lost in the distance, merging with the snow of the Sierra Nevada, Capileira. The scene gives an idea of the distances of these landscapes and the way that the small villages blend in with the oaks, chestnuts and pines that abound in the region. The shady valleys and

A map of the upper and lower Alpujarras. Above: Trevélez, at 1,650 metres above sea level.

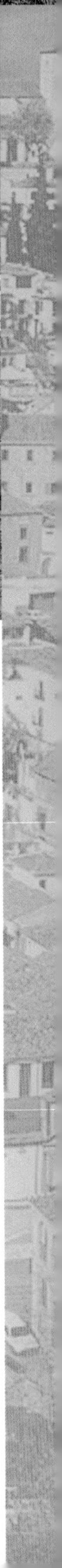

The photograph above shows a view of the village of Pampaneira, clinging to one of the higher slopes of the Alpujarra; further up is Bubión, overlooking the Poqueira ravine; and almost lost in the distance, merging with the snow of the Sierra Nevada, Capileira. The scene gives an idea of the distances of these landscapes and the way that the small villages blend in with the oaks, chestnuts and pines that abound in the region. The shady valleys and ravines, which resound to the constant rush of water, are home to cane, reeds, rushes and broom whilst the dryer mountainsides are covered with aromatic herbs such as thyme, rosemary, sage and lavender.

ravines, which resound to the constant rush of water, are home to cane, reeds, rushes and broom whilst the dryer mountainsides are covered with aromatic herbs such as thyme, rosemary, sage and lavender.

The colours of the countryside are always to the fore; the myriad hues of springtime green change during the autumn into unimaginable shades of red, yellow and orange, turning the whole of the Alpujarras into a sea of russet gold.

The most characteristic feature of these houses is their flat roofs made of slate slabs covered in a waterproof layer of slate clay, above which rise the unmistakeable profiles of the Alpujarran chimneys. These roofs are used as patios for sitting and also for drying maize, beans, figs and grapes in the sun. The white of the houses is always set off by the reds and pinks of geraniums growing in pots hanging from their balconies.